Applications and Innovations in Intelligent Systems XII

Ann Macintosh, Richard Ellis and
Tony Allen (Eds)

Applications and Innovations in Intelligent Systems XII

Proceedings of AI-2004, the Twenty-fourth SGAI International Conference on Innovative Techniques and Applications of Artificial Intelligence

 Springer

Professor Ann Macintosh, BSc, CEng
Napier University, Edinburgh, EH10 5DT, UK

Richard Ellis, BSc, MSc
Stratum Management Ltd, UK

Dr Tony Allen
Nottingham Trent University

British Library Cataloguing in Publication Data
A catalogue record for this book is available from the British Library

ISBN 1-85233-908-X
Springer is part of Springer Science+Business Media
springeronline.com

Typesetting: Camera-ready by editors
Printed and bound at the Athenæum Press Ltd., Gateshead, Tyne & Wear
34/3830-543210 Printed on acid-free paper SPIN 11006725

APPLICATION PROGRAMME CHAIR'S INTRODUCTION

A. L. Macintosh, Napier University, UK

The papers in this volume are the refereed application papers presented at ES2004, the Twenty-fourth SGAI International Conference on Innovative Techniques and Applications of Artificial Intelligence, held in Cambridge in December 2004. The conference was organised by SGAI, the British Computer Society Specialist Group on Artificial Intelligence.

This volume contains twenty refereed papers which present the innovative application of a range of AI techniques in a number of subject domains. This year, the papers are divided into sections on Synthesis and Prediction, Scheduling and Search, Diagnosis and Monitoring, Classification and Design, and Analysis and Evaluation

This year's prize for the best refereed application paper, which is being sponsored by the Department of Trade and Industry, was won by a paper entitled "A Case-Based Technique for Tracking Concept Drift in Spam Filtering". The authors are Sarah Jane Delany, from the Dublin Institute of Technology, Ireland, and Pádraig Cunningham, Alexey Tsymbal, and Lorcan Coyle from Trinity College Dublin, Ireland.

This is the twelfth volume in the *Applications and Innovations* series. The Technical Stream papers are published as a companion volume under the title *Research and Development in Intelligent Systems XXI*.

On behalf of the conference organising committee I should like to thank all those who contributed to the organisation of this year's application programme, in particular the programme committee members, the executive programme committee and our administrators Linsay Turbert and Collette Jackson.

Ann Macintosh
Application Programme Chair, AI-2004

ACKNOWLEDGEMENTS

AI-2004 CONFERENCE COMMITTEE

Dr. Tony Allen,   (Conference Chair)
Nottingham Trent University

Dr. Robert Milne,   (Deputy Conference Chair,
Sermatech Intelligent Applications Ltd   Finance and Publicity)

Dr. Alun Preece,   (Deputy Conference Chair,
University of Aberdeen   Electronic Services)

Dr. Nirmalie Wiratunga,   (Deputy Conference Chair,
Robert Gordon University, Aberdeen   Poster Session)

Prof. Adrian Hopgood   (Tutorial Organiser)
Nottingham Trent University

Prof. Ann Macintosh   (Application Programme Chair)
Napier University

Richard Ellis   (Deputy Application Programme Chair)
Stratum Management Ltd

Prof. Max Bramer   (Technical Programme Chair)
University of Portsmouth

Dr Frans Coenen,   (Deputy Technical Programme Chair)
University of Liverpool

Dr. Bob Howlett,   (Exhibition Organiser)
University of Brighton

Rosemary Gilligan   (Research Student Liaison)
University of Hertfordshire

APPLICATIONS EXECUTIVE PROGRAMME COMMITTEE

Prof. Ann Macintosh, Napier University (Chair)
Richard Ellis, Stratum Management Ltd (Vice-Chair)
Dr Robert Milne, Sermatech Intelligent Applications Ltd
Richard Wheeler, University of Edinburgh
Alan Montgomery, InferMed Ltd
Rosemary Gilligan, University of Hertfordshire

APPLICATIONS PROGRAMME COMMITTEE

CONTENTS

BEST APPLICATION PAPER

A Case-Based Technique for Tracking Concept Drift in Spam Filtering

Sarah Jane Delany[1], Pádraig Cunningham[2], Alexey Tsymbal[2],
Lorcan Coyle[2]
[1]Dublin Institute of Technology, Kevin St., Dublin 8, Ireland.
[2]Trinity College Dublin, College Green, Dublin 2, Ireland.

Abstract

Clearly, machine learning techniques can play an important role in filtering spam email because ample training data is available to build a robust classifier. However, spam filtering is a particularly challenging task as the data distribution and concept being learned changes over time. This is a particularly awkward form of concept drift as the change is driven by spammers wishing to circumvent the spam filters. In this paper we show that lazy learning techniques are appropriate for such dynamically changing contexts. We present a case-based system for spam filtering called ECUE that can learn dynamically. We evaluate its performance as the case-base is updated with new cases. We also explore the benefit of periodically redoing the feature selection process to bring new features into play. Our evaluation shows that these two levels of model update are effective in tracking concept drift.

1   Introduction

With the cost of spam to companies worldwide estimated to be ca. $20 billion a year and growing at a rate of almost 100% a year [1], spam is a problem that needs to be handled. It is a challenging problem for a number of reasons. One of the most testing aspects is the dynamic nature of spam. Something of an arms race has emerged between spammers and the spam filters used to combat spam. As filters are adapted to contend with today's types of spam emails, the spammers alter, obfuscate and confuse filters by disguising their emails to look more like legitimate email. This dynamic nature of spam email raises a requirement for update in any filter that is to be successful over time in identifying spam.

Lazy learning is good for dynamically changing situations. With lazy learning the decision of how to generalise beyond the training data is deferred until each new instance is considered. In comparison to this, eager learning systems determine their generalisation mechanism by building a model based on the training data in advance of considering any new instances. In this paper we explore the application of Case-Based Reasoning (CBR), a lazy machine learning technique, to the problem of spam filtering and present our CBR system – Email Classification Using Examples (ECUE). We concentrate in this paper on evaluating how ECUE can assist with the concept drift that is inherent in spam.

CBR offers a number of advantages in the spam filtering domain. Spam is a disjoint concept in that spam selling cheap prescription drugs has little in common with spam offering good mortgage rates. Case-based classification works well for disjoint concepts whereas Naïve Bayes, a machine learning technique that is popular for text classification, tries to learn a unified concept description.

In addition, there is a natural hierarchy of learning available to a CBR system where the simplest level of learning is to simply update the case-base with new instances of spam or legitimate email. The advantage of CBR in this first level of learning is that it requires no rebuild of the model as is necessary with other machine learning solutions to spam filtering. The second level of learning is to retrain the system by re-selecting features that may be more predictive of spam. This level of retraining can be performed infrequently and based on newer training data. The highest level of learning, performed even more infrequently than feature selection, is to allow new feature extraction techniques to be added to the system. For instance, when domain specific features are used in the system, new feature extraction techniques will allow new features to be included. In ECUE we use a similarity retrieval algorithm based on Case Retrieval Nets (CRN) [2] which is a memory structure that allows efficient and flexible retrieval of cases. The benefit of using the CRN for implementing the second and third levels of learning is that it can easily handle cases with new features; the fact that these features may be missing on old cases is not a problem.

This paper begins in Section 2 with an overview of other work using machine learning techniques for filtering spam. Section 3 discusses the problem of concept drift and existing techniques for handling concept drift. Our case-based approach to spam filtering, ECUE, is presented in Section 4, while Section 5 presents our evaluation and results of using CBR to combat the concept drift in spam. Section 6 closes the paper with our conclusions and directions for future work.

2   Spam Filtering and Machine Learning

Existing research on using machine learning for spam filtering has focussed particularly on using Naïve Bayes [3-7]. In addition there has been work using Support Vector Machines (SVMs) [3,8,9] and Latent Semantic Indexing [10]. There has also been research using memory based classifiers [4,11]. However, this work does not address the issue of concept drift which is inherent in spam and the evaluations have been on static datasets.

One technique used for tracking concept drift is ensemble learning (see Section 3.2) which uses a set of classifiers whose individual results are combined to give an overall classification. There has been some work on ensemble learning in spam filtering using boosting [1,12] and also a combination of Naïve Bayes and memory based classifiers [13]. These evaluations use static data sets and do not attempt to track concept drift.

3 The Problem of Concept Drift

This section defines concept drift and discusses approaches to handling concept drift.

3.1 Definitions and Types of Concept Drift

A difficult problem with learning in many real-world domains is that the concept of interest may depend on some *hidden context*, not given explicitly in the form of predictive features. Typical examples include weather prediction rules that may vary radically with the season or the patterns of customers' buying preferences that may change, depending on the current day of the week, availability of alternatives, inflation rate, etc. Often the cause of change is hidden, not known in advance, making the learning task more complicated. Changes in the hidden context can induce changes in the target concept, which is generally known as *concept drift* [13]. An effective learner should be able to track such changes and to quickly adapt to them.

Two kinds of concept drift that may occur in the real world are normally distinguished in the literature: (1) sudden (abrupt, instantaneous), and (2) gradual concept drift. For example, someone graduating from college might suddenly have completely different monetary concerns, whereas a slowly wearing piece of factory equipment might cause a gradual change in the quality of output parts [15]. Stanley [15] divides gradual drift into moderate and slow drifts, depending on the rate of change.

Hidden changes in context may not only be a cause of a change in the target concept, but may also cause a change in the underlying data distribution. Even if the target concept remains the same but the data distribution changes, a model rebuild may be necessary as the model's error may no longer be acceptable. This is called *virtual concept drift* [16]. Virtual concept drift and real concept drift often occur together or virtual concept drift alone may occur, e.g. in the case of spam categorization. From a practical point of view it is not important what kind of concept drift occurs as in all cases, the current model needs to be changed.

3.2 Approaches to Handling Concept Drift

There are three approaches to handling concept drift: (1) instance selection; (2) instance weighting; and (3) ensemble learning (or learning with multiple concept descriptions). In instance selection, the goal is to select instances relevant to the current concept. The most common concept drift handling technique is based on instance selection and involves generalizing from a *window* that moves over recently seen instances and uses the learnt concepts for prediction only in the immediate future. Examples of window-based algorithms include the FLORA family of algorithms [13], FRANN [17], and Time-Windowed Forgetting (TWF) [18]. Some algorithms use a window of fixed size, while others use heuristics to adjust the window size to the current extent of concept drift, e.g. "Adaptive Size" [19] and FLORA2 [13]. Many case-base editing strategies in case-based reasoning that delete noisy, irrelevant and redundant cases are also a form of instance selection [20]. Batch selection [19] taking groups of instances, may be considered as instance selection as well.

Instance weighting uses the ability of some learning algorithms such as SVMs to process weighted instances [19]. Instances can be weighted according to their age and their competence with regard to the current concept. Klinkenberg [19] shows in his experiments that instance weighting techniques handle concept drift worse than analogous instance selection techniques, which is probably due to overfitting the data.

Ensemble learning maintains a set of concept descriptions, predictions of which are combined using voting, weighted voting, or the most relevant description is selected. A number of techniques are used to identify the set of concept descriptions including feature construction [21], contextual clustering [22], sequential chunks of data [23,24] or groupings based on decreasing periods of time [15,25]. All incremental ensemble approaches use some criteria to dynamically delete, reactivate, or create new ensemble members, which are normally based on the base models' consistency with the current data.

Many learning algorithms were used for base models in systems handling concept drift. These include rule-based learning [13,16,21,24], decision trees, including their incremental versions [15,22-26], Naïve Bayes [24,25], SVMs [19], RBF-networks [17], and instance-based learning [18,20,27]. A problem with many global eager learners (if they are not able to update their local parts incrementally when needed) is their inability to adapt to local concept drift. In the real world, concept drift may often be local, e.g. only particular types of spam may change with time, while the others could remain the same. In the case of local concept drift, many global models are discarded simply because their accuracy on the current data falls, even if they still could be good experts in the stable parts of the data. In contrast to this, lazy learning is able to adapt well to local concept drift due to its local nature. Instance-based learning is sometimes criticized in that, as non-parametric learning, it needs relatively more instances to get high classification accuracy [13]. However, often it is not a problem in practice, as enough instances are available.

The most popular *benchmark data* for testing concept drift handling systems is represented by the STAGGER concepts [21] which are used to test most of the systems [13-17,21,22,25] or by a moving hyperplane [23-26]. A limitation of these is that they do not allow checking the algorithms' scalability to large problems, which is important as concept drift mostly occurs in big amounts of data arriving in the form of a stream. In addition, some real-world problems were used to test concept drift handling systems [22-24,26]. An important problem with most of the real-world datasets is that there is little concept drift in them, or concept drift is introduced artificially, e.g. by restricting the subset of relevant topics for each particular period of time [19].

4 A Case-Based Approach to Concept Drift

This section outlines ECUE, our case-based approach to spam filtering. It describes the feature selection, case retrieval and case-base editing techniques used.

In a CBR learner the examples in the training data are represented as cases in the case-base. In ECUE each email is a case represented as a vector of attributes or features. Cases are set up with binary features implemented as Boolean values. If the feature exists in the email then the case assigns the feature a value of *true*, otherwise the value of the feature is *false*. It is more normal in text classification for lexical features to carry frequency information but our evaluation showed that a binary representation works better in this domain. We expect that this is due to the fact that most email messages are short and frequency information may result in overfitting.

4.1 Feature Selection

The features for each case were identified using a variety of generic lexical features, primarily by tokenising the email into words. The emails were not altered to remove HTML tags and no stop word removal, stemming or lemmatising was performed. Email attachments were removed. Since the datasets were personal it was felt that certain headers may contain useful information, so a subset of the header information was included in the tokenisation. No domain specific features were included at this stage although previous work has indicated that the efficiency of filters can be enhanced by their inclusion [6].

Tokenising 1000 emails results in a very large number of features, (tens of thousands of features). Feature selection is necessary to reduce the dimensionality of the feature space. We used Information Gain (IG) [28] to select the most predictive features as it has been shown to be an effective technique in aggressive feature removal in text classification [29]. Our cross validation experiments, varying between 100 and 1000 features across 4 datasets, indicated best performance at 700 features.

4.2 Case Retrieval

The system uses a k-nearest neighbour classifier to retrieve the k most similar cases to a target case. The standard k-NN algorithm individually calculates the similarity of each case in a case-base to the target case. This approach is quite inefficient in domains where there is feature-value redundancy and/or missing features in cases. Because our spam cases have both of these characteristics we use an alternative similarity retrieval algorithm based on CRNs which facilitates efficient and flexible case retrieval. The CRN is equivalent, in the cases it retrieves, to the k-nearest neighbour algorithm but, particularly in this situation, is more computationally efficient.

Cases are stored within the CRN as *case nodes*. A second type of node called an *Information Entity (IE) node* represents a single feature-value pair, e.g. "viagra=true" indicating the presence of the word (feature) "viagra" within a case. Case nodes are linked to the IE nodes that represent them using *relevancy arcs*. Each relevancy arc can have a weight that reflects the importance of that IE node or feature-value pair. CRNs also have the notion of *similarity arcs* between similar feature values but this is not used in ECUE as the features are all binary.

A target case activates the CRN by connecting to the IE nodes, via relevance arcs, that represent the values of its features. This activation spreads across the net to the case nodes, each of which accumulates a score appropriate to its similarity to the target case. The case nodes with the highest activations are those most similar to the target case.

Figure 1 illustrates our CRN for spam filtering. As the features in our case representation are binary, IE nodes are only included for features with a *true* value. The relevancy arcs are all weighted with a weight of 1.

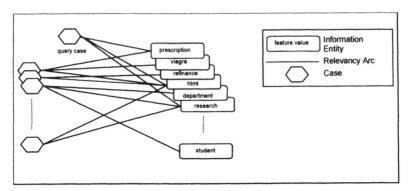

Figure 1 The CRN for spam filtering

A serious problem for spam filters is the occurrence of False Positives (FP), legitimate emails classified incorrectly as spam. An FP is significantly more serious than a False Negative (FN) (a spam email incorrectly classified as legitimate). For many people the occurrence of FPs is unacceptable. Due to this fact, the classifier used unanimous voting to determine whether the target case was spam or not. All neighbours returned had to have a classification of spam in order for the target case to be classified as spam. This strongly biases the classifier away from FPs.

4.3   Case-base Management

The approach to concept drift that we are applying is instance selection. Over time the case-base needs to be updated to include new types of spam and non-spam emails. Given the volume of emails that a single email user may get each week, there is a need to actively manage the training data. Our previous work on case-base editing techniques identified a method of case-base editing that uses the competence characteristics of a case-base to remove noisy and redundant cases. This method is called Competence-Based Editing (CBE) [30].

CBE initially builds a competence model of the case-base identifying for each case its competence properties, i.e. those cases that it contributes to classifying correctly and those it contributes to misclassifying. The technique is then a two-stage process. Using these competence properties the first stage, the competence enhancement stage, identifies and removes noisy cases. The second stage, the competence preserving stage, identifies and removes redundant cases (i.e. cases in the middle of a large cluster of cases of the same classification). The advantage of our case-editing method applied to the spam domain is that it results in a conservative pruning of the case-base which we found resulted in larger case-bases but better generalisation accuracy than typical case-editing techniques [30].

5 Evaluation

This section presents our evaluation of ECUE. Our results are presented at two levels. Firstly, we present an evaluation of the performance of the system at the first level of learning, i.e. simply updating the case-base with new examples of spam and legitimate email. Secondly, we evaluate the performance of the system when a model rebuild (i.e. when the feature selection process is redone) is carried out periodically. The evaluations were offline evaluations using emails collected over an extended period of time.

5.1 Experimental Setup

A key objective was to evaluate the performance of a CBR spam filter over a period of time to see how it handled the concept drift inherent in spam. Two datasets were used. The datasets were derived from two corpora of email, each corpus was derived from the emails sent to individuals over a period of approximately eighteen months. Dataset 1 is a collection of emails received by one individual up to and including December 2003 and Dataset 2 is a collection of emails received by a different individual up to and including January 2004. The legitimate emails include a variety of personal, business and subscribed mailing list emails. The emails were ordered in date order.

A training set of 1000 cases, 500 spam emails and 500 legitimate emails, was set up for each dataset. This training data included the last 500 spam and non spam emails received up to the end of February 2003 in the case of Dataset 1 and up to the end of January 2003 in the case of Dataset 2. This left the remainder of the data for testing. Table 1 shows the profile of the test data across each month for both datasets.

Table 1 Profile of the testing data

		Feb '03	Mar	Apr	May	Jun	Jul	Aug	Sep	Oct	Nov	Dec	Jan '04	Tot
Data Set 1	spam		629	314	216	925	917	1065	1225	1205	1830	576		8902
	non spam		93	228	102	89	50	71	145	103	85	105		1076
Data Set 2	spam	142	391	405	459	406	476	582	1849	1746	1300	954	746	9456
	non spam	151	56	144	234	128	19	30	182	123	113	99	130	1409

A case-base was set up for each training dataset using the feature selection process described in Section 4.1 with 700 features in each case. The classifier used was k-nearest neighbour with $k = 3$ using unanimous voting as discussed in Section 4.2. Each email in the testing datasets, documented in Table 1, was presented for classification in date-received order to closely simulate what would happen in a real-time situation. Results were accumulated and reported at the end of each month.

5.2 Evaluation Metrics

Since an FP is more serious than an FN, accuracy (or error) as a measure of performance, does not give the full picture in that there is no transparency with regard to the numbers of FPs and FNs occurring. Two filters with similar accuracy may have very different FP and FN rates.

Previous work on spam filtering uses a variety of measures to report performance. The most common performance metrics are precision and recall [10]. Sakkis *et al.* [5] introduce a weighted accuracy measure which incorporates a measure of how much more costly an FP is than an FN. Although these measures are useful for comparison purposes, the FP and FN rate are not clear so the true effectiveness of the classifier is not evident. For these reasons we will use the rate of FPs, the rate of FNs, and the average within class error rate, $Error = (FPRate + FNRate)/2$ as our evaluation metrics. A final justification for using this set of metrics is that it is in line with how commercial spam filtering systems are evaluated on the web and in the technical press [31].

5.3   CBR vs. Naïve Bayes

As Naïve Bayes appears to be the machine learning technique of choice for spam filtering (see Section 2) we compared ECUE with a Naïve Bayes classifier [32], the results of which are summarised here.

Experiments on a number of static datasets, (subsets of those described in Section 5.1) showed that neither one of the two classifiers Naïve Bayes or the CBR classifier outperformed the other consistently [32]. These results appear to confirm other findings on static datasets [4]

Of more interest were the evaluations performed over a period of time allowing the system to dynamically update its training data with examples of spam and legitimate email that were incorrectly classified. A number of experiments were performed, varying from making no updates to the original case-base training data to updating an edited case-base on a monthly, weekly and daily basis with those emails that were misclassified over the specified period. Case-base editing used the CBE technique discussed in Section 4.3. Our evaluation showed the best performance occurred when updating an edited case-base on a daily basis with any emails misclassified that day. These results are presented in Figure 2.

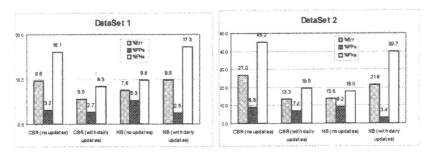

Figure 2 CBR vs. Naïve Bayes with dynamic updating

The same experiments were performed using a Naïve Bayes classifier on unedited training data. The training data could not be edited for the Naïve Bayes classifier as the editing technique is a competence-based editing technique which uses a *k*-NN classifier to determine the competence of each case in the case-base and analyses the competence properties of the cases to determine which cases should be removed. Due to the significance of FPs, the Naïve Bayes classifier was configured to be biased away from false positives by setting the classification threshold to 1.0. Figure 2 includes the results of using Naïve Bayes.

Although Naïve Bayes has a better overall error rate over the dataset as a whole with no updating, the CBR system performs better in both datasets when dynamically updating the data to learn from incorrectly classified emails. It can be seen that daily updating of the training data with misclassified emails improves performance of the CBR system but has an overall detrimental effect on the Naïve Bayes classifier. Naïve Bayes with daily updates does improve the FP rate more significantly than ECUE but the degradation of the FN rate has an overall negative effect on performance. It is worth noting that updating a system using Naïve Bayes with any new training data requires a separate learning process to recalculate the probabilities for all features. Updating a CBR system, such as ECUE, with new training data simply requires new cases to be added to the case-base.

5.4 Level 1 Learning – Continuous Updating with new Instances

The objective of this evaluation was to examine at a detailed level the performance of the system with continuous updating of an edited case-base with the misclassified emails. The detailed results are presented in Figure 3 as (*edited cb, daily updates*). In order to illustrate the performance improvements offered by case-base editing and continuous updating, Figure 3 also includes the results of the full training case-base (*full cb, no updates*) and the edited case-base (*edited cb, no updates*) when applying all the test data in date order with no updates. Finally, for comparison purposes, Figure 3 includes a more typical window-based updating procedure (*full cb, window-based daily updates*). The original (unedited) case-base of 1000 cases was used and at the end of each day those cases that had been misclassified were added to the case-base. Then the window-based update procedure was achieved as follows; for each case that was added, remove the oldest existing case of the same classification.

The graphs in Figure 3 illustrate a number of things:

- The concept drift in the data is evident in both datasets (*full cb, no updates*).
- Although case-base editing does not show a decrease in error in Dataset 2, the decrease in FPs is significant which is crucial for this domain.
- Updating the edited case-base daily with misclassified cases shows a significant improvement in overall average error across classifications in both datasets and overall FP performance is improved in both datasets.
- Although the overall FP rate is better for window-based updates than for updates to the edited case-base for Dataset 2, it is considerably worse for Dataset 1. The average error across classifications (taking into account the FN rate) is better for updates to an edited case-base across both datasets.

An issue with continuous updating on the edited case-base is case-base management; although the editing process reduces the case-base size initially the size of the case-base grows each month. For Datasets 1 and 2 the editing process reduces the initial training case-bases to 741 and 575 cases respectively. However, the resulting size of the case-base after all the data has been applied (i.e. after 10 months for Dataset 1 and 12 months for Dataset 2) is 1512 and 2518 respectively. The advantage of the window-based update procedure is that the case-base remains at 1000 cases always.

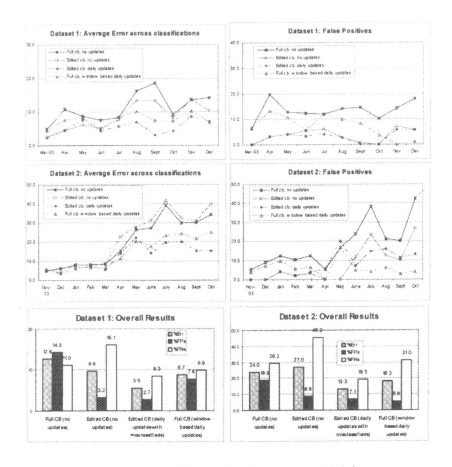

Figure 3 Results of First Level Learning - Continuous Updating

5.5 Level 2 Learning – Model Rebuild with Feature Reselection

Our next experiments involved evaluating whether the next level of learning (periodically reselecting features) improved the performance gains that we had achieved by continuous updating with misclassified cases. This level of learning involves a complete model rebuild. We chose to reselect features at the end of every 3-month period. At the reselect date, a new training set of 1000 emails was constructed. This training set consisted of the last 500 spam and 500 non-spam emails received up to the reselect date. Features were selected from this training set using the same feature selection process described in Section 4.1 above. A case-base was built from this training set and was edited using CBE. Emails for the next 3 months were classified against this new case-base.

Figure 4 presents the results of applying feature reselection to both daily updates on an edited case-base and to window-based daily updates.

The graphs in Figure 4 illustrate the following results:

- Incorporating a periodic feature reselection and model rebuild reduces the average error across classifications for both daily update procedures.
- Applying daily updates to an edited case-base and including 3 monthly feature reselection results in lower error rates than using a daily window-based update procedure with feature reselect.
- Although the error rates reduce in all cases with feature reselection, there is no consistent improvement in FP rate for either update technique.

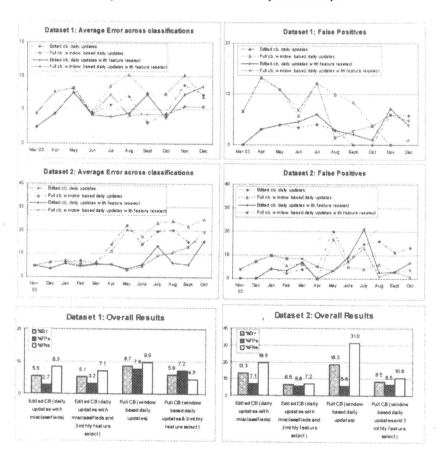

Figure 4 Results of Second Level of Learning – Feature Reselection

An advantage of including the feature reselection and case-base editing procedure for daily updates is that it controls the size of the case-base. Table 2 shows the size of the case-base after each feature selection and case-editing process occurred on the two datasets. In all but one situation, the edited case-base has not increased over the 3-month period beyond the size of the original case-base (1000 cases). Thus, the frequency with which feature reselection is performed can be configured to manage the size of the case-base.

Table 2 Case-base sizes during evaluation with feature reselection

Dataset 1		Dataset 2	
Case-base size after feature select & edit	Size after 3 months of updates	Case-base size after feature select & edit	Size after 3 months of updates
741	821	575	652
718	842	628	736
678	1055	661	845
719	798 (after 1 month)	580	971

6 Conclusions

We have shown that using a lazy learner can handle the concept drift inherent in email spam data. Our approach is to update the case-base at the end of each day with cases that were misclassified by the system that day and to periodically rebuild the case-base using the most recent cases to reselect features. This approach performs better than the typical window-based approach at both levels of model update.

A further level of learning, to define new domain specific features is also available to our system and will be evaluated in future work. The implementation of ECUE (due to the CRN) will allow new features to be included in cases to be added to the case-base at times other than model rebuilds. However, since our model rebuild involves full feature extraction and reselection, it may not be necessary to exploit the potential of the CRN to integrate cases based on different feature sets.

Future work in this area will also include a comparison of our approach to concept drift with the more common ensemble approach to handling concept drift.

References

1. Spira J. Spam E-Mail and its Impact on IT Spending and Productivity, Basex Report 2003, http://www.basex.com/poty2003.nsfl
2. Lenz M, Auriol E, Manago M. Diagnosis and Decision Support. In: M. Bartsch-Sporl, H. D. B., and Wess, S. (eds) Case-Based Reasoning Technology: From Foundations to Applications, Springer-Verlag, 1998 LNCS 104
3. Androutsopoulos I, Paliouras G, Michelakis E. Learning to Filter Unsolicited Commercial E-Mail. Tech rpt 2004/2, 2004, NCSR "Demokritos", http://www.iit.demokritos.gr/skel/i-config/publications/
4. Androutsopoulos I, Koutsias J, Paliouras G, Karkaletsis V, Sakkis G, Spyropoulos C, Stamatopoulos, P. Learning to filter spam e-mail: A comparison of a naive Bayesian and a memory-based approach. In: 4th PKDD Workshop on Machine Learning and Textual Information Access. 2000
5. Pantel P, Lin D. SpamCop: A spam classification and organization program. In: Learning for Text Categorization—Papers from the AAAI Workshop, Madison Wisconsin, 1998, 95–98. AAAI Technical Report WS-98-05

6. Sahami M, Dumais S, Heckerman D, Horvitz E. A Bayesian Approach to Filtering Junk Email. In: AAAI-98 Workshop on Learning for Text Categorization. Madison ,Wisconsin. 1998, 55-62, AAAI Technical Report WS-98-05.

7. Androutsopoulos I, Koutsias J, Konstantinos V, Chandrinos V, Paliouras G, Spyropoulos C. An evaluation of Naive Bayesian anti-spam filtering, In: Potamias G, Moustakis V, van Someren M (eds.) Proc. of the ECML 2000 Workshop on Machine Learning in the New Information Age, 2000, 9-17

8. Drucker HD, Wu D, Vapnik V. Support vector machines for spam categorization. IEEE Transactions On Neural Networks, 1999 10(5) 1048–1054

9. Kolcz A, Alspector J. SVM-based filtering of e-mail spam with content-specific misclassification costs. In: Proc. of TextDM'2001, IEEE ICDM-2001 Workshop on Text Mining, San Jose CA 2001.

10. Gee K.R. Using Latent Semantic Indexing to Filter Spam. In: Proc. of the 2003 ACM Symposium on Applied Computing (SAC), ACM, 2003, 460-464

11. Sakkis G, Androutsopoulos I, Paliouras G, Karkaletsis V, Spyropoulos C, Stamatopoulos P. A Memory-Based Approach to Anti-Spam Filtering for Mailing Lists. Information Retrieval 2004 6(1) 49-73

12. Carreras X, Marquez L. Boosting trees for anti-spam email filtering. In: Proc. 4th Int. Conf. on Recent Advances in Natural Language Processing 2001 Tzigov Chark, Bulgaria.

13. Sakkis G, Androutsopoulos I, Paliouras G, Karkaletsis V, Spyropoulos C, Stamatopoulos P. Stacking classifiers for anti-spam filtering of e-mail. In: (ed) Lee & Harman , Proc. of 6th Conf. on Empirical Methods in Natural Language Processing 2001, 44-50

14. Widmer G, Kubat M. Learning in the presence of concept drift and hidden contexts, Machine Learning 1996 23 (1) 69-101

15. Stanley K.O. Learning concept drift with a committee of decision trees, Tech. Report UT-AI-TR-03-302, Dept of Computer Sciences, University of Texas at Austin, USA, 2003

16. Widmer G, Kubat M. Effective learning in dynamic environments by explicit context tracking, In: Proc. ECML 1993, Springer-Verlag, LNCS 667, 1993, 227-243

17. Kubat M, Widmer G. Adapting to drift in continuous domains, Tech. Report ÖFAI-TR-94-27, Austrian Research Institute for Artificial Intelligence, Vienna, 1994

18. Salganicoff M. Tolerating concept and sampling shift in lazy learning using prediction error context switching, AI Review, Spec. Iss. on Lazy Learning, 1997 11 (1-5) 133-155

19. Klinkenberg R. Learning drifting concepts: example selection vs. example weighting. Intelligent Data Analysis, Special Issue on Incremental Learning Systems Capable of Dealing with Concept Drift, 2004 8 (3) (to appear)

20. Cunningham P, Nowlan N, Delany SJ, Haahr M. A Case-Based Approach to Spam Filtering that Can Track Concept Drift. The ICCBR'03 Workshop on Long-Lived CBR Systems, Trondheim, Norway, 2003

21. Schlimmer JC, Granger RH. Incremental learning from noisy data, Machine Learning, 1986 1(3):317-354

22. Harries M., Sammut C., Horn K., Extracting hidden context, Machine Learning, 32(2), 1998, 101-126.

23. Street W, Kim Y. A streaming ensemble algorithm (SEA) for large-scale classification, Proc. 7th ACM SIGKDD Int. Conf. on Knowledge Discovery and Data Mining KDD-2001, ACM Press, 2001, 377-382

24. Wang H, Fan W, Yu PS, Han J. Mining concept-drifting data streams using ensemble classifiers. In: Proc. 9th ACM SIGKDD Int. Conf. on Knowledge Discovery and Data Mining KDD-2003, ACM Press, 2003, 226-235

25. Kolter JZ, Maloof MA. Dynamic weighted majority: a new ensemble method for tracking concept drift. In: Procs. 3rd IEEE Int. Conf. on Data Mining, IEEE CS Press, 2003, 123-130

26. Hulten G, Spencer L, Domingos P. Mining time-changing data streams. In: Proc. 7th Int. Conf. on Knowledge Discovery and Data Mining, ACM Press, 2001, 97-106.
27. Aha DW, Kibler D, Albert MK. Instance-Based Learning Algorithms. Machine Learning, 1991 6:37-66
28. Quinlan J Ross. C4.5 Programs for Machine Learning. Morgan Kaufmann Publishers, San Mateo, CA, 1993.
29. Yang Y, Pedersen JO. A comparative study on feature selection in text categorization. In: Proceedings of ICML-97, 1997, 412–420
30. Delany SJ, Cunningham P. An Analysis of Case-Based Editing in a Spam Filtering System, In: Proc. of 7th European Conf. in Case-Based Reasoning, ECCBR-04, Springer Verlag, 2004 (to appear)
31. http://www.brightmail.com/accuracy.html
32. Delany SJ, Cunningham P, Coyle L. An Assessment of Case-base Reasoning for Spam Filtering. In: Working papers of 15th Artificial Intelligence and Cognitive Science Conference (AICS 2004), 2004
33. Lewis D, Ringuette M. Comparison of two learning algorithms for text categorization, In: SDAIR, (1994) 81-93.
34. Niblett. Constructing decision trees in noisy domains. In: Proceedings of the Second European Working Session on Learning, Sigma, 1987, 67-78.
35. Kohavi R, Becker B, Sommerfield D. Improving Simple Bayes. In: ECML-97 Proceedings of the Ninth European Conference on Machine Learning. 1997

SESSION 1:

SYNTHESIS AND PREDICTION

Matching and Predicting Crimes

Dr. G.C. Oatley[1], Prof. J. Zeleznikow[2] & Dr. B.W. Ewart[3]

1. School of Computing and Technology, University of Sunderland, UK

2. School of Information Systems, Victoria University, Australia

3. Division of Psychology, University of Sunderland, UK

Abstract

Our central aim is the development of decision support systems based on appropriate technology for such purposes as profiling single and series of crimes or offenders, and matching and predicting crimes.

This paper presents research in this area for the high-volume crime of Burglary Dwelling House, with examples taken from the authors' own work a United Kingdom police force.

Discussion and experimentation include exploratory techniques from spatial statistics and forensic psychology. The crime matching techniques used are case-based reasoning, logic programming and ontologies, and naïve Bayes augmented with spatio-temporal features. The crime prediction techniques are survival analysis and Bayesian networks.

1.   Introduction

The statutory requirement under the *Crime and Disorder Act (1998)* for United Kingdom police and local partnerships to undertake crime and disorder audits and produce strategies based on these audits, has provided a powerful stimulus to the mapping and analysis of crime data. [1] makes the point that the 'recent shift within British policing towards a more decentralised, proactive style has shifted the analytical focus onto analysts and intelligence officers at the police divisional level who are now expected to be the hub of the local intelligence gathering effort. For high volume crime, this has left an analytical void.'

The authors work is in this area is with the high volume crime of Burglary from Dwelling Houses (BDH) though collaboration with West Midlands Police (WMP). Software [2] was developed to interrogate the database of recorded crimes in order to explore the temporal and spatial characteristics of BDH across the entire operational command unit. The objectives were to allow police to test their beliefs about BDH trends and patterns against the empirical realities, thereby providing a more substantive empirical foundation for the development and implementation of preventative and detection strategies. Furthermore, the data provided to the project (representing the time period 1997-2001) was used to develop diverse decision support tools. Sophisticated matching and predictive abilities were developed, based on analysis of the data through techniques from statistics and artificial intelligence guided with concepts from forensic psychology and criminology.

Following a presentation of the data, and some background to initial analysis of this data (Section 2), this paper then discusses crime matching by case-based reasoning (CBR), logic programming and ontologies, and naïve Bayes augmented with spatio-temporal features (Section 3), and the crime prediction techniques of survival analysis and Bayesian networks (Section 4).

2. Data and Initial Analysis

The dataset used by the authors represented approximately three and a half years of data, containing the age and sex of the victim and offender (if known). Each crime was represented by a list of stolen property, the features shown in Table 1, and also various Home Office classifications and internal references. Of particular importance were the date stamp, and grid references (Ordnance Survey 12-number grid system), and the Boolean modus operandi (behavioural) features shown in Table 2.

There are a wealth of approaches that can be taken to this kind of data, from Geographical Information Systems (GIS), spatial statistics, statistics, artificial intelligence and forensic psychology and criminology.

An important first step with geocoded data is the 'pins in maps' approach of plotting in a GIS (for good review papers of crime mapping see: [3,4]) - the authors integrated their own mapping functionality in the final decision support system.

1. Alcohol, cigarettes, foodstuffs 2. Antiques, paintings, china, silverware 3. Audio, radio 4. Auto accessories, fuel 5. Books 6. Building material 7. Cards, cheques 8. Cash, till, safe 9. Clothing 10. Computer 11. Cosmetics, toiletries 12. Documents 13. Domestic appliance 14. Drugs, medical 15. Fancy goods 16. Firearms 17. Furniture non antiques including carpets 18. Garden 19. Jewellery 20. Keys 21. Luggage 22. Office, stamps, stationery 23. Optical, personal 24. Other, toys, musical, pushchair, mail, tack saddle etc., animal, metals 25. Pedal cycle 26. Photographic 27. Purse, wallet 28. Sporting 29. T/v, video 30. Telecom 31. Tools, hardware, plant and equipment 32. Vehicle

Table 1 Stolen property features.

GROUPING	VARIABLES
LOCATION OF ENTRY	1. Wall 2. Adjoining Property 3. Below 4. Front 5. Rear 6. Side 7. Roof 8. Window 9. Door 10. Above
ENTRY METHODS AND BEHAVIOUR	Smash 2. Cut 3. Cutting equipment 4. Duplicate Key 5. Drill 6.Force 7. Remove Glass 8. Ram 9. Insecure door/window 10. Climbed
TYPE OF DWELLING	1. Old 2. Terrace 3. Maisonette 4. Bungalow 5. Semi-detached 6. Town House 7. Flat
SEARCH BEHAVIOUR	1. Untidy Search 2. Downstairs Only 3. Many Rooms 4. Upstairs Only 5. Tidy Search 6. Search All Rooms
LOCATION OF EXIT	1. Wall, 2. Adjoining Property 3. Below, 4. Front 5. Rear 6. Side 7. Roof 8. Window 9. Door 10. Exit Same as Entry
ALARM/PHONE	1. Cut Phone 2. Tamper with Alarm 3. Alarm Activated
BOGUS OFFICIAL CRIME	Social Services 2. Bogus Official (type unknown) 3. Council 4. DSS 5. Home Help 6. Gardener 7. Other 8. Water 9. Police 10. Distraction Bogus Crime

Table 2 Modus operandi features.

Additions to simple plotting of crime locations were visual inspection of the data using Gaussian (bell-shaped) *kernel-based approximation* for the probability density function (see [5]), and the forensic psychology idea of '*prevalence, incidence and concentration*' [6].

Another very useful algorithm used was the spatial statistics check for *complete-spatial-randomness* (CSR) using *quadrat methods*. As the name suggests, CSR determines whether a set of spatial data is completely random and is the standard model against which a spatial point pattern is compared. The reasons for beginning an analysis with a test for CSR are that the rejection of CSR is a prerequisite for any serious attempt to model an observed pattern. CSR acts as a dividing hypothesis between regular and clustered patterns. Our experiments across offender data resulted in a CSR value ranging between 1.7 to 2.2 for all reasonable set quadrat sizes, indicating a high degree of clustering. In comparison the *k-function* on the same data indicates clustering at a low level but not at higher levels.

The interested reader is directed to the freely available *CrimeStat*[1] [7] software, which provides an introduction to many spatial data algorithms. Also, the Bayesian software *WinBUGS* is able to import spatial data (maps) in three common GIS formats (ArcInfo, Splus and EpiMap).

The data mining algorithms of association rules, CART trees and classification rules (from decision trees) - with or without dimensionality reduction - indicated either no significant relationships or relationships that are too complex to determine using these methods. However, feature selection for Kohonen neural networks used to cluster offenders, flagged the following variables as discriminating: 'entry-' and 'exit point', 'entry method', 'victim sex', and 'search strategy'. At face value these would be expected to be important. What may appear to be surprising is that there are no significant property stolen types listed. In a similar vein an analysis of Sunderland West Police Force data by the authors [8] showed that there was little evidence for the theory that offenders wait for certain items of property to be replaced by insurance companies and then strike again.

The statistical method of Multidimensional scaling (MDS) was postponed until a more restricted number of features had been determined – however interesting work using this approach can be found in [9].

3. Matching Crimes

The ability to link or match crimes is important to the Police in order to identify potential suspects. Pease [10] asserts that 'location is almost never a sufficient basis for, and seldom a necessary element in, prevention or detection', and that non-spatial variables can, and should be, used to generate patterns of concentration. To date, little has been achieved in the ability of 'soft' forensic evidence (e.g. the burglar's modus operandi) to provide the basis of crime linking and matching, and this section describes recent work [11] which investigates crime matching based upon the combinations of locational data with behavioural data.

3.1 Single Crimes with Similarity-Based Retrieval

A retrieve-and-propose CBR system [12] incorporated four different similarity metrics – *k-nearest neighbour* (KNN), *Tversky's contrast model* (TC), and the *cosine* and *modified-cosine rule matching functions* (CR and MCR) – see [13]. The cosine rule includes the benefit of *local* weighting

---

[1] *CrimeStat®* is a spatial statistics program for the analysis of crime incident locations, developed by Ned Levine & Associates under grants from the National Institute of Justice (grants 1997-IJ-CX-0040 and 1999-IJ-CX-0044).

for attributes, where the weight is dependent upon each particular case. Tversky's model extends the nearest neighbour algorithm and cosine rule approaches and includes a contrast between attributes that match and those that do not. [13] proposed a modification to the cosine similarity metric, which not only includes local weighting, but also computes a contrast.

The aim then was to compare the differing treatment of local and global features, and also the importance of a contrast between differing feature representations.

The case base for our experiments consisted of modus operandi, property stolen, time and location features - for each crime where the offender was known (1140 cases). In this way we propose an offender for an unsolved crime by retrieving the most similar previous crime. Four feature selection algorithms were used - Best-First, Forward Selection, Decision Table and Genetic Search – using the WEKA data mining tool.

The rank position of each offender was determined against their own crime (ideally they should be retrieved with rank position 1), and the average rank across all offenders was the measure by which to compare the similarity performance – this is admittedly a very simple metric, which does not consider the bias introduced by offenders committing varying numbers of crimes.

The results were that CR and MCR produced very similar similarity ratings. However, MCR discriminates better with ranking - average mean and median rank was always higher for all feature sets. Surprisingly KNN and TC produced the same average similarity and rank, and thus perform equally well, and they always (across all feature sets) produced higher average similarity ratings and rankings than CR and MCR. The data consisted solely of globally weighted Boolean features, and each case was measured across the same features in query and case base (no contrast). It is expected that the modified methods (especially MCR) would be more useful when the data representation is more complex. The features selected are under review also, as is the most appropriate way to weight the features.

An important consideration in this domain is that time stamping crime is difficult as the time of occurrence, for instance of a burglary or motor vehicle theft, may not be known exactly. Therefore, it is useful to view crime events as singularities of variable length along the time line. Approaches from the forensic psychology literature include the 'aoristic' [14] approach for two events X and Y, with operators such as [XbeforeY|XequalsY|XmeetsY|XstartsY|XendsY|XoverlapsY|XduringY]. This has been seen previously in the artificial intelligence literature as Aamodt's implementation of Allens' [15] temporal system in the long-established Creek semantic network-based case-based reasoning system (see [16]).

3.2 Naïve Bayes Classifier and Spatio-Temporal Features

For these experiments modus operandi (MO), temporal and geographic information on the detected burglaries (n=966) attributable to specific offenders (n=306) was used. The ability of three algorithms to match a target crime to the actual offender is evaluated. The first (RCPA) uses only MO information, the second (RPAL) only temporal and geographic data and a third algorithm (COMBIN) is a combination of the two.

The RPAL algorithm represents spatio-temporal information and is the product of *recency*, *prolificness* and *actual location* data on each crime. *Recency* is the distance in time between any previous crime and the considered crime, while *prolificness* represents the amount of previous crimes committed by an offender before the considered crime. *Actual location* is the Euclidean distance between any previous crime and the considered crime.

Each RPAL equation included parameters that were assigned values drawn from empirical findings within the literatures of forensic psychology and criminology, but were also the subject of optimisation experiments using a genetic algorithm[2]. For instance in Equation 1 for *recency*, there are three parameters that can be optimised. Similar equations for *prolificness* and *actual location* containing parameters that were optimised can be found in [24]. The objective functions used to determine the fitness of a solution considered the number of times an offender occurs in the top 30 for his/her own crime. The value 30 was based upon the value of 29 determined by previous studies [17] and represents a 'reasonable' number of offenders to search through.

Empirical or *naïve Bayes* approach (see [18]) was used for the classifier using the MO and property stolen features. Naïve Bayesian classifiers assume the effect of an attribute value on a given class is independent of the other attributes. This assumption is made to simplify computations – hence the use of the word naïve.

The general approach involves creating a matrix containing all of the crimes for all offenders, with the presence or absence of the behavioural features represented as Boolean attributes. Interpreting this matrix enabled the matching of new crimes against all the offender data.

Optimisation was also carried out over the 105 modus operandi and 32 property stolen features, using the *GAlib* genome *'GA1DBinaryStringGenome'* with each bit in the string representing the presence or absence of the feature.

$$t_{crime} \neq t_{last\_offence\_before\_crime}$$

---

[2] The optimization was carried out using the C++ genetic algorithm library *GAlib* [Wall, 1996]

$$Recency = \begin{cases} PARAM\_RECENT\_SCALE / t_{crime} - t_{last\_offence\_before\_crime}; & \text{Crime occurring today} \quad [1] \\ PARAM\_RECENT\_CLOSEST; & \text{No last crime} \\ PARAM\_RECENT\_TINY; \end{cases}$$

Where:

$PARAM\_RECENT\_SCALE=28;$

$PARAM\_RECENT\_CLOSEST=56;$

$PARAM\_RECENT\_TINY=0.0001.$

In Table 3, the ranks are presented by the RCPA, RPAL and COMBIN models for each of the three offender groups (SDs are in parenthesis).

The RPAL and COMBIN each achieve a perfect match for 24% of the crimes. For prolific offenders, matching using MO information alone is better than temporal and geographic data, although the best performance is achieved when in combination.

Model	RCPA	RPAL	COMBIN
Group 1 (committed 1-5 crimes)	195.96 (88.42)	406.26 (158.17)	35.07 (24.86)
Group 2 (committed 6-10 crimes)	35.10 (9.28)	181.45 (117.25)	12.62 (8.69)
Group 3 (committed over 10 crimes)	13.73 (7.92)	84.02 (84.41)	7.53 (7.57)

Table 3 Mean retrieval ranks.

Combining the algorithms RPAL and RCPA with their different properties within this forensic domain is an extemporized process. The lessons of this work should be used to guide the formal evaluation of such processes in the future.

3.3 Matching Series of Crimes with Logic

Several commercial systems perform link analysis, for instance *COPLINK* [19] and *FLINTS* - 'Forensic Led Intelligence System' [20]. Recent work by the authors in this area uses a logic programming language (Prolog) to generate flexible matching facilities. The data were converted into Prolog facts, such as offender('20E1/4441/98',m,14,193), where the first attribute is a reference to a crime, then sex, age, and unique offender identifier.

The property stolen and modus operandi data were converted into ontologies to permit generalization of matching, for instance 'cash' and 'cheques' can be generalized to 'money'. The ontologies are imported into the SWI-Prolog environment as RDFS. The benefit of using such an ontology (which is essentially a set of predicates) is that it is easy to view and adapt in an editor such as Protégé, and to engage a domain expert in its construction [21].

In this manner the logic programming paradigm gives an extremely flexible way of querying and examining the data. Consider the way that a *series* of crimes can be determined. To be a member of a series each crime in the list has to be *linked* with another by some 'location_link', 'property_stolen_link', 'property_description_link', 'time_link' and 'gang_link'. An example of the former is where two crimes are within a certain geographical area. The 'gang_link' is slightly more complex, locating crimes where two or more offenders were caught, offenders who obviously know each other. Several networks of offenders can be found, who either know each other directly ('strong' offenders) or through intermediary links with other offenders ('weak' offenders).

Based on these predicates it is simple to determine a series, given the set of all the links - all that remains are that the links are ordered chronologically. This then provides the data miner the possibility of examining the features of crimes in the series, also of finding out all crimes carried out by a gang, and determining an appropriate metric for crime matching. As well as being able to relax the 'friendship' (strong_offender_friends or weak_offender_friends), it is also possible to relax the criteria for 'property_stolen_link' (i.e. move up one step in the ontology), relax the geographical search area, and relax the time period between crimes. Of course all of these 'relaxing' criteria are not equivalent, and it might be pertinent on one occasion to relax the geographic catchment area, however on another occasion relax the property stolen criteria, or gang-membership.

This work is in its early stages, and it is clear that development of this approach for exploratory purposes will need to closely tie in with development with the graphical user interface.

[22] describe the benefits in using such an inductive logic programming approach to identify complex relational patterns that might indicate terrorism threats in large amounts of relational data. They have tested their approach on 'nuclear smuggling' and 'contract killing' data to great success, although optimizing the performance is an issue that is still to be addressed with large datasets.

4.   Predicting Crimes

There exists very little literature about predictive models for police decision support (see [23]).   Crime prediction with the West Midlands data is motivated by the observation that using officially reported burglaries, most houses are victimised only once and most repeat victims are 'hit' twice only in a 12 month period.   If police wait until the second victimisation, it appears from official statistics that it would be too late – the likelihood of a third burglary is small. The first issue described in this section is survival analysis which [24] used to explore if modus operandi distinguishes houses burgled once only from those suffering a revictimisation. This is important to the implementation strategy of both preventative and detection resources. The second issue described in this section is a Bayesian belief network, which predicts the likelihood of burglary as a combination of varying kinds of forensic information.

4.1   Survival/Failure Time Analysis

Survival/failure time analysis, developed primarily in the health sciences, deals with the issue of censored observations, which arise whenever the dependent variable of interest represents the time to a terminal event, and the duration of the study is limited in time. For example, it is possible to study the 'survival' of victims of a given crime, given the current point in time.   Binary logistic regression with the *'Single victimisations'* and *'First in a series of victimisations',* as the dependent groups were executed with the set of crime scene variables of Tables 1 and 2.

Comparing non repeats with 'quick' repeats (i.e. within 365 days), the use of force, searching behaviour, type of property, place of entry, place of exit, alarm activation and use of bogus official strategy are discriminating features.   In this way we are able to identify the features of a 'first' burglary which are predictive of a revictimisation. Survival analysis was employed to examine if a burglar's behaviour could be used to identify which properties within this high risk group were likely to be burgled 'sooner rather than later'   Examining the proportions of the group that are revictimized within specified time intervals reveals the temporal pattern of repeat burglaries. This is represented at each time period by the *hazard rate* and the *probability density*.   The former is of the *rate* of being revictimized at the midpoint of a time interval, while the latter is *probability* of being revictimized by the midpoint. [25] found the risk of a repeat was highest within a month (28 days) of the first crime. To facilitate comparison, the time intervals here are taken in increments of 56 days. Cox regression examines the association of modus operandi variables and the timing of revictimizations.   The period (in days) to the second victimisation is the 'survival time' while the crime scene variables are the covariates. Separate analyses are conducted for each group of variables. Nineteen properties were revictimised on the same day (i.e. within hours of the first burglary) and so have a survival time of zero days. These would normally be dropped by SPSS as they have non positive time values. Their inclusion was achieved by giving each a time value of one day.

The highest probability of revictimization occurs within the first time interval. The probability of not surviving (i.e. being revictimized) to the mid point of the 0-56 day interval is 0.0058. The two subsequent intervals each have a probability density of 0.0026. The lowest probability of repeat burglaries is found in the longest interval beginning 336 days from the first crime.

Interval Start Time (in days)	No. of Properties Entering the Interval	No. of Properties Suffering a Repeat During the Interval	Probability Density	Hazard Rate
0	606	196	.0058	.0069
56	410	87	.0026	.0042
112	323	87	.0026	.0056
168	236	63	.0019	.0055
224	173	66	.0019	.0084
280	107	73	.0022	.0185
336	34	34	.0010	.0357

Table 4 Probability densities and hazard rates of revictimization.

In Table 4, there are successive 56 day intervals for properties comprising the Twelve Month Repeats group. The rate of reconvictimization is greatest within the longest time intervals. The hazard rate (0.0069) for the shortest time interval is the fourth highest across the seven intervals. The interval beginning at 56 days after the first burglary has the lowest hazard rate (0.0042).

Grouping	Variables	Beta Value	Significance	Mean Time (days) to Revictimization
Entry Methods and Behaviour	7. Remove Glass	-0.57	0.03	P = 73, A=146
	8. Ram	-1.55	0.003	P= 26, A=144

Search Behaviour	6. Search All Rooms	-0.25	0.06	P = 131, A=154
Location of Exit	8. Window	0.35	0.05	P = 168, A=133

Table 5 Crime scene variables which survival analyses reveals are significantly and marginally significantly associated with the time to revictimisation.

Table 5 presents the significant crime scene covariates. The mean time to revictimization is presented for those properties where the variable is present (code P) and for properties where the factor is absent (code A). Ramming and removing glass to gain entry are strongly associated with early revictimisation. A search of all rooms is a marginally significant indicator of relatively early revictimisation. In contrast, exit by a window is significantly associated with a longer period between the first and subsequent burglary.

4.2 Bayesian Network

Bayesian belief networks (see [26]) specify joint conditional probability distributions. They allow class conditional independencies to be defined between subsets of variables. Bayesian belief networks provide a graphical model of causal relationships on which learning can be performed. The developed network can be seen in Figure 1.

'Premise crime history' is the number of previous crimes suffered by this premise. 'Prevalence, incidence and concentration' represent the status of the area. 'Property stolen' had been explored by the Police using a frequency count – with 'AUDIO/RADIO' and 'JEWELLERY' being demonstrated to be the most significant variables. The remaining feature is 'Modus operandi features', which was subjected to analysis through binary logistic regression analysis. The specific details of this approach can be found in [2].

The results of the Bayesian network (for instance calibration) are not presented, indeed this approach has never been validated - this is because it contained so many arbitrary decisions and was intended as a prototype 'proof of principle' demonstration, although considerable thought was given to how this network was embedded in the final decision support system for use by police officers [27].

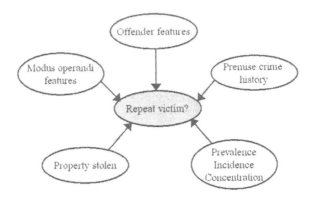

Figure 1 OVER Project Bayesian network.

5. Conclusions and Future Directions

Using a wide range of techniques it is possible to discover useful information to assist in crime matching, not only of single crimes, but also of series of crimes.   Techniques from artificial intelligence (Kohonen networks, logic programming, CBR and feature selection, genetic algorithms and empirical Bayes) and forensic psychology have proven more or less useful, and also differ in requirements for explicit encoding of domain knowledge. Modified cosine rule matching function will be investigated more thoroughly as the case description becomes more complex.

The logic programming approach however has been crafted explicitly for this problem domain and provide great potential for exploring the data, for instance matching *series* of crimes against previous series of crimes. More thought will be given to modelling as ontologies, and the automated generation of ontologies, structures that can more easily engage domain experts.

The RPAL algorithm and offender features are not complicated, but proved very useful in the experiments. Further thought will be made regarding the inclusion of new features.

A desirable feature of an analysis is that it is robust, and none of the approaches we have considered are predictive in any robust sense except survival analysis, naïve Bayes, and Bayesian belief networks. Future work will continue with these, and also look to develop a full Bayesian model. Because of the additionally desirable features of the Dempster-Shafer model of uncertain reasoning, this will also be explored.

Acknowledgements

The authors acknowledge the support of West Midlands Police for data, and Matthew Wall of MIT for GAlib.

References

1. Hirschfield, A., 2001. Decision support in crime prevention: data analysis, policy evaluation and GIS. *In: Mapping and Analysing Crime Data – Lessons from Research and Practice*, A., Hirschfield & K, Bowers (Eds.). Taylor and Francis, 2001, pp. 237-269.

2. Oatley, G.C., & Ewart, B.W., 2003. Crimes Analysis Software: 'Pins in Maps', Clustering and Bayes Net Prediction. *Expert Systems with Applications* 25 (4) Nov 2003 569-588

3. Soomro, T.R., Naqvi, M.,R. & Zheng, K., 2001. GIS: A Weapon to Combat the Crime. In: Proceedings of SCI 2001/ISAS 2001 (International Conference on Information Systems, Analysis and Synthesis): Part I.

4. COPS 2004. Community Oriented Policing Services home page. http://www.cops.usdoj.gov. Online, accessed 2004

5. Bishop. 1995. Neural Networks for Pattern Recognition, Clarendon Press, Oxford.

6. Pease, K., 1998. Repeat Victimisation: Taking Stock. Police Research Group. Crime Detection and Prevention Series, Paper 90. London, Crown Copyright

7. Levine, N., 2002. CrimeStat: A Spatial Statistics Program for the Analysis of Crime Incident Locations (v 2.0). Ned Levine & Associates, Houston, TX, and the National Institute of Justice, Washington, DC. May 2002.

8. Ewart, B.W., Inglis P., Wilbert, M.N. & Hill, I., 1997. An analysis of time intervals of victimisation. *Forensic Update* 50, pp 4-9, 1997

9. Green, E. J., Booth, C. E., & Biderman, M. D. 1976. Cluster analysis of burglary M/O's. *Journal of Police Science and Administration*, 4, 382-388.

10. Pease, K., 2001. What to do about it? Lets turn off our minds and GIS. In: Mapping and Analysing Crime Data – Lessons from Research and Practice, A., Hirschfield & K, Bowers (Eds.). Taylor and Francis, London and New York, 2001, pp. 225-237.

11. Ewart, B.W., Oatley, G.C., & Burn K., 2004. Matching Crimes Using Burglars' Modus Operandi: A Test of Three Models. Forthcoming.

12. Oatley, G.C., 2004. Case-based reasoning (chapter). In: D., Addison & J., MacIntyre (Eds.), Intelligent Computing Techniques; A Review, Springer-Verlag, ISBN: 1-85233-585-8

13. Gupta, K. M., & Montazemi, A. R., 1997. Empirical Evaluation of Retrieval in Case-Based Reasoning Systems Using Modified Cosine Matching Function. Transactions on Systems, Man, and Cybernetics – Part A: Systems and Humans, 27(5), pp. 601-612.

14. Ratcliffe J.H., 2002. Aoristic signatures and spatio-temporal analysis of high volume crime patterns. *J. Quantitative Criminology* Vol. 18, No. 1, March

15. Allen J.F., 1983. Maintaining Knowledge about Temporal Intervals. *Communication of ACM* Vol.26, 123-154, (1983).

16. Jaere, M.D., Aamodt A., & Skalle, P., 2002. Representing temporal knowledge for case-based prediction. In: S., Craw & A., Preece (Eds.) Proceedings of ECCBR 2002, Springer Verlag, LNAI 2416, pp. 174-188

17. Yokota, K., & Watanabe, S., 2002. Computer based retrieval of suspects using similarity of modus operandi. International Journal of Police Science and Management 2002 Vol. 4, Pt. 1, pp. 5-15.

18. Carlin, J.B. and Louis, T.A. 2000. Bayes and Empirical Bayes Methods for Data Analysis (2nd edition), New York: Chapman and Hall.

19. Chen, H., Chung, W., Xu, J.J., Wang, G., Qin, Y., & Chau, M., 2004. Crime data mining: a general framework and some examples. IEEE Computer April 2004, Vol 37, No. 4

20. Leary, R.M. 2003. New Intelligence of the 21st Century: How Smart is it? *Forensic Technology News* November: 6.

21. Noy, N.F., Grosso, W. & Musen, M.A., 2000. Knowledge-Acquisition Interfaces for Domain Experts: An Empirical Evaluation of Protege-2000. Twelfth International Conference on Software Engineering and Knowledge Engineering (SEKE2000), Chicago, IL.

22. Mooney, R.J., Melville, P., Rupert, Tang, R.T, Shavlik, J., Dutra, I., Page, D., & Costa, V.S., 2004. Inductive Logic Programming for Link Discovery. In: H. Kargupta, A., Joshi, K., Sivajumar, & Y., Yesha (Eds.), Data Mining: Next Generation Challenges and Future Directions, AAAI Press, 2004

23. Oatley, G.C., MacIntyre, J., Ewart, B.W., & Mugambi, E., 2002. SMART Software for Decision Makers KDD Experience. *Knowledge Based Systems* 15 (2002) 323-333.

24. Ewart, B.W., & Oatley, G.C., 2003. Applying the concept of revictimization: using burglars' behaviour to predict houses at risk of future victimization. *International Journal of Police Science and Management* 5 (2) 2003

25. Polvi, N., Looman, T., Humphries, C., & Pease, K., 1991. The Time Course of Repeat Burglary Victimization. *British Journal of Criminology* 31 (4) 411-414

26. Pearl, J., 1988. Probabilistic Reasoning in Intelligent Systems: Networks of Plausible Inference. Morgan Kaufmann Publishers, Inc, 1988.

27. Zeleznikow, J., 2002. Designing decision support systems for crime investigation. In: *Proceedings. of the Fifth International Conference on Forensic Statistics (ICFS5)*, Isola di San Servolo, Venice, Italy, August 30 - September 2, 2002

Story Plot Generation based on CBR

Pablo Gervás, Belén Díaz-Agudo, Federico Peinado, Raquel Hervás

Dep. Sistemas Informáticos y Programación, Universidad Complutense de Madrid

Madrid, Spain

{pgervas,belend}@sip.ucm.es,fpeinado@fdi.ucm.es,

Abstract

In this paper we present a system for automatic story generation that reuses existing stories to produce a new story that matches a given user query. The plot structure is obtained by a case-based reasoning (CBR) process over a case base of tales and an ontology of explicitly declared relevant knowledge. The resulting story is generated as a sketch of a plot described in natural language by means of natural language generation (NLG) techniques.

1 Introduction

With the advent of information technology, many domains have achieved productivity improvements due to the introduction of computers. The film industry has seen some of its tasks radically affected – like the generation of special visual effects, or the computer assisted animation. On related work areas, such as the generation of film scripts, there has been no comparable improvement. A number of films in industry have benefited from IT tools for script-writing, such as and Dramatica[1] or WritePro[2], but there has been little progress towards automation of the process of draft generation.

Automatic construction of story plots has always been a long standing goal in the entertainment industry, specially in the more commercial genres that are fuelled by a large number of story plots with only a medium threshold on plot quality, such as TV series or video games. Although few professionals would contemplate full automation of the creative processes involved in plot writing, many would certainly welcome a fast prototyping tool that could produce a large number of acceptable plots involving a given set of initial circumstances or restrictions on the kind of characters that should be involved. Subsequent selection and revision of these plot sketches by professional screen writers could produce revised, fully human-authored valid plots.

In this paper we present a system for automatic story generation that reuses a case base of existing stories to produce a new story that matches a given user query. The plot structure is obtained by a case-based reasoning (CBR) process over the case base and an ontology of explicitly declared relevant knowledge (Section 3). The resulting story is generated as a sketch of a plot described in natural language by means of natural language generation (NLG) techniques (Section 4).

---

[1] http://www.screenplay.com/products/dpro/index.html
[2] http://www.writepro.com/

2 Related Work

This section, outlines previous relevant work on story generation and natural language generation applied to narrative texts.

2.1 Computational Plot Generation

There have been various attempts in the literature to obtain a computational model of story generation by considering the role of planning in story generation. Tale-Spin [15], IDA (I-Drama Architecture) [13] and Fairclough and Cunningham [9] explore with different approaches the way in which plot generation can be interpreted as a planning process.

Of the various approaches to plot generation, some have applied CBR explicitly to the plot generation process. Minstrel [19] included a CBR process to model the creative process of generating a story line. Fairclough and Cunningham [9] developed an interactive multiplayer story engine that applies case-based planning and constraint satisfaction to control the characters and make them follow a coherent plot. In [4] poetry generation is chosen as an example of the use of the COLIBRI system. COLIBRI assists during the design of KI-CBR systems that combine cases with various knowledge types and reasoning methods. It is based on CBROnto [6, 7], an ontology that incorporates reusable CBR knowledge, including terminology plus a library of reusable Problem Solving Methods (PSMs).

Our work is based on ideas from the work of Vladimir Propp [17]. Propp derives a morphological method of classifying tales about magic, based on the arrangements of "functions". This provides a description of the folk tales according to their constituent parts, the relationships between those parts, and the relations of those parts with the whole. The main idea is that folk tales are made up of ingredients that change from one tale to another, and ingredients that do not change. According to Propp, what changes are the names - and certain attributes - of the characters, whereas their actions remain the same. These actions that act as constants in the morphology of folk tales he defines as *functions*. For example, some Propp functions are: Villainy, Departure, Interdiction, Interdiction Violated, Acquisition of a Magical Agent, Guidance, Testing of the hero, etc. There are some restrictions on the choice of functions that one can use in a given folk tale, given by implicit dependencies between functions: for instance, to be able to apply the *Interdiction Violated* function, the hero must have received an order (*Interdiction* function).

There have been various attempts to apply this work to story generation. The GEIST project [10] uses a simplified version of Propp's morphology. Fairclough and Cunningham's [9] interactive multiplayer story engine operates over a way of describing stories based on Propp's work.

2.2 Natural Language Generation

The most natural format for presenting a plot to users is narrate it in natural language. Obtaining a high quality natural language text for a story is itself a subject of research even if the plot is taken as given [3]. This paper is considered a first approximation to the overall task, and it focuses on the interface between the CBR module and the NLG module.

Recent overviews of NLG [18] define a number of basic tasks to be carried out when generating a natural language text: *content determination* - finding what to say -, *document structuring* - organizing what is to be said -, *sentence aggregation* - grouping together the parts that allow it -, lexicalization - selecting the words that will realize each concept -, *referring expression generation* - choosing the right expression to refer to each element in its actual context - and *surface realization* - turning the result into a linear natural language sentence. Different solutions can be applied to resolve each of this tasks.

Text generation in this paper is done by means of NLG based on templates. Texts follow conventionalized patterns which can be encapsulated in *schemas* [14], template programs which produce text plans. Schemas are derived from a target text corpus by breaking them up into messages, organising the messages into a taxonomy, and identifying how each type of message is computed from the input data.

The specific architecture of the NLG module presented here is implemented using cFROGS [1], a framework-like library of architectural classes intended to facilitate the development of NLG applications. cFROGS identifies three basic design decisions: what set of modules to use, how control should flow between them, and what data structures are used to communicate between the modules.

3 A CBR System for Composing Plot Plans

The plot generation module of the system presented here is based on a Knowledge Intensive CBR approach to the problem of generating story plots from a set of cases consisting of analyzed and annotated fairy tales. Our system operates in two phases: an initial one that applies CBR to obtain a plot plan from the conceptual description of the desired story provided by the user, and a final phase that transforms the resulting plot plan into a textual rendition by means of template based NLG. Readers interested specifically in the plot generation process are referred to [5], where this initial stage is described in detail. This section provides only a brief outline of those parts of the plot generation process that are relevant to the NLG module.

3.1 The System Knowledge

Knowledge representation in our system is based on a basic ontology which holds the various concepts that are relevant to story generation. Propp's character functions are used as basic recurrent units of a plot. In order to be able to use them computationally, they have been translated into this ontology that gives semantic coherence and structure to our cases [16]. This initial ontology is subject to later extensions, and no claim is made with respect to its ability to cover all the concepts that may be necessary for our endeavour.

We have implemented this ontology using the last release of the Protégé ontology editor that was developed at Stanford University [8]. It can manage ontologies in OWL [2], a new standard that has recently reached a high relevance. The choice of OWL as a representation language provides the additional advantage, that it is designed to work with inference engines like RACER [11].

Although the functions of the *dramatis personae* are the basic components, we also have other elements. The ontology also provides the background knowledge required by the system, as well as the respective information about characters, places and objects of our world.

The ontology is used to complement the specific knowledge of the cases, and it is used by the CBR system to measure the semantical distance between similar cases or situations, and maintaining an independent story structure from the simulated world. The domain knowledge of our application is the classic fairy tale world with magicians, witches, princesses, etc. The current version of the ontology contains a number of basic subconcepts to cover this additional domain knowledge that needs to be referred from within the represented function. Next we summarize the most important concepts of our ontology.

- **Propp functions.** Propp's character functions act as high level elements that coordinate the structure of discourse. Each function has constraints that a character that is to perform it must satisfy. The contents of a function are the answers to the Wh-questions: what, when, where, who (the characters of the function) and why.

- **Moves.** Morphologically, a tale is a whole that may be composed of *moves*. A move is a type of development proceeding inside the history, and it can refer different Propp's functions. One tale may be composed of several moves that are related between them. We represent tales and their composing moves using structured descriptions. A tale is related with an ordered sequence of complete moves. We represent the temporal sequence between these moves using the CBROnto temporal relations.

- **Character.** The roles in the story must be filled by characters (for instance, who performs a function). Each character is defined by a set of relationships with other characters, objects in his possession, location... These characters are one of the elements that the user can choose to customize a story.

- **Properties of the characters** By properties or attributes of the characters, we mean the totality of all the external qualities of the characters: their age, sex, status, external appearance, peculiarities of this appearance, dwelling (described by a relation with a place),... These attributes provide the tale with its brilliance, charm and beauty. However, one character in a tale is easily replaced by another (permutability law) [17].

- **Roles.** Propp describes a number of 'spheres of action' that act as roles that certain characters have to fulfill in the story (like villain, hero,..).

- **Places and objects.** Certain locations (outdoors, indoors, countries, cities...) and symbolic objects (towels, rings, coins...) can be significant to

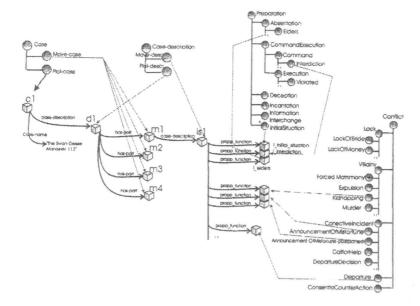

Figure 1: Case Structure

the way a story develops, and any sort of substitution during adaptation must take this into account. Our ontology must have the ability to classify such locations and objects.

- **Descriptions.** Since our system generates text by filling in templates with selected descriptions that correspond to instances of particular concepts, it was considered convenient to have these descriptions represented in the ontology in such a way that their relations with the relevant concepts can also be modelled and the inference mechanisms available can be employed in their selection.

- **Cases.** Cases are built up of a selection of stories from the original set of the Afanasiev compilation originally used by Propp. Within the defined case structures we represent the plots of the fairy tales. Cases are described with attributes and values that are pre-defined, and structured in an object-oriented manner (see Figure 1).

We facilitate the case structure authoring tasks by proposing a framework to represent cases that is based on the CBROnto terminology. Besides, we define a reasoning system (based on generic CBR PSMs) that works with such representations [7].

Cases are built based on CBROnto case representation structure [6, 7] using the vocabulary from the domain ontology. The semantic constraints between scene transitions are loosely based on the ordering and co-occurrence constraints established between Proppian functions.

As an example of the type of stories that are being considered, the following outline of one of the tales that Propp analyses is given below [3]. The main events of the plot are described in terms of character functions (in bold) :

> *The Swan Geese (113 of Afanasiev Collection).* **Initial situation** (a girl and her small brother). **Interdiction** (not to go outside), **interdiction violated, kidnapping** (swan geese take the boy to Babayaga's lair), **Competition** (girl faces Babayaga), **Victory, Release from captivity, Test of hero** (swan geese pursue the children), **Sustained ordeal** (children evade swan geese), **Return.**

3.2 The CBR Module

We use the descriptive representation of the tale plots with a CBR system, that retrieves and adapts these plots in several steps and using the restrictions given in the query.

3.2.1 Query specification, similarity assessment and case retrieval

We propose an interactive case retrieval process taking into account progressive user inputs. A query determines some of the components of the tale we want to build. For example, its characters, descriptive attributes, roles, places, and the Propp functions describing the actions involved in the tale. The system retrieves the more similar case with the restriction of Propp morphology and characters available. As CBROnto provides with a general test-bed of CBR methods we have made different tests with different similarity measures between the complex descriptions that represents the plots [7].

Each retrieved case constitutes a plot-unit template. The retrieved case components are *hot-spots* (or flex points) that will be substituted with additional information obtained from the context, i.e. the query, the ontology and other cases, during the adaptation process. Similarity measures should guarantee that (when possible) all the query elements are valid elements to be allocated in the retrieved cases.

For instance, let us say we want a story about a *princess*, where **murder** occurs, where an **interdiction** is given and **violated**, there is a **competition**, and a **test of the hero**. We can use that information to shape our query. The system retrieves the case story number 113, Swan-Geese (described earlier).

Retrieval has occurred using structural similarity over the ontology (described in [7]) because the structure of this story satisfies straight away part of the conditions (interdiction, competition, test of hero) imposed by the query. No murder appears, but there is a *similar* element: a kidnapping. **Kidnapping** and **murder** are similar because they are different types of villainies; so, they are represented as children of the same concept **Villainy** in the ontology (see Figure 2).

---

[3]Complete text in http://gaia.sip.ucm.es/people/fpeinado/swan-geese.html

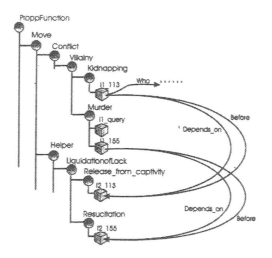

Figure 2: Substitution example

3.2.2 Adaptation

The retrieval process provides with the plot skeleton where the system makes certain substitutions. More creative results may be achieved by generating a solution as a mixture of the ingredients from various cases. During the adaptation of our *plot case*, we use additional retrieval steps (defining adequate queries) over the case base of *move cases* (that are part of the plot cases, see Figure 1) to find appropriate substitutes maintaining the dependencies and temporal relations.

In our example, the system should suggest an adaptation where **murder** is substituted for the **kidnapping**. However, the **kidnapping** in the retrieved case has *dependencies* with the **release from captivity** that appears later on (which is a **liquidation of lack** according to the ontology) (see Figure 2). To carry out a valid adaptation, the adaptation process is forced to define a query and retrieve cases in which **murder** appears with a *similar* dependency (i.e. dependency with another **liquidation of lack**).

The following case is retrieved (only a part of which is relevant to the issue):
> (*155 of Afanasiev Collection*). (...) **Absentation** of the hero (brother goes hunting), **Deception** of the villain (beautiful girl entices him), **Murder** (girl turns into lioness and devours him), (...) **Consent to counteraction** (other brother sets out), **Competition** (faces beautiful girl), **Victory** (kills lioness), **Resurrection** (revives brother), **Return**.

In this case there is a dependency between the **murder** and the **resuscitation**. The adaptation system can therefore substitute the kidnapping-release pair in the first retrieved case with the murder-resuscitation pair in the second,

cf0 Initial situation (a knight and his beloved princess).	what: ∅ where: l0 who: (ch0,ch1)
cf1 Interdiction (not to go forest).	what: action(ch2,ch1,s0,warn), (clause(s0,rep,neg), action(ch1,x,l1,go)) where: l0 who: (ch2,ch1)
cf2 Interdiction violated	what: action(ch1,l1,go) where: (l0,l1) who: (ch1)
cf3 Murder (a lioness devours her)	what: action(ch3,ch1,devour) where: l1 who: (ch3,ch1)
cf4 Competition (knight faces the lioness)	what: action(ch0,ch3,face) where: l1 who: (ch0,ch3)
cf5 Victory (kills lioness)	what: action(ch0,ch3,kill) where: l1 who: (ch0,ch3)
cf6 Resurrection (revives the princess)	what: action(ch0,ch1,resurrect) where: l1 who: (ch0,ch1)
cf7 Return	what: action(ch0,l0,return) where: (l1,l0) who: ch0

Table 1: Plot plan for *The Lioness (new fairy tale)*.

obtaining a better solution for the given query. Additional adaptations can be carried out to substitute the hero of the first case (the girl) or the prisoner (the boy) for the princess specified in the query.

The resulting plot, showing how the two cases are combined, could be a story like the one shown in Table 1. Details are discussed in the next section.

4 The Natural Language Generation Module

Processing the plot plan in order to obtain a readable rendition of it involves operations like joining sentences together wherever this gives more fluency to the text, substituting character identifiers for pronouns or definite descriptions wherever appropriate, or selecting specific words to use in realizing templates whenever options are available. The NLG involved in this process is simple, based on templates rather than a full grammar. However, it provides a marked improvement in the readability of resulting texts.

4.1 Input Data for the NLG Module

If the CBR process of the first stage has taken place successfully, the second stage will accept as input a data structure satisfying the following constraints:

- The case that has been selected during retrieval, has been pruned or combined with other cases retrieved during adaptation and strung into a case sequence that makes up a plot skeleton.

- The character functions, acting as templates for the basic units of the plot, have been filled in during adaptation with identifiers for the characters described in the query

We will refer to it as a *plot plan*. A plot plan is structured in terms of instances of character functions. Each instance of a character function contains references to specific instances of other concepts in the ontology. To avoid ambiguity problems during processing, each instance of a concept in the ontology must have a unique identifier. Table 1 presents an example of the plot plan for the result obtained by the CBR module for the example discussed earlier. For readability, wh-questions that are not directly relevant to the plot have been ommitted. Cross indexing with instances in the ontology is indicated by an identifier (cf* for character functions, l* for locations, ch* for characters...).

The amount of information available in the ontology for the various concepts now involved in the plot plan is very large. Additionally, rendering such a story into text must take into account contextual dependencies that arise progressively as subsequent character functions are described in sentences. For these reasons, transcription of the plot plan into text is broken down into small fragments of text corresponding to single character functions.

Each character function is processed separately. When processing a given character function, the NLG module accesses only the information available in the ontology corresponding to:

1. The instance of the character function that appears in the text

2. The instances of all elements of the ontology that appear in the instantiation of the character function

3. The instances of all elements of the ontology that appear in the instantiations in 2.

Let us take the cf3 instance of the *Murder* character function appearing in Table 1 as an example. The following information about it, provided by the CBR module by navigating the ontology according to the above rule, is available to the NLG module:

- The events related with this character function take place at some location: an instance of *location* that is a dark forest outside the castle

- Two *characters* are involved: a lioness and the princess

- The lioness has the following *atributes*: she plays the *role* of villain in the story, she is hungry and fierce, and she lives in the forest

- The princess has the following *atributes*: she plays the role of *victim* in the story, she is blonde and pretty, has parents, is in love with a knightt, and lives in the castle

All this information is processed by the *Conceptual Representation* stage of the cFROGS architecture, and the required data are converted into an internal

Table 2: Output of the stages of the NLG module

Content Determination	Discourse Planning	Sentence Aggregation
character(ch1,princess) character(ch3,lioness) location(l1,forest) role(ch3,villain) attribute(ch3,hungry) attribute(ch3,fierce) action(ch3,ch1,devour)	character(ch3,lioness), attribute(ch3,hungry) character(ch3,lioness), attribute(ch3,fierce) character(ch3,lioness), character(ch1,princess), action(ch3,ch1,devour)	character(ch3,lioness), attribute(ch3,hungry), attribute(ch3,fierce) character(ch3,lioness), character(ch1,princess), action(ch3,ch1,devour)

Ref. Expression Gen.	Lexicalization	Surface Realization
character(ch3,lioness), ref(ch3,def), attribute(ch3,hungry), attribute(ch3,fierce) character(ch3,pron), character(ch1,princess), ref(ch1,def), action(ch3,ch1,devour)	"lioness" "a" "hungry" "fierce" L(x)+" was "+L(y)+" and "+L(z) "she" "princess" "the" L(x)+" devoured "+L(y)	"The lioness was hungry and fierce." "She devoured the princess.".

representation Draft data structure chosen by the designers. This data structure presents the advantage of allowing simultaneous representation at multiple levels – for instance semantic representations, documental representations, and rhetorical representations.

Some text has been generated before this character function, which acts as the context in which it will appear in the final story. To deal with this, the NLG module also keeps a record of the results of processing all previous character functions of the same plot. This is stored as an additional Draft data structure, containing the *discourse history*. This discourse history is initially empty, and it is stored by the NLG module and updated each time a new character function is processed.

4.2 Stages of the NLG Module

The NLG module carries out its task in six stages: content determination, discourse planning, sentence aggregation, referring expression generation, lexicalization, and surface realization. Each one of these stages corresponds to a basic task in rendering the instance of the character function as text. An example of the output at each stage for our example is presented in Table 2.

4.2.1 Content Determination

This stage checks the information that is available for the given instance of the character function against a record of the semantic information that has already been rendered as text for previous character functions of the same plot plan. Its main goal is to filter out of the rendition of the present character function the information that has already been conveyed in the rendition of the previous ones.

Because the discourse history is represented as a Draft data structure, the system has access to the semantic information that acted as input in previous character functions, even though they have already been processed into text.

For the example character function described above, a lot of the information available will have already been imparted in the transcription of earlier character functions, and so is filtered out of the contents to be processed for the current one. For instance, most of the information about the princess will already be known to the reader at this stage and is ommitted. The lioness, however, enters the story at this stage, and so will have to be described. The location is not new either, since the princess moved there in the previous character function, so its description will be ommitted.

4.2.2 Discourse Planning

The discourse planning stage has to organise all the information that has been selected as relevant into a linear sequence, establishing the order in which it is to appear in the final text.

This is achieved by means of simple heuristics that give priority in the sequence to some concepts of the ontology over others. For instance, whenever they are all to be included in a text rendition, characters are treated first, then location, then any relatives of the character are mentioned, then objects present are mentioned, then finally the actions in the character function are narrated. For the example above, the available information is reordered according to the heuristic.

4.2.3 Sentence Aggregation

This stage takes care of regrouping any elements in the current draft that may be aggregated to provide better fluency of the text. The algorithm employed looks for concepts appearing as object of similar verb constructions that occur adjacently in the discourse plan, and substituting them for a single verb construction with a plural object.

In the example, the system spots a possible rhetorical grouping of two of the entries, joining the descriptive facts about the lioness as a conjunction.

4.2.4 Referring Expression Generation

This stage checks the current version of the draft against the lexical information already used in the rendition of any previous character functions of the same plot plan. The goal is to ensure that each instance of a concept appearing in the current character function is referred to in terms that: (1) are sufficient for the reader to identify with the current one any previous appearances of the same concept, and (2) are not exactly the same as those used in the immediately preceding sentence, to improve the fluency of the text.

Few alternatives are available for a system handling limited world information such as ours. The current version of this stage focuses on substitution of nouns for pronouns whenever the name has recently been mentioned in the text. The window of occurrence that is contemplated is restricted to a character function unless there is a possibility of confussion.

An additional task handled at this stage is selection of definite or indefinite articles to accompany singular nouns. Following Heim [12], a simple mechanism is implemented that opts for indefinite articles whenever the referent has not appeared before in the story and definite articles everywhere else.

For the example, a definite article is used for the lioness in her first appearance, because she has already been mentioned earlier. The following reference to her uses a pronoun. The princess is given a definite article because she has already appeared (not a pronoun, since earlier occurrences where in other character functions).

4.2.5 Lexicalization

This stage selects words to describe the concepts involved in the current draft. Depending on the different syntactic roles that concepts are associated to, the actual terms to be used can be of three types:

- Concepts that are static object (characters, locations, objects...) are associated to specific lexical terms

- Concepts that involve verbs (whether introduced explicitly by instances of character functions or implicitly required to provide linguistic structure to descriptions of available static objects) are associated with templates corresponding to the structure of the sentences to be built with them

- Concepts related to linguistic features (definite/indefinite markers, pronouns...) are given the correct form

Templates partly solve the need for having an explicit grammar, but the ontology provides the required information to solve issues like number and gender agreement.

The example presents the type of lexical elements identified for the instances under consideration.

4.2.6 Surface Realization

This stage is in charge of using the terms selected in the previous stage to fill in the templates. Additionally, it carries out a basic ortographic transformation of the resulting sentences. Templates are converted into strings formatted in accordance to the orthographic rules of English - sentence initial letters are capitalized, and a period is added at the end.

5 Conclusions

Although the system is not fully-implemented yet, the progress so far points to a reasonable solution for Story Generation. Our approach follows the lines of structuralist story generation, which distinguishes it from more transformational work [15, 13]. Unlike the uses of Proppian functions described for other systems [9], our approach represents character functions with more granularity. This allows the establishment of relations between characters and attributes and the functions in which they appear. Dependencies between character functions are modelled explicitly, so they can be checked and enforced during the process of plot generation without forcing the generated plots to be structurally equivalent to the retrieved cases.

The heuristics currently used for the NLG module are intended as tentative approximations, and further work is planned in which the results of the system are evaluated for readability by means of reading tests by a group of volunteer users. The heuristics would then be refined to achieve maximal user satisfaction.

The system architecture is general in as much as one accepts Propp's set of character functions as complete. In the face of disagreement, the ontology is easy to extend, and, as mentioned before, it is not intended to be complete as it is. Under these conditions, the approach described in this paper may be extend to work in other domains.

In future work we intend to address the possible interactions between the two stages. Once these issues have been solved, the integration of the generator with software applications for script writing – along the lines of classics - such as Dramatica and WritePro- can be contemplated.

Acknowledgements

The work was partially funded by the Spanish Committee of Science & Technology (TIC2002-01961). The third author is supported by a FPI Predoctoral Grant from Complutense University of Madrid.

References

[1] R. H. and P. Gervás. Using design patterns to abstract a software architecture for natural language generation. In S. Juknath and E. Jul, editors, *ECOP 2004 PhD workshop*, 2004.

[2] S. Bechhofer and F. van Harmelen et al. OWL web ontology language reference. W3C http://www.w3.org/TR/2004/REC-owl-ref-20040210/, 2004.

[3] C. B. Callaway and J. C. Lester. Narrative prose generation. *Artificial Intelligence*, 139(2):213–252, 2002.

[4] B. Díaz-Agudo, P. Gervás, and P. González-Calero. Poetry generation in COLIBRI. In S. Craw and A. Preece, editors, *ECCBR 2002, Advances in Case Based Reasoning*. Springer LNAI, 2002.

[5] B. Díaz-Agudo, P. Gervás, and F. Peinado. A case based reasoning approach to story plot generation. In *ECCBR'04*, Springer-Verlag LNCS/LNAI, Madrid, Spain, 2004.

[6] B. Díaz-Agudo and P. A. González-Calero. An architecture for knowledge intensive CBR systems. In *Advances in Case-Based Reasoning - (EWCBR 2000)*. Springer-Verlag, 2000.

[7] B. Díaz-Agudo and P. A. González-Calero. A declarative similarity framework for knowledge intensive CBR. In *Procs. of the (ICCBR 2001)*. Springer-Verlag, 2001.

[8] J. G. et al. The evolution of Protégé: An environment for knowledge-based systems development. Technical report, Stanford University, 2002.

[9] C. Fairclough and P. Cunningham. A multiplayer case based story engine. In *4th International Conference on Intelligent Games and Simulation*, pages 41–46. EUROSIS, 2003.

[10] D. Grasbon and N. Braun. A morphological approach to interactive storytelling. In M. Fleischmann and W. Strauss, editors, *Artificial Intelligence and Interactive Entertainment, Living in Mixed Realities*, 2001.

[11] V. Haarslev and R. Moller. *RACER User s Guide and Reference Manual Version 1.7.7*. Concordia University and Univ. of Appl. Sciences in Wedel, November 2003.

[12] I. Heim. *The Semantics of Definite and Indefinite Noun Phrases*. PhD thesis, University of Massachusetts, 1982.

[13] B. Magerko. A proposal for an interactive drama architecture. In *AAAI Spring Symposium on Artificial Intelligence and Interactive Entertainment*, Stanford, CA, 2002. AAAI Press.

[14] K. R. McKeown. The text system for natural language generation: An overview. In *20th Annual Meeting of the ACL*, pages 261–265, 1982.

[15] J. R. Meehan. Tale-spin and micro tale-spin. In R. C. Schank and C. K. Riesbeck, editors, *Inside computer understanding*. Erlbaum Lawrence Erlbaum Associates, Hillsdale, NJ, 1981.

[16] F. Peinado, P. Gervás, and B. Díaz-Agudo. A description logic ontology for fairy tale generation. In *Language Resources for Linguistic Creativity Workshop, 4th LREC Conference.*, Lisboa, Portugal, 2004.

[17] V. Propp. *Morphology of the Folktale*. University of Texas Press, 1968.

[18] E. Reiter and R. Dale. *Building Natural Language Generation Systems*. 2000.

[19] S. R. Turner. Minstrel: A computer model of creativity and storytelling. Technical Report UCLA-AI-92-04, Computer Science Department, 1992.

Studying Continuous Improvement from a Knowledge Perspective

Dr. Steve Davison
Mimica Limited
steve.davison@mimica.co.uk
www.mimica.co.uk

Dr. John L. Gordon
Applied Knowledge Research Institute
john@akri.org
www.akri.org

John A. Robinson
BAE SYSTEMS
john.a.robinson@baesystems.com
www.baesystems.com

Abstract

This paper describes a project undertaken at BAE SYSTEMS to study the process of Continuous Improvement (CI) from a knowledge perspective. We used the Knowledge Structure Mapping (KSM) technique to identify ways of managing the underlying knowledge resource in order to share and disseminate best practice and thereby increase the effectiveness of CI on site. A secondary goal was to investigate the potential for applying KSM to other areas of the business. We provide background to the project, a discussion of the approach taken along with initial results and conclusions.

1.   Introduction

This paper concerns a project undertaken at BAE SYSTEMS to study the way that Continuous Improvement (CI) is actually implemented by staff in a particular work cell. CI is a strategic activity within a business that faces major competitive pressures to reduce manufacturing costs and timescales, whilst increasing quality and productivity. This study was intended to supplement its knowledge about how CI is currently working and how CI itself could be improved. Traditional process studies tend to focus on what happens and less so on how it happens, the latter being the focus of this novel study.

Knowledge Structure Mapping (KSM) is the main technique that we use within the framework of a Structural Knowledge Audit (SKA) [3, 6]. SKA provides a complete methodology within which KSM can be applied with confidence and includes detailed definitions of each of the key stages of an audit, including the important preparatory work that must be undertaken to establish the context for the actual KSM.

1.1 Background for the Study

The Samlesbury Factory in Lancashire is at the heart of Eurofighter Typhoon production. Manufacture in this and almost all other areas of aerospace demands constant innovation and improvement. Technological advances mean that advanced aircraft need to come into service much faster than they used to which means that manufacturing methods and assembly lines need to reach near optimum performance much sooner. Even at these levels, improvements must always be sought and general lessons learned must be studied to provide improved methods for future projects.

CI in aerospace manufacture needs to be more than a manufacturing approach, it needs to be a way of life.

BAE SYSTEMS staff at Samlesbury have, for many years, been closely involved in the work carried out by the Applied Knowledge Research Institute (AKRI), the research arm of Blackburn College. This has meant that the company is fully aware of developments made within AKRI and in many cases has contributed to those developments.

This combination of business need and knowledge research involvement meant that BAE SYSTEMS was able to consider novel approaches to existing problems that had not been tested before.

1.2 Why Apply Knowledge Structure Mapping to Continuous Improvement?

Making a link between KSM and CI may not appear obvious at first sight. However, BAE SYSTEMS were involved in some initial trials of the early work on KSM in 1998 and through its internal improvement processes it is constantly looking for ways to improve. The early trials of KSM in the factory were very successful, leading to significant cost savings in one manufacturing area. BAE SYSTEMS were aware of the developments to KSM that had been achieved since then and therefore the company was in a good position to consider the application of KSM to CI from a well-informed perspective[5].

Part of Eurofighter Typhoon Manufacture is the Advanced Manufacturing Technology (AMT) cell. This cell carries out complex, high technology and high precision automated machining operations on aircraft frames. The cell has a well-motivated staff who are used to adapting to change, solving problems and improving performance to match more and more demanding schedules. The staff from this cell have worked with a CI mentality for some time and have developed their own techniques that are additional to those used within the rest of the factory.

The factory at Samlesbury had also recently appointed a new manager in charge of the development of CI across the site. This meant that CI would be studied with fresh eyes and improvements to CI would be sought.

The four key areas that met to make this project both possible and desirable were in summary:

1. A serious demand for CI and a need to disseminate Best Practice

2. A participatory knowledge of KSM

3. An active and well motivated cell with CI experience

4. A new site wide initiative in CI

An additional factor was that the company could use the project also as an opportunity to evaluate the effectiveness of applying KSM to specific business issues. This was an important additional factor because although KSM had been used successfully several years earlier, this was intended to address a specific business need and no attempt was made at the time to evaluate the approach in a more general business context.

2. The Knowledge Structure Mapping

A Knowledge Structure Map (KSM) is intended to provide several things that support the management and development of a knowledge resource. A KSM also represents an excellent way of studying a concept from a knowledge perspective. Detailed descriptions of KSM, its intended uses and how it supports management have been dealt with in more detail elsewhere [3]. The aim here is to show how a KSM is an appropriate way to study the area of CI.

2.1 Outputs from a KSM Investigation

One of the main claims about a KSM is that it provides people with a way of visualising and taking informed decisions about an invisible asset, a knowledge resource. Within this context, a knowledge resource is considered to be only that knowledge that is contained in the heads of people and not information in books, documents or computer and network systems. A KSM project provides:

1. A map of boxes and connecting links. Each box represents a specific piece of knowledge and each link shows learning dependency.

2. Data about each knowledge node that represents the informed opinion of experts relating to several pre-defined parameters.

3. Analysis of data and map structure using a software tool that provides answers to questions that can be posed based using it range of analytical features.

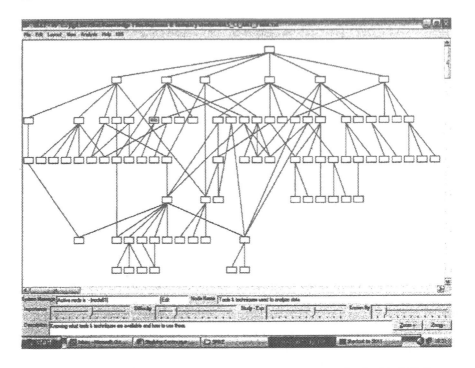

Figure 1 The complete KSM for Continuous Improvement in the AMT Cell.

Figure 1 is a screen shot from the tool 'SKAT' that is used to build, analyse and view KSMs. SKAT is a software tool developed by the AKRI to meet the specific requirements of Knowledge Structure Mapping and analysis. It has a number of features in common with other knowledge acquisition tools, as well as several not available elsewhere. For example, it has a range of sophisticated map layout algorithms that produce a highly readable and logical layout with minimal manual intervention. Overall, it greatly facilitates the mapping and data collection process and saves considerable time in analysing the results. The main part of figure 1 shows the complete KSM for CI from the project. The map is scaled down to fit on the screen and therefore shows no other data such as node names. Text boxes below the map show the name of the node selected on the map (shaded grey) and a brief description of the knowledge represented there. Four sliders provide values for each of four parameters for the selected node. These values were assigned at the interview stage and validated with an overall domain expert who is called a 'knowledge leader' during the project.

Analysis is available through the menu system and either provides data through map colour and shading or through separate graphs, tables and report windows. The map, both electronic version and large A0 plot, the raw data, the analytical outputs and more general observations and recommendations are combined in a final project report. Observations and recommendations concentrate on a knowledge perspective of the study and should not offer advice that is outside the scope of the study. People in receipt of the knowledge centred observations may be helped to integrate this new information with their existing information and knowledge of an organisation or concept.

The report and its associated information and advice are intended to make a difference to the way that the knowledge area is developed and improve performance or protect and develop valuable resource.

2.2　The Value of a Knowledge Centred Approach

It is well known that difficult problems and situations can be enlightened if a different view is taken of them. The 'cognitive interview' used by some police forces for eye-witness testimony, succeeds because it helps people to consider the same scene from many different views and in several different ways. This has been shown to help witnesses recall more information more accurately than for a simple linear interview [1, 4].

In general, organisations take a process approach to their activities, that is they find it relatively easy to discuss what "things" they do, the order in which those things occur and the typical decisions involved in doing one thing instead of another. In contrast, asking businesses what knowledge is applied when doing "something" or making a decision about which of a range of things to do next, is clearly much harder. The knowledge acquisition "bottleneck" is a well known issue in knowledge engineering.

Various knowledge engineering approaches have been devised to address this problem but there remain a number of fundamental issues, not least of which is the perceived threat of such activities to those involved in the exercise. Worries about loss of ownership and reduced job security can be very real barriers to successful knowledge acquisition.

The methodology associated with building a KSM forces a knowledge-based approach but it does this by considering structure, rather than the actual knowledge itself. For example, if you were to develop a KSM for a travel company you would probably find out that knowing what major competitors were offering as special promotions was an important piece of knowledge. An interviewee may or may not actually "have" that particular knowledge and it does not need writing down in detail to be useful. For the purposes of developing a KSM we just need to know that it exists, how it relates to other pieces of specific travel industry knowledge and to collect other data about it such as its importance to the knowledge area in question.

This technique therefore eases the knowledge acquisition bottleneck considerably since interviewees do not have to divulge the detailed knowledge. Secondly, they can contribute even if they don't have the knowledge themselves, they just need to know that it exists. Both of these factors mean that the approach is far less threatening to interviewees, more consistent and reliable. However, we are not suggesting that the approach should replace conventional knowledge engineering techniques. In fact our analysis may point to areas of knowledge that could be most usefully protected or developed using a Knowledge Based Systems (KBS) approach. Developing a KSM can quickly highlight the most appropriate and high risk knowledge areas thereby increasing the potential success of a KBS development.

It achieves this by considering human knowledge acquisition and how new knowledge relies on prerequisite existing knowledge in order to create full understanding. When a KSM is constructed, process is only referred to in order to help the interviewee identify knowledge. Generally, process becomes less and less important as interviews proceed. Therefore, a KSM provides a valuable bridge between the process-oriented perspective common in organisations and the knowledge-centred perspective adopted by knowledge engineering practitioners.

Taking our particular knowledge-centred approach also helps a study to focus. When investigating a concept such as 'problem solving' for instance, it can be difficult to decide how to tackle this, where to start and how to proceed. If the task becomes one of constructing a KSM that shows what you need to know in order to know about problem solving, then the activity becomes very focused, the deliverables assured and the analysis and recommendations follow on logically. Using the method means that there is little difference in producing maps for say, running a country, launching a new product or knowing how to negotiate. All use the same methodology although the necessary resources and expertise may be more difficult to find in certain cases.

3. The CI Investigation

This section will describe how the investigation was carried out and what decisions were taken at the outset and as the study developed. Stages from initial plans to delivery of results will be considered.

3.1 Defining the Study Focus

The drive to initiate discussion about this project came from the on going need to improve Eurofighter Typhoon manufacturing. However, initial meetings took place without a pre-conceived project focus. There were however several management objectives at this stage. These were:

1. To shed new light on the manufacturing activity

2. To focus on the Advanced Manufacturing Technology (AMT) Cell

3. To obtain maximum business benefit from any project undertaken.

Discussion at initial meetings centred on these objectives but it became clear that a parallel objective would also be to evaluate the KSM approach for future projects. During discussion it emerged that there was also a new site initiative to develop a more structured and consistent approach to CI and this was accompanied by the appointment of a new site manager in that post. This lead to the realisation that the AMT cell staff were already developing new approaches to CI and implementing their own version of it.

A study of CI in the AMT cell would satisfy each of the objectives above and also provide a forum to evaluate the KSM approach. It was possible that results from the project could be of benefit across the site and not just within the confines of the AMT cell. This would be made more likely in light of the new managerial appointment.

The remaining task was to firm up the precise quest that the study would follow. This meant deciding precisely what the knowledge related question would be that the map would reflect. The statement entered into the description box of the main (top) knowledge node would be:

What you know in order to understand everything about continuous improvement (CI) in the Advanced Manufacturing Technology Cell (AMT)

The map itself would represent the structure of the knowledge that formed the learning dependency of this top knowledge node. The data collected about each item of knowledge would relate to the focus or top knowledge area.

3.2   Forming the Team

The SKA methodology involves interviewing several experts from the knowledge area in question. The knowledge held by the experts must span the entire knowledge area in question but it need not all be held by one individual. Typically, between 4 and 10 experts are interviewed.

Within this team of experts, it is necessary to identify one individual that will take on the role as 'knowledge leader', a term used only because it was not easy to think up a better one. The knowledge leader has a more general role and also acts as an arbiter to settle conflicts in views and answer questions that arise during the work. The knowledge leader therefore needs to have a good overall knowledge of the whole area and should not have a particular bias such as may result in a person that works in one part of the knowledge area. The knowledge leader therefore usually has some overview or supervisory role across the knowledge area and would also have considerable experience in the area and exposure to it.

Each person will normally be interviewed twice. The first time will be within the whole group and the interview will be a group interview. The second interview will be as an individual contributor. The knowledge leader would also have these interviews but would be seen several more times during and at the end of the interview period to validate data and resolve conflict.

Once the knowledge leader was identified for this project, that person was extremely helpful in identifying appropriate people from the work cell to join the team and be interviewed. This support ensured that the best experts were selected, that the knowledge they held covered the whole knowledge area and provided a balanced view.

There was of course a wider team than this. The additional people had a more strategic interest and were part of the group that identified the project and set the work in motion. This extended team were not interviewed but were actively involved in defining the project parameters and were at the report presentation. This part of the team were also responsible for taking the project findings forward and defining appropriate business response. This could be summarised as the Management/Leadership group.

3.3   The Study Approach

It is not appropriate to outline the complete methodology here but a brief description of the activities undertaken in the data collection phase of the project will be given. The main difficulty with eliciting the information to construct a KSM is that the people that are to be interviewed are not used to thinking about what they do in terms of knowledge. This also means that they do not really know how to respond during interviews and they also are not sure what information is actually being collected. Because of these factors, the first day of project activity is devoted entirely to group sessions where all of the team (not the extended team) must be present.

Initially two presentations are given. The objective of the first is to help the participants to consider knowledge and separate what they think knowledge is from the other things that they know about such as processes. The objective of the second presentation is to explain precisely what will happen during the project, how interviews will be conducted, what information will be collected, how it will be recorded and what the outputs of the project will be. During the same day a group interview is carried out. This group interview has a specific purpose. That is to elicit the top level of the knowledge structure. This top level should completely define the knowledge area so that subsequent interviews elicit knowledge that is prerequisite of the top level nodes but not the target node directly.

This first day prepares the team in several ways. It helps them to refocus on knowledge more easily when their individual interview is carried out. It allows them to see how the map will unfold and what the questions, etc. will be like. It also allows them to think about their own knowledge within the context of the developing map in advance of their interview. When each team member is interviewed separately, there are few surprises. They are also happy with the idea that the map will grow during the interview and that the map will be nearer to its completed form when their interview is finished because of the information they have provided. The map provides a strong focus for the interviews and also records progress in a unique way as a series of incremental graphical snap-shots.

At intervals of two or three interviews, the knowledge leader is asked to consider data such as the relative values that team members have assigned to parameters. The knowledge leader may also be asked to resolve knowledge structure issues such as do you really need to understand 'x' in order to fully understand 'y' or are these really separate pieces of knowledge. Clearly the interviewers are trained in how to pose such questions correctly.

At the start of each interview the interviewee will be updated on the changes that have taken place since that person last saw the map (probably at the group interview). For early interviews, this can easily be done in front of the computer screen but as the map develops, it is more rewarding to print larger intermediate maps to speed up this updating process. At later stages, the interview may be conducted in front of this large plot of the map rather than in front of the computer screen. The last person from the team to see the map during this elicitation phase will be the knowledge leader.

When all data is collected (i.e. 4 key parameters gathered for each node) and the map structure formed, the analytical phase begins.

3.4 Analysing and Evaluating Results

There are three elements that provide data for the analysis. These are:

- A notes file containing relevant knowledge related comment picked up during the interviews

- The numeric data collected during parameter assignment and

- The structural organisation of the KSM.

A report also contains three main elements:

- A results section outlining the actual findings and presenting information from the three elements listed above

- An analysis section where reasons for the data are sought and where data is viewed in combination with other parts of the data

- An observations or recommendations section where higher level observations and conclusions are extracted from the results and analysis. These will be knowledge focused.

Much of the data that is used for the results section of the report is derived directly from the software tool SKAT. This can produce raw data, tables, graphs and comma separated files for import to a spreadsheet. An appendix in the report contains the full data tables of parameters ordered in different ways such as the most important knowledge first or the highest risk knowledge first etc. The results section of the report will contain extracts from these full tables.

The tool also provides some analytical features directly. One of these is the ability to consider how all parameters have been assigned values collectively. This allows managers to consider, for instance, how much of this knowledge area is known by more than 10% of the staff. The other feature is an experimental reporting feature that will be discussed further in the next section. At present, the aim of the tool is to provide as much information as possible so that the person constructing the report is able to do a comprehensive job. Future plans are to increase the support that the tool provides to the analysis and report generation aspects of the work.

3.5 Report Delivery

When the report is complete, the report, a large (A0) KSM colour coded for knowledge risk and any other specific outputs from the work are handed over at a full team presentation. This presentation is a fly through the report with reference to important elements of the work using the tool SKAT. The aim of this presentation is to briefly re-establish the context, quickly present the results, show how the results were analysed and explain the conclusions, observations and recommendations from the work.

The results are usually presented to the extended team that includes all of those involved in the data collection phase and all of those with strategic input and interest. The presentation usually takes about 2 hours including some discussion. Following this a further meeting is held between the people carrying out the work and that part of the team with the strategic view. This meeting is to compare the actual outcomes of the project with the expectations documented before the practical work started. The objective of the meeting is to begin to derive actions that will implement the most relevant findings of the work and consider what difference this will make to the organisation.

4. Project Results

This section will present a flavour for the results, analysis and conclusions only. The work was an actual commercial project and it would be inappropriate to present results in detail, even if space permitted.

4.1 The Results

Typically, the results for this project were primarily taken from SKAT output. A table of the highest risk knowledge is presented here to provide a flavour for these results. Table 1 shows the highest risk knowledge areas from the CI project.

Node-Name	Importance	Difficulty	Study-Exp	Known-By
Identify discreet actions	9	8	9	1
Analyse customer feedback	9	8	9	1
Identify areas for improvement	10	8	9	3
Identifying inefficient actions	7	8	8	0
Individual strengths and weaknesses	9	7	7	0
Encourage involvement and responsibility	9	8	6	0
Maintenance of motivation	10	7	6	0
Team composition	9	5	7	0

Table 1: Highest risk knowledge areas from the CI project

Risk in this instance is calculated from a combination of the parameters shown in the table. The precise meaning of the parameters and the reasons for using these parameters is covered in other work [3].

4.2   Analysis of the Results

The map elicited during this project was not one of the larger maps when compared with other business projects but the information contained within it, non the less revealing. An as yet experimental automated reporting facility in the tool generated the following brief, whole map report.

The knowledge structure map for CI in AMT cell contains 84 nodes and 107 arcs. The map addresses the issue of:- What you know in order to understand continuous improvement (CI) in the Advanced Manufacturing Technology Cell (AMT)

A complexity value of 1.27 for this map is typical of Knowledge structure maps.

There are 14 significant overlapping structures and the most significant of these is the overlap between CI Process and Identify areas for improvement. Other significant overlapping structures include Design Improvements and Identify areas for improvement, CI Process and Design Improvements, CI data analysis and Identify areas for improvement, CI Process and CI data analysis, in order of significance. The integrated nature of this knowledge resource suggests that initiatives to help more people achieve a greater understanding of more of the knowledge area would be effective and rewarding.

This text was derived by the software tool and is presented above without change. It shows that analysis is able to consider knowledge sub areas and how the knowledge within these sub areas may overlap with other sub areas. This can be a very useful analytical facility for managers. The tool is also able to present such information in a more visually acceptable way. This facility is able to generate reports for individual knowledge nodes. A report for one of these nodes is as follows:

> *Node report for - Process*
>
> *This node is situated at map layer 4 of 6 layers.*
>
> *Process shows a significant prerequisite knowledge structure. Process is a knowledge area that is supportive of many other areas. The node is an integrated part of the knowledge structure.*
>
> *Process is a fairly important node that is considered to be very difficult to replace. It is thought to be acquired chiefly from experience with an element of study and is known by quite a number of people from this knowledge area. Because of these factors, Process is an element of knowledge at medium risk within this knowledge area.*
>
> *The following documentation was provided by knowledge area experts during map construction: { The process is the "thing" we are trying to improve. A more general definition of the process rather than an in depth knowledge of every action }*

The analytical capabilities of the tool are still limited but these are the subject of further research and development. The tool does however provide adequate raw data and assistance to support the person responsible for report compilation in his or her work. One of the more novel deliverables from this project was the derivation of a process flow chart for CI. This is not a standard deliverable but was appropriate in this specific case. Each element of the process flow for CI was extracted from the KSM and association between the flow diagram and the KSM made additional contribution to the results and the understanding of the work. This diagram also featured in one of the more concrete recommendations to management that making CI more accessible and explicit in this way would lead to continuous improvement of the CI process itself.

4.3   Observations and Recommendations

The report contained 8 main observations or recommendations. There is not space to include the full details of all of these here but a brief outline will be provided along with a more detailed discussion on one area in particular.

1. Some of the knowledge identified as 'difficult to replace' is also derived chiefly from study. A series of internal dissemination events targeted at the selected knowledge topics would help disseminate this knowledge.

2. The effects of previous attempts by the company to address areas such a motivation and idea generation have been short lived. A programme of incremental input using suggested 'gadgets'[1] could provide continuity and development and therefore sustenance.

3. The study challenges the efficiency of the current reward scheme. The map shows that the scheme requires a considerable knowledge input and therefore it may cost as much as it generates. This should be evaluated.

4. The CI process should also be looked upon as a new knowledge generator. The element missing is a way of recognising this by archiving new knowledge and making it accessible for the future rather than simply implementing the findings.

5. The process that is the target for CI forms a central and integrated part of the KSM and is essential to many other CI knowledge areas. This means that efforts to improve CI are likely to be more effective if carried out internally rather than if external consultants were to take over CI responsibility.

6. The knowledge of 'what things to measure for CI' should be given a higher priority because of its key role. Project findings suggest that staff simply accept this knowledge as a given feature rather than as a feature to be challenged and developed.

7. Many of the more difficult and intangible knowledge areas from the KSM have observational skills as a prerequisite. Currently nothing is done to address this. Input from noted experts in this area, such as the police force, could be valuable.

8. The CI process map derived from the KSM can provide several benefits:

    a. Highlight areas where knowledge development is currently poor.

    b. Highlight areas where the process needs clarification.

    c. Be extended to show how a knowledge resource can be integrated with CI.

    d. Show precisely where company initiatives fit in and their effect.

    e. Enable CI to also become a target for Continuous Improvement.

---

[1] e.g. credit card sized check lists and reminders on approaches to thinking, reasoning and problem solving.

60

One area in particular stimulated most comment and debate. This was the synthesised process map described in the final observation, and shown in Figure 2.

This process diagram gave the company a new insight into CI, demonstrating two clear routes for improvements to come through. Inevitably, because we were not undertaking a process audit directly, there are several areas where the diagram needed improvement. However, it provided new insights into how improvements are developed, and in particular the clear differentiation between systematic, measurement-oriented improvements (the left-hand leg of the diagram) and creative observation-led improvements (the right-hand leg).

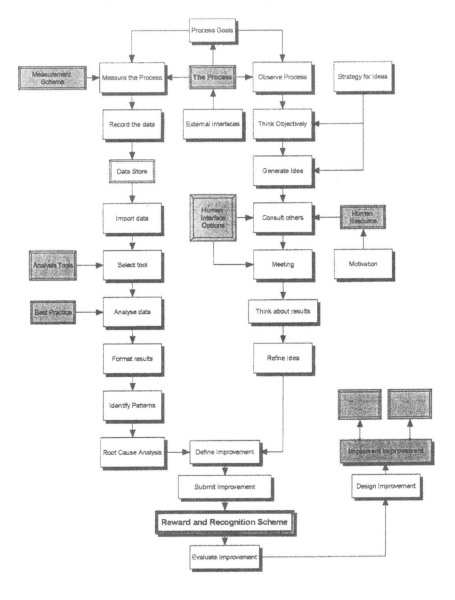

Figure 2 Process map of CI synthesised from a knowledge perspective

5. Initial Business Reaction

A number of the staff involved in the audit were initially sceptical of yet another management *initiative*. This has been encountered in earlier audits and is one of the reasons that great care is given to gaining the support of the team in the earliest stages. Practically, this meant holding a half-day introductory presentation that explained the approach, the aims and objectives of the audit and how individuals would be encouraged to contribute. It cannot be overstated how important this aspect of the audit process is and in the end we not only had enthusiastic contribution from all team members but many had suggestions for other areas where the approach could be applied.

All staff involved in the project found that KSM offered a novel and stimulating approach to the study of an important business issue. Some of the recommendations were in areas where work is already being undertaken, for instance in general staff development. Even so, the analysis provided a valuable alternative perspective on these areas. The audit process itself had several interesting side effects, a key one being that staff became much more aware of existing initiatives, systems and available approaches to solving problems. It also acted as a motivating exercise that stimulated many new ideas outside the immediate remit of the project.

The most immediate area of use for the findings was in the development of the site wide CI programme. In particular, the synthesised process map provided valuable insight into the development of a common process. Feedback from BAE SYSTEMS suggested that the knowledge approach to defining the CI process had uncovered aspects of the process that were not well understood or documented. In particular, developing management support for the more *creative* right-hand route of the process was relevant to the new processes being formalised across the site.

A few weeks after the delivery of the final presentation and workshop, the AMT team requested that we returned to provide more guidance into putting other recommendations in practice. This highlights one of the key aspects of the audit process, which is the need to incorporate recommendations about the knowledge resource into an overall business strategy.

In discussion with the team, a number of recommendations were ruled out for immediate attention on the basis of budget and resource constraints. After further debate three main actions were identified:

1. Feed recommendations into next phase of staff development planning.

2. Develop an A5 card showing the knowledge required by a new machine operator.

3. Develop a more managed and efficient approach to generating and evaluating improvement suggestions.

Another area that is being explored, based on demand from the team, is that of developing a new intranet front-end to engineering documents, indexed and organised according using the structure of the knowledge map generated in the project. This front-end could provide a more logical interface to existing and new documents, making it easier and quicker to locate useful information. As a side effect, the learning dependency structure of the knowledge map, means that new staff should be able to tailor their learning approach to suit their own individual needs, taking into account their existing pre-requisite knowledge.

A significant new project has also been proposed to develop a comprehensive training plan for a new engineering maintenance department. This new department will have approximately 160 staff and hence identifying the detailed training requirements using a systematic approach like SKA could result in significant cost savings and reduced training time.

6. Conclusion

KSM offered a novel and stimulating approach to the study of an important business area as well as highlighting the potential to address a wide range of knowledge focussed business issues. It provided a new perspective on existing problems and also generated some surprising results that caused the team to rethink some of their ideas about how continuous improvement actually works in practice. Encouragingly, the initial scepticism of some team members was replaced by a genuine enthusiasm for the approach and recognition that some results were unlikely to have been found using alternative analytical techniques.

By making the knowledge of the team explicit in the form of a knowledge structure map, it was possible to see:

1. exactly what know-how is being applied in continuous improvement,

2. the extent and complexity of the dependencies and

3. understand where the key risk areas were.

Analysis of the map and other information collected during the audit did give rise to some surprising results, particularly the synthesis of a continuous improvement process from a knowledge-perspective and novel ways in which some business issues could be addressed. This latter category included finding ways to make more effective observations and it was proposed that BAE SYSTEMS seek advice from the police who are highly trained in this area.

One of the most interesting results from the project was the development of a process map for CI that demonstrated clearly that improvements are generated in two distinct ways, which require separate support and encouragement by management. In particular, finding ways to encourage better observation and creative thinking were highlighted as key to this aspect of CI across the site.

Inevitably one must question the cost benefit of any new approach. Actual savings in time, effort and cost will only be achieved by selecting the critical observations and implementing them in the light of current business strategy. Importantly, results from the audit include a detailed set of parameters about the state of the knowledge resource, and these can be re-evaluated continuously to measure improvements over time and therefore the effectiveness of KSM.

This project demonstrated that analysing a problem from a knowledge perspective could both enhance other approaches and provide novel insights into business problems. It was rewarding to see that the AMT team took ownership of the project and its results. It was recognised as being a valuable way of sharing and disseminating know-how as well as stimulating and motivating the team to find new ways to solve problems.

Ultimately, the quantified measures of success will only come about through careful implementation of key recommendations in the final report. This particular part of BAE SYSTEMS have no doubt that in the long term, a strategic commitment to sharing and disseminating know-how using SKA will enhance quality and reduce costs.

References

1. Canter D. Alison L. (eds) Offender Profiling Series: Vol 1 - Interviewing and Deception, Ashgate Publishing Limited, 1999

2. Gordon J.L., Creating Knowledge Maps by Exploiting Dependent Relationships, in Knowledge Based Systems, Vol13, pp71-79, Elsevier Science, 2000

3. Gordon J.L., Creating Knowledge Structure Maps to support Explicit Knowledge Management. Applications and Innovations in Intelligent Systems VIII. pp33-48. Springer, 2000

4. Milne, R., and Bull, R. Back to basics: A componential analysis of the original cognitive interview mnemonics with three age groups. Applied Cognitive Psychology, 16, 1-11, 2002

5. Gordon J.L. Perceptions of the Business Knowledge Resource. Applications & Innovations in Intelligent Systems X. Eds Macintosh, Ellis & Coenen, pp225-246, Springer, 2002

6. Davison, S.J. & D. Hatch (2003), Structural Knowledge Auditing - a novel management process, The Chemical Engineer, Consultants and Contractors File, June 2003.

ReTAX+: A Cooperative Taxonomy Revision Tool

Sik Chun (Joey) Lam, Derek Sleeman, and Wamberto Vasconcelos
Department of Computing Science
The University of Aberdeen, Aberdeen, AB24 3UE, UK
{slam, sleeman, wvasconc}@csd.abdn.ac.uk

Abstract

ReTAX is a system that assists domain experts to accommodate a new item in an established taxonomy; it suggests a number of ways in which that can be achieved namely; modifying the new entity, the taxonomy, or both. Further, a set of refinement operators are used to guarantee the consistency of the resulting taxonomy. ReTAX+ is a system which provides the user with additional functionalities as they build a new taxonomy or reuse an existing taxonomy. Specifically, it provides functions to enable a user to add, edit or delete the values associated with class attributes; additionally, it provides functions to add a class, delete a class, merge two classes, and split a class. Again consistent with the philosophy of ReTAX, ReTAX+ offers the user, when relevant, a number of options to achieve his objectives. For example, deleting a class is a fairly radical step and various decisions need to be made about the resulting "orphaned" instances and sub-classes.

1. Introduction

Our ultimate goal is to build a sophisticated Ontology Development and Maintenance environment. However, we made a conscious decision to first build a sophisticated taxonomy development tool; having achieved that objective we are now analysing the various enhancements which will be needed to ReTAX+'s functions to provide a comparable environment for handling ontologies. The basic approach of the original ReTAX system [1] is that it accepts as inputs a pre-established taxonomy and a new item to be classified. The system has a clear set of rules to determine whether a taxonomy is well formed, and an associated set of operators to achieve consistency. In fact, a new item can be accommodated onto a taxonomy by modifying the new entity, changes to the taxonomy or a combination of both. Whilst still retaining those features the enhanced system ReTAX+ now also provides an taxonomy maintenance environment in which attributes can be added, deleted and edited; similarly, a class can be added, deleted, merged with another class, or a class can be split. Again ReTAX+ is a cooperative system which suggests, at various stages, options; it is the user who makes the selections.

The paper is organised as follows: Section 2 presents an overview of the related work. Section 3 describes the system architecture. Section 4 provides some preliminary definitions on ontological analysis. In Section 5, the operations on attributes and classes and refinement strategies are presented. Finally, the implementation of system, the next steps, and a conclusion are given.

2. Related Work

Many tools for building ontologies have been developed in the last few years[1]. Four popular ontology editors are compared in this section: OntoEdit, WebODE, Protégé and OilEd, each of which covers a wide range of ontology development processes. We mainly focus on their developed evaluation services and the support for (semi-) automatic ontology improvement.

OntoEdit[2] employs Ontobroker[3] as its inference engine. It is used to process axioms in the refinement and evaluation phases [5]. However, it lacks transparency during refinement and evaluation, as the user does not obtain explanations why a particular change is necessary; the user only obtains information about the numbers of resulting changes, but not the details [6]. WebODE[4] uses the ODEClean [7] approach to evaluate the concept taxonomy by exposing inappropriate and inconsistent modeling choices according to the meta-properties. The errors in the taxonomy appear in a separate window and are high-lighted in the graph [2]. However, there is no functionality provided for users to correct the reported errors; nor can the system make the changes easily. Protégé[5] has a powerful plug-in PROMPT[6]. This tool guides users through the merging process, presenting them with suggestions for which operations should be performed, and then performs certain operations automatically [8]. However, its focus lies on ontology merging and alignment, rather than ontology evaluation. OilEd[7] uses the reasoning support ontology system - FaCT, which checks class consistency and infers subsumption relationships [9]. Only these sources of errors are indicated but no explanation or suggestion for users to resolve inconsistencies are given.

All four tools have inference mechanisms, but only offer partial support for (semi-) automatic ontology refinement, even though they make the ontology easier to understand and modify [5]. Also there is no information provided for users to analyse the reasons for conflicts which arise. This means the feedback cannot directly help users revise the ontologies effectively.

---

[1] http://www.ontoweb.org/download/deliverables/D13_v1-0.zip
[2] http://www.ontoprise.de/home
[3] Ontobroker is an the inference engine produced by ONTOPRISE
[4] http://delicias.dia.fi.upm.es/webODE/
[5] http://protege.stanford.edu/
[6] http://protege.stanford.edu/plugins/prompt/prompt.html
[7] http://oiled.man.ac.uk/

It is generally agreed that the developers of ontologies need a great deal of support as this is seen as a complex process. Generally, ontology management tools provide facilities to add, edit and delete classes, subclasses and instances. We did a comparative review of the facilities provided by these four systems when the user attempts to delete a class, its subclasses and instances. OntoEdit pops up a window which indicates how many classes, relations, instances and values of instances will be deleted. WebODE also pops up a window which indicates the classes, attributes, relations or other references which will be deleted, and the subclasses which will be re-allocated to the root of the ontology. In Protégé, a class with instances cannot be deleted; a class without instances but with subclasses can be deleted (the subclasses are deleted as well). In OilEd, a class which is referenced by other classes or attributes or relations cannot be deleted.

However, in ReTAX+, a class with subclasses can be deleted, and the user is prompted, by a list of options, to choose how to handle the orphaned subclasses, attributes and instances (explained in Section 5.3.2). We concluded that proactive support for class and relationship identification is necessary during the refinement phase, and the editor should allow the user control of these processes [6].

3. System Architecture

ReTAX+ is designed as a 3-tier architecture: front end (user interface), middle (inconsistency detection and refinement strategies), and back end (output results).

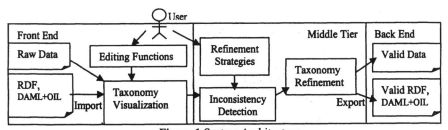

Figure 1 System Architecture

The ReTAX+ front end reads data from a text file, which contains the definitions of classes and attributes, and attribute values. An RDF file can also be imported to the system. The back end processes the refined taxonomy which can be stored in a text file or exported to an RDF file.

The middle tier is responsible for detecting inconsistencies in the taxonomy using consistency rules (explained in Section 5.3), and then implementing the refinements. Any invalid classes are displayed in different colours. In order to assist the user to modify the inconsistent structure, we implemented a process with the following characteristics:
- It explains and indicates the source and reasons for inconsistencies;
- The user is given a set of possible refinement strategies. For example, in the case of deleting a class, the user is given options for how to re-classify the orphaned subclasses, instances and attributes.

4. Definitions for Ontological Analysis

Previous efforts at organising taxonomies have focused on the semantics of the taxonomic relationship [10]. Our approach, however, concentrates on the properties (i.e. attributes) involved in the taxonomic relationship, rather than the semantics of the relationship itself. Therefore, only the properties of the class determine its consistency in the whole hierarchy structure; while their structural relationship (e.g. partition, generalization) and semantic meanings are not taken into account.

In this paper, we present and formalize the attributes and the taxonomy structure using set theory. We then demonstrate how they can be used for conceptual modelling. The following section gives formal definitions.

4.1 Taxonomy

A taxonomy is a finite set of frames, called *classes*, together with a finite set of arcs, called *relationships*, that join some or all of these classes. In a tree, classes lower down in the hierarchy can be seen as specialisations of the classes higher up in the hierarchy. The hierarchy reflects class-subclass relationship. There is a numeric threshold value τ, which is a cut-off between dominant and subsidiary attributes. Its value is changeable by the user, however its default value is 0.5.

Definition 1: A taxonomy T is a triple $T = \langle C, \tau, \rho \rangle$ where

- ❏ $C = \{C_1, C_2, ..., C_n\}$ is a finite set of classes C_i, $1 \leq i \leq n$
- ❏ $\tau \in \Re$, is a real number representing a threshold value, $1 \leq \tau \leq 0$
- ❏ $\rho: C \times C$ formally represents the class-subclass relationships among the classes of the taxonomy, such that if $(C, C') \in \rho$ then C' is a subclass of C

4.2 Class & Attributes

All classes have the same attributes in a taxonomy, the values of attributes are what distinguish one class from other classes. The following three points explain why we decided all classes should have the same attributes:

1. Speed up design by reusing attributes

   When a class or sub-class is created, the user only needs to provide the attribute values, which are inherited from the root or parent, rather than creating new attributes to describe the class. The inheritance of attributes reduces the design effort.

2. Minimize the accidental design and structure errors

   This avoids the user introducing any duplicated attributes (e.g. an attribute which already exists in other classes) and the same semantical attributes (e.g. attributes which are essentially synonyms).

3. Extend the description of taxonomy to be more complete

   When an attribute is appended to a class, it is propagated to the whole taxonomy; the descriptions of other classes are extended with the extra attribute.

In order to increase the differentiation of an individual class from the whole hierarchy, each attribute has a discriminatory relevance index (which we abbreviate as *dri*) indicating the taxonomic significance or discriminatory power of an attribute. The attribute values could be either a set of integers, string, or classes, this attribute is called the "ordered-set"; or a range of integers, called "integer-range", which has the lowest and the highest limit of the range.

Definition 2: A class C is a pair $C = \langle c, A \rangle$ where
- ❑ c is the name of the class
- ❑ A is the set of attributes of the class.

Definition 3: The attributes A of a class are represented as a set of triples $\langle a, V, d \rangle$ where
- ❑ a is the attribute name
- ❑ $d \in \mathfrak{R}$, is a real number representing its dri value, $1 \leq d \leq 0$
- ❑ V is either a set of attribute values $\{v_1, v_2, ..., v_n\}$ or an integer pair $\langle r_L, r_H \rangle$

$$V = \begin{cases} \langle r_L, r_H \rangle, \text{ then } A \text{ is an integer-range type attribute,} \\ \qquad \text{where } r_L \text{ and } r_H \text{ is the lowest and highest limit of the range} \\ \\ \{v_1, v_2, ..., v_n\}, \text{ then } A \text{ is an ordered-set type attribute,} \\ \qquad \text{where } v \text{ can be an integer, string or class} \end{cases}$$

Definition 4: The subsidiary attributes of a class are the subset of attributes whose dri values are less than the given threshold value τ, that is,

$\text{sub}(\langle c, A \rangle) \subseteq A,$
$\text{sub}(\langle c, A \rangle) = \{\langle a, V, d \rangle \mid \langle a, V, d \rangle \in A, d < \tau\}$

Definition 5: The dominant attributes of a class are the subset of attributes whose dri values are greater than or equal to the given threshold value τ, that is,

$\text{dom}(\langle c, A \rangle) \subseteq A,$
$\text{dom}(\langle c, A \rangle) = \{\langle a, V, d \rangle \mid \langle a, V, d \rangle \in A, d \geq \tau\}$

5. Operations on Taxonomy

Taxonomy development is necessarily an interactive process [6]. There are a number of factors which require taxonomy refinement [6]:

1. The original taxonomy often includes errors.
2. The accepted domain knowledge or the users requirements change and hence it is necessary to revise the corresponding taxonomy.

Therefore, the system has to cope with taxonomy modifications, and has to ensure consistency of the taxonomy whenever it is changed [3]. Our approach is to implement semi-automatic taxonomy refinements, that is the system requires the user to choose an appropriate refinement strategy from a number of options and the system then implements the chosen changes. The current set of refinements is:
- Maintenance of the τ and dri values
- Adding, deleting and editing attributes
- Adding, deleting, splitting and merging classes

5.1 Maintenance of τ and dri

If a taxonomy keeps expanding, either its width or depth increases, it may be necessary to change the τ value. The adjustment of τ has an important effect on the taxonomy, the τ arbitrary value could result in an excessive number of dominant attributes or none. To avoid these adverse effects, the system presents change information in an orderly way, and describes any potential problems to the user when he adjusts the τ value [6]. After comprehending the information, the user commits or cancels the change. Once the change is activated, the system generates a list of suggestions and propagates changes to alleviate the side effects.

We realise that it might be difficult for the user to assign numeric values to attributes, to differentiate them into dominant and subsidiary features. Furthermore, during the design of a taxonomy such values can experience constant changes with repercussions throughout the taxonomy. We are currently investigating means to provide automatic support for this task, whereby the user would simply alert ReTAX+ about the status of an attribute, i.e., if it should be a dominant or a subsidiary feature. The system should then automatically assign a *dri* value to the attribute which would make that attribute subsidiary or, indeed, dominant, reflecting the user's preference. When a class is created ReTAX+ assign a default value of zero to the *dri* of all attributes, making them all subsidiary.

5.2 Manipulation of Attributes

Whenever an attribute of a class is modified, the change needs to be propagated to its superclasses and subclasses. The following sections describe these mechanisms.

5.2.1 Editing an attribute

The attribute values of an ordered-set type attribute can be deleted or added to; that of an integer-range type attribute can be modified.

Algorithm 1a: Ordered-set type attribute $\langle a, \{v_1, v_2, ..., v_n\}, d \rangle$
When a new attribute value v is added to an ordered set type attribute of a class, this value is added to its super-classes and sub-classes as well. Its sibling classes are unaffected with the addition. When an attribute value v is deleted from the ordered set type attribute, this value is deleted from its sub-classes, but its super-classes are not affected.

Algorithm 1b: Integer-range type attribute $\langle a, \langle r_L, r_H \rangle, d \rangle$
The range of an integer range type attribute of a class is constrained by that of its parent. When the integer range of the attribute is narrowed, the range of its sub-class is narrowed as well; if the range of the class is widened, then the ranges of the superclasses need to be widened but the ranges of the subclasses do not need to be changed (see Figure 2).

5.2.2 Adding an attribute

This extends the description of a taxonomy by adding a new attribute. Only a dominant attribute can be introduced to a class, so that it can be used to distinguish among the siblings.

When a new attribute is added to a class, the user can either assign a *dri* value, or indicate the current dominant attribute; in this case the system sets the *dri* value of the new attribute to be slightly higher than the *dri* value for the current dominant attribute. The new attribute is propagated to the whole taxonomy. The *dri* value in both its superclasses and subclasses decreases, as its importance is gradually decreased. The *dri* value for those classes which are not its superclasses, subclasses and siblings are zero by default.

Algorithm 2: The new attribute, A_{new}, its attribute values and *dri* are given by the user, and are added into a set of sibling classes C_s respectively. The subclasses of C_s inherit the same attribute values as C_s; the superclasses of C_s have the integrated attribute values of C_s. The *dri* value both in the subclasses and superclasses are less than the threshold value τ. The attribute value is null in other classes; their *dri* value is zero by default.

5.2.3 Deleting an attribute

This removes an attribute $\langle a, V, d \rangle$ from a taxonomy T.

Algorithm 3: Only an attribute which is subsidiary in every class in a taxonomy can be deleted. If the user wants to delete a dominant attribute of a class, then he has firstly to change the *dri* value of the attribute so that it is designated as a subsidiary attribute. Indeed this has to be done for all the nodes in the taxonomy, before an attribute can be deleted.

5.3 Manipulation of Classes

In this section, we describe the "Add a new class", "Delete a class", "Merge two classes" and "Split a class" functions, they are performed to improve the structure according to the user requirements. The user is informed which classes, instances and attributes are affected after these operations are initiated.

5.3.1 Adding a new class

One of the functions of ReTAX+ is to assist the user in accommodating a new class in an established taxonomy. Following the addition of the new class, the taxonomy may no longer be valid, in which case the system has to refine the taxonomy and possibly the class to ensure the new class is appropriately located.

Algorithm 4: When a class is created, ReTAX+ assigns a default value of zero to the *dri* of all attributes, making them all subsidiary. The user is required to fill the attribute values which are constrained by the attribute values of the root. He indicates the exact values of *dri* if he knows the importance of each attribute. Perhaps, he can just indicate the dominant attribute whose *dri* values will then be assigned by the system automatically. The new class must have at least one dominant attribute, otherwise, it has no characteristics and cannot be added in the taxonomy. Hence, the system searches for the most likely parent and adds the new class as its child. Otherwise, find the class whose dominant attribute is the same as the new class's dominate attribute, and add the class as its siblings. If no sibling is found, add the class as a child of the root. As a final step the taxonomy needs to be re-validated.

5.3.2 Deleting a class

When a class in the hierarchy is deleted, there are several concerns to be resolved. One is what to do with the orphaned sub-classes; and what to do with the class's instances; thirdly, what to do when other classes have cited the to-be-deleted class as one of their attribute values. For each concern, we provide a set of possible strategies for users to choose based on their own preferences. For the orphaned sub-classes and those attributes whose value is the deleted class, see Algorithm 5. For the class's instances, they may either be deleted or reconnected to its super-class [4].

Algorithm 5: A class is deleted from a taxonomy, its orphaned sub-classes can either be deleted or reconnected to its super-class or the root. Suppose there is an attribute in a class the values of which are references to classes within the taxonomy. If the user deletes a class which appears as one of the values of this attribute, then the values of the attribute must be either deleted or altered: the reference to the deleted class is changed to a reference to the parent class (see Figure 3).

```
Edit_Attribute ( T, v, ⟨a, V, d⟩, C, T' ) {   // v: a new attribute value input by the user
   switch(attribute-type)
   case (ordered-set-attribute):
      action = user's action either add or delete
      switch(action)
         case(add):
            C = ⟨c, A'⟩, A'= A ∪ {⟨a, V∪v, d⟩} − {⟨a, V, d⟩}
            for each Cₖ ∈ C do
               if ((Cₖ, C) ∈ ρ or (C, Cₖ) ∈ ρ)  // Cₖ is a superclass or subclass
                  Cₖ = ⟨c, A'⟩, A'= A ∪ {⟨a, V∪v, d⟩} − {⟨a, V, d⟩}
         case(delete):
            v = the attribute value will be deleted by the user
            C = ⟨c, A'⟩, A'= A ∪ {⟨a, V−v, d⟩} − {⟨a, V, d⟩}
            for each Cₖ ∈ C do
               if ((C, Cₖ) ∈ ρ)  // Cₖ is a subclass
                  Cₖ = ⟨c, A'⟩, A'= A ∪ {⟨a, V−v, d⟩} − {⟨a, V, d⟩}
   case (integer-range-attribute):
            ⟨r'_L , r'_H⟩ = v // v is a new integer range input by the user
            C = ⟨c, A'⟩, A'= A ∪ {⟨r'_L, r'_H⟩} − {⟨r_L, r_H⟩}  //updated with the new range
            for each Cₖ ∈ C do {
               ⟨r_{kL}, r_{kH}⟩ ∈ Aₖ, ⟨c, Aₖ⟩ = Cₖ
               if ( (C, Cₖ) ∈ ρ ) {                 // Cₖ is a subclass
                  if ( r'_L > r_{kL} ) r'_{kL} = r'_L  else r'_{kL} = r_{kL}
                  if ( r'_H < r_{kH} ) r'_{kH} = r'_H  else r'_{kH} = r_{kH}
                  Cₖ = ⟨c, A'⟩, A'= A ∪ {⟨r'_{kL}, r'_{kH}⟩} − {⟨r_{kL}, r_{kH}⟩}  //updated  subclass
               } else if ( (Cₖ, C) ∈ ρ ) {  // Cₖ is a superclass
                  if ( r'_L < r_{kL} ) r'_{kL} = r'_L  else r'_{kL} = r_{kL}
                  if ( r'_H > r_{kH} ) r'_{kH} = r'_H  else r'_{kH} = r_{kH}
                  Cₖ = ⟨c, A'⟩, A'= A ∪ {⟨r'_{kL}, r'_{kH}⟩} − {⟨r_{kL}, r_{kH}⟩}  //updated  superclass
               }
            }
         }
   T' = ⟨∪ₖ Cₖ, τ, ρ⟩
}
```

Figure 2: Algorithm 1: Editing an Attribute

5.3.3 Merging two classes

The operation of merging classes is to create a new class from two existing classes which in some ways overlap. In our approach, only the properties (i.e. attributes) of classes are used to measure the similarity.

Algorithm 6: Once the similarity between two classes is larger than the threshold value, (it is set to 0.5 by default, although a user can change it according to her needs.), the two classes can be merged to create a new class, which includes the attribute values of the two classes. Their instances and children are re-classified to the newly created class. Similar to the "Delete a Class" section, when the two classes are merged all references to the original classes which occur as attribute values in other classes, have to be replaced by the name of the merged class.

Cosine Similarity

We define an algorithm that assesses similarity by comparing the attribute values of the classes. Cosine similarity is used to calculate the similarity between two classes, its value is always between 0 and 1.

$$\text{Cosine Similarity} = \frac{\text{Number of terms in Common}}{\text{Normalized}}$$

The *cosine similarity function* [11] between these objects, CS_{XY}, treats the set of attributes as components of an M-dimensional vector, and the similarity is the cosine of the angle between these vectors (their dot product divided by their magnitudes). This similarity is given by the expression:

$$CS_{XY} = \frac{\sum_{i=1}^{L} (X_i * Y_i)}{\sqrt{\sum_{i=1}^{L} X_i^2 \sum_{i=1}^{L} Y_i^2}} \quad , \text{ where X and Y are two vectors}$$

The original function is modified to fit our approach. As all classes have the same attributes (but different attribute values), the attributes cannot distinguish the difference between classes. In this case, the comparison of classes is done by the attribute values of each class, then, the dot product of classes takes the attribute values into account. Thus the revised formula is:

Given: $C_A = \langle c_a, A_a \rangle$, $C_B = \langle c_b, A_b \rangle$, $\langle a_i, V_{ai}, d_{ai} \rangle \in A_a$, $\langle a_i, V_{bi}, d_{bi} \rangle \in A_b$, $1 \le i \le n$

$$\text{Cosine\_Similarity}(C_A, C_B) = \frac{\sum_{i=1}^{n} \{AV(\langle a_i, V_{ai}, d_{ai} \rangle)* d_{ai}\} \{AV(\langle a_i, V_{bi}, d_{bi} \rangle)* d_{bi}\}}{\sqrt{\sum_{i=1}^{n} d_{ai}^2 \sum_{i=1}^{n} d_{bi}^2}}$$

Method of calculating attribute values:

Attribute value for attributes in A_a: $AV(\langle a, V_a, d_a \rangle) = \dfrac{|V_a \cap V_b|}{|V_a|}$

Attribute value for attributes in A_b: $AV(\langle a, V_b, d_b \rangle) = \dfrac{|V_a \cap V_b|}{|V_b|}$

```
Delete_Class(T, C, T' ){   // a class C to be deleted
  Attribute_Whose_Value_C (T, C, T' ) //edit attributes whose value is referring to class C
  for each C_k ∈ C do
        if ( (C, C_k) ∈ ρ )    C_sub = ∪ C_k       // C_sub is a set of subclasses
  switch( class_choice )
        case (delete ):      C' = C − C_sub − C
        case (reconnect-to-the-root ):
           for each C_k ∈ C do
                    if ( (C, C_k) ∈ ρ ) {           // C_k is a subclass
                        set ( C_root , C'_k ) ∈ ρ , where C_root = root ( T )
                        C'_sub = ∪ C'_k       // C'_sub is a set of reconnected subclasses
                    }
            C' = C ∪ C'_sub − C_sub − C
        case (reconnect-to-the-super-class ):
           for each C_k ∈ C do
                    if ( (C, C_k) ∈ ρ ) {           // C_k is a subclass
                        set ( C_super , C'_k ) ∈ ρ , where ( C_super , C ) ∈ ρ
                        C'_sub = ∪_k C'_k.      // C'_sub is a set of reconnected subclasses
                    }
        T' = ⟨ C ∪ C'_sub − C_sub − C , τ, ρ ⟩
}
```

Figure 3. Algorithm 5: Deleting a Class

5.3.4 Splitting a class

Any class can be split into two or more classes.

Algorithm 7: A class is split into m new classes, the attributes of the split classes are the same as the original class by default, and therefore, the user is required to either create a new dominant attribute or edit their dominant attributes, so as to distinguish them. The subclasses will be re-classified according to their dominant attributes. Similar to the "Delete a Class" section, all references in the attribute lists to other classes will need to be updated appropriately.

5.4 Refinement Strategies

It is important to ensure that any taxonomy has a consistent structure, which we do in ReTAX by specifying a number of consistency rules. (Ideally we would also like to ensure that the taxonomy accurately models some aspect of the world, but this is far harder to achieve, as is involves an evaluation of the semantics of the taxonomy.) Here, we define three consistency rules for taxonomies, the system then checks for inconsistencies based on the rules, and suggests appropriate refinement strategies to the user to achieve a consistent taxonomy. The rules constrain the attributes and relationships among the classes.

Rule 1. All the children siblings of a class are more specific than their parent

$$R1 (T) =_{def} \forall C \big((V \subset V_P | \exists \langle a, V, d \rangle \in dom (C), \exists \langle a, V_P, d_p \rangle \in dom (C_p)) \wedge$$
$$(V' \subseteq V'_P | \forall \langle a', V', d' \rangle \in A , \forall \langle a', V'_p, d_p' \rangle \in A_p ,$$
$$V \neq V', \ V_P \neq V'_P , (C_p, C) \in \rho , C \in C, C_p \in C)$$

Rule 1 basically determines the membership of a class in the taxonomy [1]. All the attribute values of a child are inherited from its parent, these values may be either the same as the corresponding attribute of its parent or a specialization of the corresponding attribute. In order to discriminate the child from its parent, there must be at least one dominant attribute which is more specific than its parent. This rule is violated if one of the attribute values of the child is not found in its parent, or none of attribute values in the child are more specific than its parent.

Rule 2. All the children of a particular class are distinct

$$R2(T) =_{def} \forall C \left(V \perp V_s \mid \exists \langle a, V, d \rangle \in \text{dom}(C), \exists \langle a, V_s, d_s \rangle \in \text{dom}(C_s), \right.$$
$$\left. \forall C_s \in \boldsymbol{C}_{sibling}, \boldsymbol{C}_{sibling} \subset \boldsymbol{C}, (C_p, C) \in \rho, (C_p, C_s) \in \rho \right)$$

For each class, there exists at least a dominant attribute whose value is disjoint with its sibling classes. This rule is violated when a child or instance can belong simultaneously to two classes at the same level of the hierarchy.

Rule 3. There is at least one dominant attribute in each class. Every class has at least one dominate attribute to describe its characteristics.

$$R3(T) =_{def} \forall C \left(\text{dom}(C) \neq \varnothing \mid C \in \boldsymbol{C} \right)$$

Definition 6 The taxonomy is consistent if and only if none of above rules are violated, that is,

Consistent $(T) \leftrightarrow R1(T) \wedge R2(T) \wedge R3(T)$

5.4.1 Consistency Checking

While checking inconsistencies, the user can choose the appropriate refinement strategies from those suggested by the system, and the user is often required to provide additional information to complete the operation.

Roles of Sets and Elements:

$C = \langle c, A \rangle,$ $\langle a, V, d \rangle \in A$;

$C_{parent} = \langle c_p, A_p \rangle,$ $\langle a, V_p, d_p \rangle \in A_p$;

$C_{sibling} = \langle c_b, A_s \rangle,$ $\langle a, V_s, d_s \rangle \in A_s$; $C_{sibling} \in \boldsymbol{C}_s, \boldsymbol{C}_s \subset \boldsymbol{C}$

$C_{sub} = \langle c_{sub}, A_{sub} \rangle,$ $\langle a, V_{sub}, d_{sub} \rangle \in A_{sub}$; $C_{sub} \in \boldsymbol{C}_{sub}, \boldsymbol{C}_{sub} \subset \boldsymbol{C}$

     where $(C_{parent}, C) \in \rho, (C_{parent}, C_{sibling}) \in \rho, (C, C_{sub}) \in \rho$

We now present four situations contradicting the taxonomy rules, and we show how the inconsistencies are resolved.

1. There is no dominant attribute in a class (Rule 3 is violated).

   Algorithm 8: Check if there is a subsidiary attribute in the class which is distinct among all the siblings. If found, set it to be dominant by increasing its *dri* to be higher than the threshold value τ. Otherwise, the system asks the user to add a new attribute A_{new} to the sibling classes.

2. The values of a dominant attribute in a class are the same as its siblings (Rule 2 is violated).

   Algorithm 9: The user decides either to set that attribute in its siblings to be subsidiary (by decreasing the *dri* below the threshold value), or decides to edit its attribute values to make it distinct from its siblings (see Figure 4).

3. A dominant attribute of a child class is more general than its parent (Rule 1 is violated).

   Algorithm 10: The user decides either to set the dominant attribute to be subsidiary, or edit the dominant attribute to be more specific than its parent.

4. An attribute value in a child class is not found in its parent (Rule 1 is violated).

   Algorithm 11: This new attribute value in a child class is added to its parent and its superclasses.

5.4.2 Redundancy Checking

The first three rules are the constraints that guarantee the well form of the taxonomy. However, it may not be enough just to assist domain experts building a consistent taxonomy. The usability, usefulness and quality of the taxonomy are important requirements, especially when one has to develop or expand a taxonomy. There are two subsidiary checks to eliminate redundant information in the taxonomy. When redundant information is detected, the user is reminded that that value may not be useful. He can choose either to delete or retain that value, which will be highlighted in a distinct colour if it is retained.

Redundant attribute value — A child inherits all attributes of its parent class. The values of all attributes of a class must appear in at least one of its children. If a value of an attribute does not appear in at least one subclass, then the user should be reminded that that value may be redundant.

$$R4(T) =_{def} \forall\, C\left(\, V_p = \cup_k V_k \mid \forall\, \langle c, A_k\rangle \in C_{sub}, \langle a, V_p, d_p\rangle \in A_p, \langle a, V_k, d_k\rangle \in A_k,\right.$$
$$\left.(\langle c_p, A_p\rangle, \langle c, A_k\rangle) \in \rho\,,\, 1 \leq k \leq |C_{sub}|\,,\, C_{sub} \subset C\,\right)$$

Redundant attribute — Every attribute in a taxonomy should act as a dominant attribute in at least one class. This is because each attribute in the taxonomy should be used to distinguish at least one class, otherwise, it is redundant. The system informs the user there is such an attribute that is subsidiary in all classes in the taxonomy, and asks him either to delete or retain that attribute.

$$R5(T) =_{def} \forall\, \langle a, V, d\rangle\left(\, d \geq \tau \mid \langle a, V, d\rangle \in A, C = \langle c, A\rangle, \exists\, C \in C\,\right)$$

6. Implementation

ReTAX+ is implemented in JAVA. It provides a user friendly interface to create and manage taxonomies. Figure 5 shows its interface components.

6.1 Planned Enhancements

Enhancing the User Interface: However, the step-wise guidance for the refinements needs to be improved; we aim to minimize the user's inputs by giving him options to choose from (e.g. a Yes/No option).

Refinement Logging: The taxonomy refinement audit trail can help experts keep track of the changes they make. Whenever a change is made to a taxonomy, the meta-information, such as change of description, reason of change, cost of change, time of change and identity of the editor are all recorded in a log file [4]. The detailed log of all performed changes not only supports the reversibility requirement (explained below), but also allows other experts to appreciate the reasons for the changes made.

Reversibility Functionality: There are numerous circumstances where the user needs to reverse the effects of changes. The reversibility functionality allows undoing changes at the user's request [4], thus, the user can choose one of the options without worrying whether an inconsistent taxonomy might result.

7. Conclusion

In this paper, we presented the ReTAX+ framework for creating and managing taxonomies. The framework includes functions for editing classes and attributes, merging and splitting classes and inconsistency refinements. To enable the user to obtain the taxonomy most suitable for his needs, we introduce a list of possible refinement strategies, enable him to resolve the inconsistencies as best suites his requirements. Our hope is that the taxonomies which are produced by ReTAX+ will be of a higher quality and hence they will be reused in a number of different applications.

```
Siblings_Not_Distinct ( T, C , action,  T' ){
        //action = set the attribute to be subsidiary or edit the dominant attribute
        boolean same = false;
        for each Csk ∈ Cs do {        //update its sibling classes
            if ( V = Vsk | ⟨a, Vsk, dsk ⟩ ∈ dom(Csk ) ){
               switch ( action)
                  case(set-to-be-subsidiary ):
                     set dsk' < τ
                     Ask' = A ∪  {⟨a, Vsk d'sk ⟩} − {⟨a, Vsk, dsk ⟩}
                     Cs' = Cs ∪ {⟨c, Ask'⟩} − {⟨c, Ask⟩}
                     same = true;
                  case (edit-attribute):
                     Edit_Attribute ( T, ⟨a, Vsk, dsk ⟩ , Csk, T' )
            }
        }
        if(same){        //update C itself, if its attributes are the same as its siblings
            switch ( action)
               case(set-to-be-subsidiary ):
                  set d' < τ
                  A' = A ∪  {⟨a, V, d'⟩} − {⟨a, V, d ⟩}
                  C' = C ∪ {⟨c, A'⟩} − {⟨c, A⟩}
               case (edit-attribute):
                  Edit_Attribute ( T, ⟨a, V, d ⟩ , C, T' )
               T' = ⟨C'∪Cs' − Cs , τ, ρ ⟩
        }
}
```

Figure 4. Algorithm 9: Siblings are not distinct

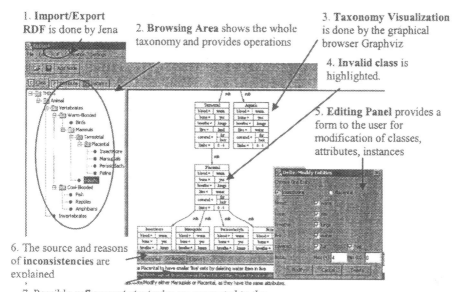

1. Import/Export
RDF is done by Jena

2. Browsing Area shows the whole taxonomy and provides operations

3. Taxonomy Visualization is done by the graphical browser Graphviz

4. Invalid class is highlighted.

5. Editing Panel provides a form to the user for modification of classes, attributes, instances

6. The source and reasons of inconsistencies are explained

7. Possible refinement strategies are suggested to the user to make modifications on the taxonomy

Figure 5. Screen Shot of ReTAX+ User Interface

References

[1] E. Alberdi, D. Sleeman, "ReTAX: a step in the automation of taxonomic revision". In Artificial Intelligent 91, p257 – 279, 1997

[2] O. Corcho, M. Fernández-López, A. Gómez-Pérez, O. Vicente, "WebODE: an integrated workbench for ontology representation, reasoning and exchange". In: 13th International Conference on Knowledge Acquisition and Knowledge Management, 2002

[3] Y. Sure, "On-To-Knowledge – Ontology based Knowledge Management Tools and their Application". In: German Journal Kuenstliche Intelligenz, Special Issue on Knowledge Management (1/02), 2002

[4] L. Stojanovic, A. Maedche, B. Motik, N. Stojanovic, "User-driven Ontology Evolution Management", In Proceedings of the 13th European Conference on Knowledge Engineering and Knowledge Management EKAW, Madrid, Spain, 2002.

[5] R. Mizoguchi, "Ontology Engineering Environments", Handbook of Ontologies, chapter 14, Springer, 2004

[6] L. Stojanovic, B. Motik, "Ontology Evolution within Ontology Editors", In ECON: Evaluation of Ontology-based Tools, 2002

[7] N. Guarino, C. Welty, "Evaluating Ontological Decisions with OntoClean", In: Communications of the ACM, Feb 2002

[8] F. N. Natalya, M. A. Musen, "The PROMPT suite: interactive tools for ontology merging and mapping". In: International Journal of Human-computer Studies, 2003

[9] Y. Sure, J. Angele, S. Staab, "OntoEdit: Guiding Ontology Development by Methodology and Inferencing", 2002

[10] R. Brachamn, "What IS-A Is and Isn't: An Analysis of Taxonomic Links in Semantic Networks", IEEE Computer, page 30-36, 1983

[11] B. T. Luke, "Distances in Clustering", Online Lecture Notes, 2003

SESSION 2:

SCHEDULING AND SEARCH

A Non-Binary Constraint Ordering Approach to Scheduling Problems

Miguel A. Salido[1], Federico Barber[2]

[1]DCCIA, Universidad de Alicante, Spain

DSIC, Universidad Politécnica de Valencia, Spain

{msalido, fbarber}@dsic.upv.es

Abstract

Nowadays many scheduling problems can be modelled as Constraint Satisfaction Problems (CSPs). A search algorithm requires an order in which variables and values should to be considered. Choosing the right order of variables and values can noticeably improve the efficiency of constraint satisfaction.

Furthermore, the order in which constraints are studied can improve efficiency, particularly in problems with non-binary constraints. In this paper, we propose a preprocess heuristic called *Constraint Ordering Heuristic* (COH) that classifies the constraints so that the tightest ones are studied first. Thus, inconsistencies can be found earlier and the number of constraint checks can significantly be reduced.

1 Introduction

Nowadays, many scheduling problems can be efficiently modelled as Constraint Satisfaction Problems (CSPs) and solved using constraint programming techniques. Some scheduling problems can be modelled naturally using non-binary constraints [15]. Although, researchers have traditionally focused on binary constraints [19], the need to address issues regarding non-binary constraints has recently started to be widely recognized in the constraint satisfaction literature. Thus, to define heuristics to solve non-binary CSPs becomes relevant.

One approach to solving CSPs is to use a depth-first backtrack search algorithm [5]. Using this approach, scheduling problems can be solved through the iterative selection of an operation to be scheduled next (i.e. variable selection) and the tentative assignment of a reservation (i.e value) to that operation. If in the process of constructing a schedule, a partial solution is reached that can not be completed without violating some of the constraints, one or several assignments need to be undone. This process of undoing earlier assignments is referred to as *backtracking*. It deteriorates the efficiency of the search procedure and increases the time needed to find a solution. While the worst-case complexity of backtrack search is exponential, several heuristics to reduce its average-case complexity have been proposed in the literature [7]. However, determining which algorithms are superior to others remains difficult. Theoretical analysis provides worst-case guarantees which often do not reflect average performance. For instance, a backtracking-based algorithm that incorporates features such as variable ordering heuristics will often in practice have substantially better performance than a simpler algorithm without this feature [13], and yet the two share the same worst-case complexity. Similarly, one algorithm may be better than another on problems with a certain characteristic, and worse on another category of problem. Ideally, we would be able to identify this characteristic in advance and use it to guide our choice of algorithm.

Many of the heuristics that improve backtracking-based algorithms are based on *variable ordering* and *value ordering* [16], due to the additivity of the variables and values. However, constraints are also considered to be *additive*, that is, the order of imposition of constraints does not matter, all that matters is that the conjunction of constraints be satisfied [2].

Thus, a scheduling problem can be modelled as a CSP, and using some of the current ordering heuristics, it can be solved in a more efficient way by some of the backtracking-based search algorithms (Figure 1).

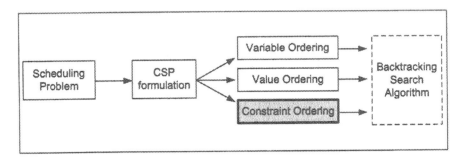

Figure 1: Constraint Ordering

In spite of the additivity of constraints, only some works are reported on binary constraint ordering mainly for arc-consistency algorithms [12], and even less work has been done on non-binary constraint ordering (for instance in disjunctive constraints [18]). Only some heuristic techniques classify the non-binary constraints by means of the arity. However, less arity does not imply a tighter constraint. Moreover, when all non-binary constraints have the same arity, or these constraints are classified as hard and soft constraints, these techniques are not useful.

In this paper, we propose a heuristic technique called *Constraint Ordering Heuristic* (COH) that can easily be applied to any backtracking-based search algorithm and that classifies the constraints so that the tightest ones are studied first. This is based on the *first-fail* principle, which can be explained as

"To succeed, try first where you are more likely to fail"

In this way, the tightest constraints are selected first for constraint checking. Thus, the search space is pruned soon and inconsistent tuples can be found earlier because it is not necessary to check these inconsistent tuples with the rest of the constraints with the corresponding savings in constraint checking.

In the following section, we formally define constraint satisfaction problems and describe two well-known ordering algorithms. In section 3, we present an example of non-binary scheduling problem. Section 4 describes the Constraint Ordering Heuristic. In section 5, we present the computational complexity. The results of the evaluation are presented in section 6. Finally, in section 7, we present our conclusions.

2 Definition and Algorithms

Briefly, a constraint satisfaction problem (CSP) consists of:

- a set of variables $X = \{x_1, x_2, ..., x_n\}$

- each variable $x_i \in X$ has a set D_i of possible values (its domain)

- a finite collection of constraints $C = \{c_1, c_2, ..., c_k\}$ restricting the values that the variables can simultaneously take.

A solution to a CSP is an assignment of values to all the variables so that all constraints are satisfied; a problem with a solution is termed *satisfiable* or *consistent*. The objective in a CSP may be to determine whether a solution exists, that is, if the CSP is consistent, one, many or all solutions, or an optimal, or a good solution by means of an objective function defined in terms of certain variables.

In some scheduling problems it is desirable to find all solutions in order to give the user the ability to search the design space for the best solution, particularly when various parameters are difficult to model [8]. Some techniques such as value ordering are not valid to solve this type of problems.

Two ordering algorithms are analysed in [16, 2]: variable ordering and value ordering. Let's briefly look at these two algorithms.

2.1 Variable Ordering

The experiments and analyses by several researchers have shown that the ordering in which variables are assigned during the search may have substantial impact on the complexity of the search space explored. The ordering may be either a static ordering, or dynamic ordering. Examples of static ordering heuristics are *minimum width* [9] and *maximum degree* [6], in which the order of the variables is specified before the search begins, and it is not changed thereafter. An example of dynamic ordering heuristic is *minimum remaining values* [13], in which the choice of next variable to be considered at any point depends on the current state of the search.

Dynamic ordering is not feasible for all search algorithms, e.g., with simple backtracking, during the search, there is no extra information available that could be used to make a different choice of ordering from the initial ordering. However, with forward checking, the current state includes the domains of the variables as they have been pruned by the current set of instantiations. Therefore, it is possible to base the choice of the next variable on this information.

2.2 Value Ordering

Comparatively little work has been done on algorithms for value ordering even for binary CSPs [11]. The basic idea behind value ordering algorithms is to select the value for the current variable which is most likely to lead to a solution. Again, the order in which these values are considered can have substantial impact on the time necessary to find the first solution. However, if all solutions are required or the problem is not consistent, then the value ordering does not make any difference. A different value ordering will rearrange the branches emanating from each node of the search tree. This is an advantage if it ensures that a branch which leads to a solution is searched earlier than a branch which leads to a dead-end. For example, if the CSP has a solution, and if a correct value is chosen for each variable, then a solution can be found without any backtracking.

Suppose we have selected a variable to instantiate: how should we choose which value to try first? It may be that none of the values will succeed. In that case, every value for the current variable will eventually have to be considered and the order does not matter. On the other hand, if we can find a complete solution based on the past instantiations, we want to choose a value which is likely to succeed and unlikely to lead to a conflict.

3 Example of Non-binary Scheduling Problem

In this section, we summarize a well-studied non-binary problem in the electric power industry: optimally scheduling preventive maintenance of power generating units within a power plant. This non-binary scheduling problem can be cast as a non-binary constraint satisfaction problem. The problem of scheduling off-line preventive maintenance of power generating units is of substantial interest to the electric power industry. A typical power plant consists of one or two dozen power generating units which can be individually scheduled for preventive maintenance. Both the required duration of each unit's maintenance and a reasonably accurate estimate of the power demand that the plant will be required to meet throughout the planning period are known in advance. The general purpose of determining a maintenance schedule is to determine the duration and sequence of outages of power generating units over a given time period, while minimizing operating and maintenance costs over the planning period, subject to various constraints. A maintenance schedule is often prepared in advance for a year at a time, and scheduling is done most frequently on a week-by-week basis. The power industry generally considers shorter term scheduling, up to a period of one or two weeks into the future, to be a separate problem called *unit commitment*. As a problem for an electric power plant operator, maintenance scheduling must take into consideration such complexities as local holidays, weather patterns, constraints on suppliers and contractors, national and local laws and regulations, and other factors that are germane only to a particular power plant. More details of this model can be seen in [10], and similar models are presented in [1]

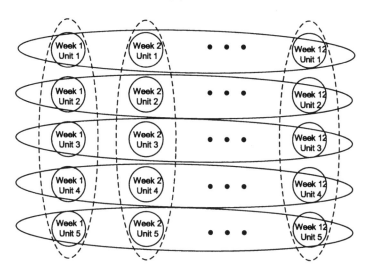

Figure 2: A diagrammatic representation of a maintenance scheduling constraint satisfaction problem. Each circle stands for a variable representing the status of one unit in one week. The dashed vertical ovals indicate constraints between all of the units in one week: meeting the minimum power demand and optimizing the cost per week. The horizontal ovals represent constraints on one unit over the entire period: scheduling an adequate period for maintenance.

The maintenance scheduling problem can be visualized as a matrix (Figure 2). Each entry in the matrix represent the status of one generating unit for one week. A unit can be in one of the three states: ON, OFF, or MAINT.

A valid maintenance schedule must meet many requirements, which arise naturally from the definition. First, the schedule must permit the overall power demand of the plant to be met for each week. Thus the sum of the power output capacity of all units scheduled to be on must be not less than the predicted demand, for each week. Then, the schedule must satisfy the following inequalities (non-binary constraints):

$$\sum_i z_{it} k_i \geq D_t \qquad \text{for each time period } t \qquad (1)$$

where $z_{it} = 1$ if $x_{it} = on$, and 0 otherwise, where x_{it} is the status (ON, OFF, or MAINT) of unit i in period t, k_i is the power output capacity of unit i and D_t is the energy (output) demand in period $t : 1, .., W$.

Additional requirements are that maintenance must start and be completed within the prescribed window, and the single maintenance period must be continuous, uninterrupted, and of the desired length. The following conditions must hold true for each unit i. This gives rise more non-binary constraints. For example, no more than M units can be scheduled for maintenance simultaneously. Thus, the following non-binary constraint must be satisfied:

$$\sum_i y_{it} \leq M \qquad \text{for each time period } t \qquad (2)$$

where $y_{it} = 1$ if $x_{it} = MAINT$, and 0 otherwise.

After meeting all the constraints, the objective is to find a schedule which minimizes the maintenance and operating cost during the planning period. Furthermore, it may also be necessary to reschedule the projected maintenance midway through the planning period. In this case, a new schedule which is as close as possible to the previous schedule may be desired, even if such a schedule does not have minimal cost.

Generally, formalizing a maintenance scheduling problem as a constraint satisfaction problem entails deciding on the variables, the domains, and the constraints which will represent the above requirements of the problem. The goal is to develop a scheme that is conducive to finding a solution {a schedule} speedily. The formulation must trade off between the number of variables, the number of values per variable, and the arity of the constraints. In general, problems having fewer variables, smaller value domains, and constraints of smaller arity will tend to be easier to solve. Since real-life problems are often large, these three conditions cannot be met simultaneously, and compromises must be made to achieve a satisfactory representation as a constraint satisfaction problem. How to best make these compromises and how the choices made affect the performance of an algorithm are important directions for further research. As we pointed out in the introduction, in this paper, we will classify the problem constraints so that the tightest constraints are selected first for constraint checking. For example in this non-binary scheduling problem, the set of inequalities presented in (1) can be classified from the tightest one to the loosest one. The tightest inequality constraint will be $\sum_i z_{ip} k_i \geq D_p : D_p = min\{D_1, ..., D_W\}$ and the loosest one will be $\sum_i z_{il} k_i \geq D_l : D_l = max\{D_1, ..., D_W\}$. Thus, inconsistent tuples can be found earlier and the search space can be pruned soon with the corresponding savings in constraint checking.

Thus, inconsistent tuples can be found earlier with the corresponding savings in constraint checking.

4   Constraint Ordering Heuristic (COH)

Currently, several constraint satisfaction techniques have been developed to directly manage non-binary scheduling problems as transforming techniques have many drawbacks. Some main drawbacks are:

- Transforming a non-binary into a binary CSP produces a significant increase in the problem size, so the transformation may not be practical [3, 14] particulary in large scheduling problems.

- A forced binarization generates unnatural formulations, which cause extra difficulties for CSP solver interfaces with human users [4].

As current techniques manage non-binary constraints in a natural way [4], new heuristics can be applied to these constraints to reduce the search space. As we pointed out in introduction some of these heuristics classify the non-binary constraints by means of the arity. However, when all non-binary constraints have the same arity (maximum arity), these techniques are not useful.

In this section, we propose a heuristic technique called *Constraint Ordering Heuristic* (COH) to classify the non-binary constraints, independently of the arity so that the tightest constraints are studied first. Inconsistencies can then be found earlier and the number of constraint checks can be significantly reduced.

4.1   Specification of COH

COH is an easy preprocess heuristic based on the sampling from a finite population in statistics, where there is a population, and a sample is chosen to represent this population. In our context, the population is composed of the points (states) lying within the convex hull of all initial solutions generated by means of the Cartesian product of variable domain bounds. The sample is composed by $s(n)$ random and well distributed points (s is a polynomial function) in order to represent the entire population.

As in statistic, the user selects the size of the sample $s(n)$. COH studies how many states $st_i : st_i \leq s(n)$ satisfy each constraint c_i. Thus, each constraint c_i is labeled with p_i: $c_i(p_i)$, where $p_i = st_i/s(n)$ represents the probability that c_i satisfies the whole problem. Thus, COH classifies the constraints in ascending order of the labels p_i so that the tightest constraints are classified first (see Figure 3). Therefore, COH translates the initial non-binary CSP into an ordered non-binary CSP so that it can be studied by a CSP solver.

We present the pseudo-code of COH below.

Constraint Ordering Heuristic

Inputs: A set of n variables, $X_1, ..., X_n$;
For each X_i, a set D_i of possible values (the domain)
A set of constraints, $C_1, ..., C_k$.
Outputs: A set of ordered constraints, $C_{ord1}, ..., C_{ordk}$.
1.- From the entire number of points generated by the Cartesian Product of the variable domain bounds, COH selects a well distributed sample with $s(n)$ points.
2.- With the selected sample of points ($s(n)$), COH studies how many points st_i : $st_i \leq s(n)$ satisfy each constraint c_i. c_i is labelled with p_i such that $p_i = st_i/s(n)$.
3.- COH classifies the constraints in ascending order of the labels p_i.

Example (The 4-Queens Problem): This well-known problem is an example of discrete problem with four variables, and seven constraints.

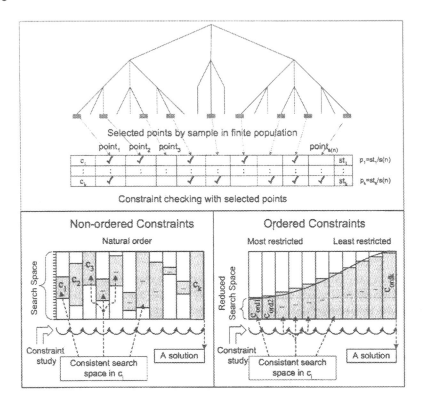

Figure 3: From non-ordered constraint to ordered constraint

Figure 4 shows the initial CSP and the possible solutions (2,4,1,3) and (3,1,4,2) obtained using BT and BT+COH. COH checks how many tuples (from a given sample: $s(n) = n^2 = 16$ tuples $\{(1,1), (1,2), \cdots, (4,3), (4,4)\}$) satisfy each constraint and classifies them afterwards. We can observe that some constraints are tighter than others (c_1, c_4, c_6 satisfy less valid tuples). BT must check 224 constraints to obtain both solutions, while BT+COH must only check 168. It can be observed that BT+COH studies first the tightest constraints c_1, c_4, c_6. These constraints are enough to obtain both solutions and the following only must be checked to be consistent.

$$(2,4,1,3) \leftarrow c_1 : (2,4), c_4 : (4,1), c_6 : (1,3)$$
$$(3,1,4,2) \leftarrow c_1 : (3,1), c_4 : (1,4), c_6 : (4,2)$$

In section 5, we present a more exhaustive evaluation of the n-queens problem.

z1, z2, z3, z4 : 1..4
$c1: |z1-z2| \neq 1$
$c2: |z1-z3| \neq 2$
$c3: |z1-z4| \neq 3$
$c4: |z2-z3| \neq 1$
$c5: |z2-z4| \neq 2$
$c6: |z3-z4| \neq 1$
alldifferent(z_i)

Possible Tuples: (1,1)(1,2)(1,3)(1,4)(2,1)(2,2)(2,3)(2,4)(3,1)(3,2)(3,3)(3,4)(4,1)(4,2)(4,3)(4,4)

Natural Order	Constraint Checks: 224	Valid tuples
$c_1: |z_1-z_2|=1$	(1,3)(1,4)(2,4)(3,1)(4,1)(4,2)	6
$c_2: |z_1-z_3|=2$	(1,2)(1,4)(2,3)(3,4)(2,1)(4,1)(3,2)(4,3)	8
$c_3: |z_1-z_4|=3$	(1,2)(1,3)(2,3)(2,4)(3,4)(2,1)(3,1)(3,2)(4,2)(4,3)	10
$c_4: |z_2-z_3|=1$	(1,3)(1,4)(2,4)(3,1)(4,1)(4,2)	6
$c_5: |z_2-z_4|=2$	(1,2)(1,4)(2,3)(3,4)(2,1)(4,1)(3,2)(4,3)	8
$c_6: |z_3-z_4|=1$	(1,3)(1,4)(2,4)(3,1)(4,1)(4,2)	6

Constraint Ordering	Constraint Checks: 164	Valid tuples
$c_1: |z_1-z_2|=1$	(1,3)(1,4)(2,4)(3,1)(4,1)(4,2)	6
$c_4: |z_2-z_3|=1$	(1,3)(1,4)(2,4)(3,1)(4,1)(4,2)	6
$c_6: |z_3-z_4|=1$	(1,3)(1,4)(2,4)(3,1)(4,1)(4,2)	6
$c_2: |z_1-z_3|=2$	(1,2)(1,4)(2,3)(3,4)(2,1)(4,1)(3,2)(4,3)	8
$c_5: |z_2-z_4|=2$	(1,2)(1,4)(2,3)(3,4)(2,1)(4,1)(3,2)(4,3)	8
$c_3: |z_1-z_4|=3$	(1,2)(1,3)(2,3)(2,4)(3,4)(2,1)(3,1)(3,2)(4,2)(4,3)	10

Figure 4: 4-queens Problem with Constraint Ordering Heuristic

5 Analysis of COH

COH selects a sample composed of $s(n)$ points, so the spatial cost is $O(s(n))$. COH checks the consistency of the sample with each non-binary constraint, so its temporal cost is $O(ks(n))$. Then, COH classifies the set of constraints in ascending order. Its temporal complexity is $O(klogk)$. Thus, the temporal complexity of COH is $O(max\{ks(n), klogk\})$.

6 Evaluation of COH

In this section, we compare the performance of COH with some well-known CSP solvers: Chronological Backtracking (BT), Generate&Test (GT), Forward Checking (FC) and Real Full Look Ahead (RFLA) [1], because they are the most appropriate techniques for observing the number of constraint checks.

As we have pointed out in introduction determining which algorithms are superior to others remains difficult. Algorithms and heuristics have often been compared by observing their performance on benchmark problems, such as the n-queens puzzle, or on suites of random instances generated from a simple,

---

[1]Backtracking, Generate and Test, Forward Checking and Real Full Look Ahead were obtained from CON'FLEX, which is a C++ solver that can handle non-binary constraint with discrete and continuous domains. It can be found in: http://www-bia.inra.fr/T/conflex/Logiciels/adressesConflex.html.

uniform distribution. The advantage of using a benchmark problem is that if it is an interesting problem (to someone), then information about which algorithm works well on it is also interesting. The drawback is that if an algorithm beats to any other algorithm on a single benchmark problem, it is hard to extrapolate from this fact. An advantage of using random problems is that there are many of them, and researchers can design carefully controlled experiments and report averages and other statistics. A drawback of random problems is that they may not reflect real life situations.

This empirical evaluation was carried out with both different types of problems: benchmark problems and random problems.

Benchmark problems

The n-queens problem is a classical search problem to analyse the behaviour of algorithms. In a previous section, the 4-queens problem was internally studied.

The 4-queens problem is the simplest instance of the n-queens problem with solutions. The problem is to place four queens on a 4×4 chessboard so that no two queens can capture each other. That is, no two queens are allowed to be placed on the same row, the same column, or the same diagonal. In the general n-queens problem, a set of n queens is to be placed on an $n \times n$ chessboard so that no two queens attack each other.

Table 1: Number of constraint check saving using our model with GT , BT, FC and RFLA in the n-queens problem.

	GT+COH	BT+COH	FC+COH	RFLA+COH
queens	*Constraint Check Saving*	*Constraint Check Saving*	*Constraint Check Saving*	*Constraint Check Saving*
5	2.1×10^4	2.4×10^2	150	110
10	4.1×10^{11}	3.9×10^7	1.4×10^5	9.3×10^4
20	1.9×10^{26}	3.6×10^{18}	9.6×10^{14}	6.03×10^{11}
50	2.4×10^{70}	3.6×10^{52}	3.1×10^{44}	1.6×10^{32}
100	2.1×10^{143}	2.1×10^{106}	4.5×10^{93}	1.8×10^{66}
150	5.2×10^{219}	3.7×10^{161}	6.8×10^{142}	2.1×10^{100}
200	9.4×10^{295}	8.7×10^{219}	9.9×10^{198}	2.2×10^{134}

In Table 1, we present the amount of constraint check saving in the n-queens problem using Generate and Test with COH (GT+COH), Backtracking with COH (BT+COH), Forward Checking with COH (FC+COH) and Real Full Look Ahead with COH (RFLA+COH). Here, our objective is to find all solutions. The results show that the amount of constraint check saving was significant in GT+COH and BT+COH due to the fact that COH classified the constraints in the appropriate order, so that the tightest constraints were checked first, and inconsistent tuples were discarded earlier. Furthermore, the amount of constraint check saving was also significant in FC+COH and RFLA+COH in spite of being more powerful algorithms than BT and GT.

Table 2: Number of constraint checks in problems $< 3, c, 20 >$

problems	Result	Backtracking constraint checks	Backtracking+COH constraint checks
$< 3, 3, 20 >$	S	5190.5	1832.1
$< 3, 3, 20 >$	F	27783	9761
$< 3, 5, 20 >$	S	12902.9	2990.8
$< 3, 5, 20 >$	F	46305	9761
$< 3, 7, 20 >$	S	21408.3	3253.2
$< 3, 7, 20 >$	F	64827	9761
$< 3, 9, 20 >$	S	32423.8	4256.5
$< 3, 9, 20 >$	F	83349	9761
$< 3, 11, 20 >$	S	44452.4	4214.3
$< 3, 11, 20 >$	F	101871	9761
$< 3, 13, 20 >$	S	52339.2	4938.5
$< 3, 13, 20 >$	F	120393	9761
$< 3, 15, 20 >$	S	60352.9	5250.7
$< 3, 15, 20 >$	F	138915	9761

Random problems

As we pointed out, benchmark sets are used to test algorithms for specific problems, but in recent years, there has been a growing interest in the study of the relation among the parameters that define an instance of CSP in general (i.e., the number of variables, domain size and arity of constraints). Therefore the notion of randomly generated CSPs has been introduced to describe the classes of CSPs. These classes are then studied using empirical methods.

In our empirical evaluation, each set of random constraint satisfaction problems was defined by the 3-tuple $< n, c, d >$, where n was the number of variables, c the number of constraints and d the domain size. The problems were randomly generated by modifying these parameters. We considered all constraints as global constraints, that is, all constraints had maximum arity. Thus, each of the tables shown sets two of the parameters and varies the other one in order to evaluate the algorithm performance when this parameter increases. We evaluated 100 test cases for each type of problem and each value of the variable parameter. The number of constraint checks is presented in Tables 2, 3 and 4.

In Table 2, we present the number of constraint checks in problems solved with BT and BT+COH, where the number of constraints was increased from 3 to 15 and the number of variables and the domain size were set at 3 and 20, respectively: $< 3, c, 20 >$. The results show that the number of constraint checks was significantly reduced in BT+COH in consistent problems (S) as well as in non-consistent problems (F). It must be taken into account that BT must check 138915 constraints in non-consistent (F) problems with 15 constraints, while BT+COH must only check 9761.

Table 3: Number of constraint checks in consistent problems using backtracking filtered with arc-consistency

		Backtracking-AC	Backtracking-AC+COH
problems	*Result*	*constraint checks*	*constraint checks*
< 5, 3, 10 >	S	2275.5	798.5
< 5, 5, 10 >	S	14226.3	2975.2
< 5, 7, 10 >	S	35537.4	5236.7
< 5, 9, 10 >	S	50315.7	5695.5
< 5, 11, 10 >	S	65334	5996.3
< 5, 13, 10 >	S	80384	6283.5
< 5, 15, 10 >	S	127342	8598.6

In Table 3, we present the number of constraint checks in problems where the number of constraints was increased from 3 to 15 and the number of variables and the domain size were set at 5 and 10, respectively: $< 5, c, 10 >$. In this case the *arc-consistency* filtering algorithm was applied before BT and BT+COH in order to observe the behaviour of COH in previously filtered problems. Therefore, this table presents the evaluation of BT-AC and BT-AC+COH. In this case, we only present the consistent problems, because most of the non-consistent problems were detected by the arc-consistency algorithm. The results show that the number of constraint checks were reduced in all cases.

In Table 4, we present the evaluation of BT-AC and BT-AC+COH in problems where the domain size was increased from 5 to 35 and the number of variables and the number of constraints were set at 3 and 5 respectively: $< 3, 5, d >$. As in the above tables, the number of constraint checks was reduced when COH classified the constraints.

Table 4: Number of constraint checks in consistent problems with backtracking filtered with arc-consistency

		Backtracking-AC	Backtracking-AC+COH
problems	*Result*	*constraint checks*	*constraint checks*
< 3, 5, 5 >	S	78.9	17.7
< 3, 5, 10 >	S	150.3	33.06
< 3, 5, 15 >	S	196.3	41.26
< 3, 5, 20 >	S	260.5	55.1
< 3, 5, 25 >	S	344.8	68.9
< 3, 5, 30 >	S	424.6	85.9
< 3, 5, 35 >	S	550.4	110.1

7 Conclusion and future work

In this paper, we propose a heuristic technique called *Constraint Ordering Heuristic* (COH) that can be applied to any backtracking-based search algorithm to solve large scheduling problems. This heuristic classifies the constraints so that the tightest ones are studied first in order to first check the constraints that are more likely to fail. Thus, inconsistent tuples can be found earlier with the corresponding savings in constraint checking. Also, hard scheduling problems can be solved more efficiently overall in problems where many (or all) solutions are required. Furthermore, this heuristic technique has also been modelled by a multi-agent system [17] in which agents are committed to solve their own subproblems.

For future work, we are working on a combination of COH with a variable ordering heuristic in order to manage efficiently more complex scheduling problems.

References

[1] T.M. Al-Khamis, S. Vemuri, L. Lemonidis, and J. Yellen, 'Unit maintenance scheduling with fuel constraints', *IEEE Trans. on Power Systems*, 933–939, (1992).

[2] R. Barták, 'Constraint programming: In pursuit of the holy grail', *in Proceedings of WDS99 (invited lecture), Prague, June*, (1999).

[3] C. Bessire, 'Non-binary constraints', *In Proc. Principles and Practice of Constraint Programming (CP-99)*, 24–27, (1999).

[4] C. Bessire, P. Meseguer, E.C. Freuder, and J. Larrosa, 'On forward checking for non-binary constraint satisfaction', *Artifical Intelligence*, 205–224, (2002).

[5] J.R. Bitner and E.M. Reingold, 'Backtracking programming techniques', *Communications of the ACM 18*, 651–655, (1975).

[6] R. Dechter and I. Meiri, 'Experimental evaluation of preprocessing algorithms for constraints satisfaction problems', *Artificial Intelligence*, **68**, 211–241, (1994).

[7] R. Dechter and J. Pearl, 'Network-based heuristics for constraint satisfaction problems', *Artificial Intelligence*, **34**, 1–38, (1988).

[8] T.C. Denk and K.K. Parhi, 'Exhaustive scheduling and retiming of digital signal processing systems', *in IEEE Transactions on Circuits and Systems-II: Analog and Digital Signal Processing*, **45**, 821–837, (1998).

[9] E. Freuder, 'A sufficient condition for backtrack-free search', *Journal of the ACM*, **29**, 24–32, (1982).

[10] D. Frost and R. Dechter, 'Maintenance scheduling problems as benchmarks for constraint algorithms', *Annals of Mathematics and Artificial Intelligence*, **26**, 149–170, (1999).

[11] P.A. Geelen, 'Dual viewpoint heuristic for binary constraint satisfaction problems', *In proceeding of European Conference of Artificial Intelligence (ECAI'92)*, 31–35, (1992).

[12] I.P. Gent, E. MacIntyre, P. Prosser, and T Walsh, 'The constrainedness of arc consistency', *Principles and Practice of Constraint Programming*, 327–340, (1997).

[13] R. Haralick and Elliot G., 'Increasing tree efficiency for constraint satisfaction problems', *Artificial Intelligence*, **14**, 263–314, (1980).

[14] J. Larrosa, *Algorithms and Heuristics for total and partial Constraint Satisfaction*, Phd Dissertation, UPC, Barcelona, 1998.

[15] L. Ros, T. Creemers, E. Tourouta, and J. Riera, 'A global constraint model for integrated routeing and scheduling on a transmission network', *in Proc. 7th International Conference on Information Networks, System and Technologies*, Minsk, Belarus, (2001).

[16] N. Sadeh and M.S. Fox, 'Variable and value ordering heuristics for activity-based jobshop scheduling', *In proc. of Fourth International Conference on Expert Systems in Production and Operations Management*, 134–144, (1990).

[17] M.A. Salido and F. Barber, 'Distributed constraint satisfaction problems for resource allocation', *In Proceeding of AAMAS Workshop on Representation and approaches for Time-Critical Decentralized Resource/Role/Task Allocation*, 95–104, (2003).

[18] M.A. Salido and F. Barber, 'A Polynomial Algorithm for Continuous Nonbinary Disjunctive CSPs: Extended DLRs', *Knowledge Based Systems. Ed. Elsevier Science*, **16**, 277–285, (2003).

[19] E. Tsang, *Foundation of Constraint Satisfaction*, Academic Press, London and San Diego, 1993.

A Heuristic Based System for Generation of Shifts with Breaks

Johannes Gärtner
XIMES Corp.
Vienna, Austria

Nysret Musliu
Technische Universität Wien
Vienna, Austria

Wolfgang Slany
Technische Universität Graz
Graz, Austria

Abstract

In this paper a system for the automatic generation of shifts with breaks is presented. The problem of generating shifts with breaks appears in many areas of workforce scheduling, like in airline companies, airports, call centers etc. and is of high practical relevance. A heuristics algorithm for solving this problem is described. It is based on greedy assignment of breaks in shifts and repair steps for finding the best position of breaks inside of shifts. The commercial product in which the algorithms are included is used in practice. Computational results for a real life problem in a large European airport are given.

1 INTRODUCTION

Workforce scheduling is necessary in many industries like , e.g., industrial plants, hospitals, public transport, airlines companies. The typical process for planning and scheduling of a workforce in an organization consists of several stages. The first stage is to determine the temporal requirements for staffing levels. After these temporal requirements are defined, usually in the next phase the shifts are constructed. In this phase also the staffing level for each shift is determined. Then the total number of employees needed is calculated based on the average number of working hours for a certain period of time, usually one week.

In Table 1 an example of such temporal requirements is given. In this example the temporal requirements are given for one week. Based on these requirements and some constraints about the possible start and length of shifts, the aim in the shift design problem is to generate legal shifts that meet in the best way the temporal requirements. Additionally in some situation generation of breaks for each employee may be required. The detailed description of the problem we consider in this paper is given in the next section.

The shift design problem we consider in this paper is similar to a problem which has been addressed in literature as shift scheduling problem. Typically for this problem it is required to generate shifts and number of employees for each shift for a single day. The aim is to obtain solutions without under-staffing

Table 1: Possible temporal requirements for one week

Time interval/day	Mon	Tue	Wed	Thu	Fri	Sat	Sun
07:00-11:00	5	5	5	5	5	1	1
11:00-14:30	10	10	10	10	10	4	4
14:30-20:30	12	12	12	12	12	4	4
20:30-06:00	14	14	14	14	14	4	4

and to minimize number of employees. The shift scheduling problem has been addressed mainly by using Integer Programming (IP). Dantzig [3] developed the original set-covering formulation. In this formulation for each feasible shift exist one variable. Feasible shifts are enumerated based on possible start, length, breaks and time windows for breaks. When the number of shifts increases rapidly this formulation is not practical. Bechtold and Jacobs [2] proposed a new integer programming formulation. In their formulation, the modelling of break placements is done implicitly. Authors reported superior results with their model compared to the set covering model. Their approach however is limited to scheduling problems of less than 24 hours per day. Thompson [7] introduced a fully implicit formulation of shift scheduling problem. A comparison of different modelling approaches is given in by Aykin [1].

Note that the problem of shift design we consider in this paper differs in several aspects from the problem of shift scheduling addressed in these papers. First, we consider generation of shifts for a week. We consider also minimizing of number of shifts and in our problem under-staffing may be allowed to some degree. For solving this problem the local search techniques based in tabu search were proposed and implemented ([6]). Further improvement of these algorithms is presented in [5]. The local search algorithms have been included in the commercial product called Operating Hours Assistant(OPA).

In this paper we describe extension of this system considering generation of shifts together with breaks for each employee. Generation of breaks makes the problem of generation of shifts much more complex, correspondingly the automatic generation of shifts with breaks is a very important issue for schedulers as good solutions can reduce significantly the costs of organizations. In Section 4 we apply the system to a real problem of a large airport in Europe. Note that experienced professional planners can construct solutions for practical problems by hand. However, the time they need is sometimes very long (one hour to several days for very large instances), and, because of the large number of possible solutions, the human planners can never be sure how strong their solution differs from the best one. Therefore, the aim of automating the generation of shifts with breaks is to make possible the generation of good solutions in a short time, thereby reducing costs and finding better solutions for problems that appear in practice.

2 PROBLEM DESCRIPTION

First we describe problem of generation of shifts without breaks as considered in [6]. Then the extension of this problem by including breaks is presented.

Instance:

- n consecutive time intervals $[a_1, a_2), [a_2, a_3), \ldots [a_n, a_{n+1})$, all with the same length *slotlength* in minutes. Each interval $[a_i, a_{i+1})$ has an adjoined numbers w_i indicating the optimal number of employees that should be present during that interval. Time point a_1 represents the begin of the planning period and time point a_n represents the end of the planning period. The format of time points is: *day:hour:minute*. For simplicity the temporal requirements are usually represented using longer time intervals. See one possible representation of temporal requirements for one week in Table 1.

- y shift types $v_1, \ldots, v_y$. Each shift type v_j has the following adjoined parameters: v_j.min-start, v_j.max-start which represent the earliest and latest start of the shift and v_j.min-length, v_j.max-length which represent the minimum and maximum lengths of the shift. In Table 2 an example of shift types is given.

- An upper limit for the average number of working shifts per week per employee.

Table 2: Possible constraints for shift types in the shift design problem

Shift type	Earliest begin	Latest begin	Shortest length	Longest length
M	05:00	08:00	07:00	09:00
D	09:00	11:00	07:00	09:00
A	13:00	15:00	07:00	09:00
N	21:00	23:00	07:00	09:00

Problem:

Generate a set of k shifts $s_1, \ldots, s_k$. Each shift s_l has adjoined parameters s_l.start and s_l.length and must belong to one of the shift types. Additionally, each real shift s_p has adjoined parameters $s_p.w_i, \forall i \in \{1, \ldots, C\}$ (C represents number of days in the planning period) indicating the number of employees in shift s_p during the day i. The aim is to minimize the four components given below:

- Sum of the excesses of workers in each time interval during the planning period.

- Sum of the shortages of workers in each time interval during the planning period.

- Number of shifts k.

- Distance of the average number of duties per week in case it is above a certain threshold.

For the extended problem which includes also the generation of breaks, it is necessary to generate a predetermined number of breaks for each employee. In this case for each shift type the possible break types should be defined by the decision maker. The break type determines feasible time windows of breaks inside of the shift. In the system described in this paper we consider break types with following features: minimal length of break, maximal length of break, minimal and maximal distance of start of break from the shift begin, and minimal distance of end of break from the end of the shift. One or more breaks may be required to be generated for each shift and employee. The objective of the problem remains as described previously.

This is a multi criteria optimization problem. The criteria have different importance depending on the situation. We use for this problem the objective function, which is a scalar function which combines the four weighted criteria. Note that we consider the design of shifts for a week (less days are also possible) and assume that the schedule is cyclic (the consecutive element of the last time slot of the planning period is the first time slot of planning period).

3 APPLICATION DESCRIPTION

Generation of shifts with breaks is one of most important features of the latest version of Operating Hours Assistant (OPA) (version 2.0). This system is suitable for use in different kind of organizations, like call centers, airports, etc. It facilitates an appropriate planning of working hours, staffing requirements and generation of optimal shifts which fulfill the legal requirements and also minimize over and under staffing in the organization. Good solution in this stage of workforce scheduling can reduce significantly the cost of organization and also are important for later stage in workforce scheduling (generation of workforce schedules). In this paper we will concentrate on one of main features of OPA 2.0, which is the generation of shifts with breaks. The current version is based on the previous version which included local search algorithms for generation of shifts without breaks and also the tools for definition of temporal requirements, and constraint about the shifts, as well preferences of user considering different criteria. For a description of these algorithms see [6, 4]. Then we give a description of the heuristics for generating breaks.

3.1 Generation of breaks

We consider the generation of breaks as a separated stage from the generation of shifts. For each shift there should be generated a fixed number of breaks. However, each employee can have different breaks, i.e., if one shift has more employees the number of breaks which the shift will contain will be $NumberOfEmployees * NumberOfFixedBreaksPerShift$.

For generation of breaks we rely in the solution produced by the local search (included in version 1.0 of OPA ([6])). Intuitively one possibility would be to consider breaks in the phase of generating shifts with the local search techniques. However, this would imply a tremendous increase of neighborhood solutions that should be generated during each iteration in the local search. Indeed, if we would have applied only two simple moves in breaks (change length of break and shifting of break to the left or right), for each shift with n employee, where each employee should have m breaks, one needs to generate $m \times n * 2$ neighborhood solution for a particular shift. To avoid so large number of neighborhood solutions we consider generation of breaks only after the shifts are generated.

For generation of breaks after generation of shifts we propose a heuristic method which is based in combination of greedy search with the local improvement based technique. The algorithm for the generation of shifts with breaks consists of the following steps:

1. Generate shifts without breaks

2. Convert solutions to shifts with one employee per day

3. Generate the difference in temporal requirements (difference curve)

4. Assign fixed breaks to shifts based on greedy algorithm

5. Apply repair steps to breaks

6. Create solution with shifts and multiple employees

The first step in solving this problem is a procedure based on the local search algorithms. This procedure is not a subject of this paper and we describe it only briefly. This procedure is based on the iterative improvement of the initial solution based on repair steps. Repair steps were used to explore the neighborhood of solutions for this problem. In order to generate the neighborhood and accept the solution for the next iteration, basic principles of the tabu search technique are used. However, while tabu search can find acceptable solutions for this problem, the complete exploration of the neighborhood (using all defined moves) in each iteration is very time consuming. To make search more effective a new approach based on using of knowledge about the problem in combination with tabu search is used. For a detailed description of these algorithms see [6].

The solution generated in the first phase contains shifts which can have more than one employee in more than one day. Next, the solution should be converted in shifts which can contain maximal one employee assigned to each particular day. Based on the solution without breaks and given temporal requirements from the problem the difference in temporal requirements (we call it difference curve, as in OPA the temporal requirements are presented graphically with some curve) is found. Next, the greedy algorithm for assigning of breaks to shifts is applied. The pseudo code of greedy algorithm is presented below:

For each shift in Solution

    For i=1 to NumberofBreaksToBeAssigned

        FindLegalRegionOfBreak
        FindBestPositionOfBreak
        DeterminLengthOfBreak

    Next

Next

The legal region of each break is found based on the constraints about the length and possible begin of a break inside of shift. The best position of each break is found based on the difference curve. The main idea is to locate the break with a greedy procedure in the best position in which the weighted sum of undercover and overcover is minimized. For example, in case there is a region where the overcover is very high that is a good position for a break as in this way the over cover is decreased. The length of a break is set in this step to be as short as possible. The last step in the generation of breaks is to apply some repair steps to the breaks which are already assigned. The basic repair steps which are used are enlargement of length of breaks and changing the break position to the left or right (within the legal region of a break). After fixing positions of breaks inside of the shifts, the solution with shifts which have multiple employees is created, by joining the duties of shifts which have the same starting time and length. The shift which is created by joining several shifts will contain also all breaks of joined shifts. Representing a solution in this form eases the construction of workforce schedules (assigning of shifts to particular employee), which is usually the next phase in the workforce scheduling process.

Note that the step of generating breaks does not have any impact on the number of shifts which were generated in the first phase. Considering undercover and overcover, in case there exist some overcover the quality of the solution can be increased during the generation of breaks.

4 APPLICATION USE

In this section we illustrate use of the system with the problem which appeared in one of largest airport in Europe. Although the extension of system for generation of shifts with breaks has been only recently implemented, the system has been already successfully used to solve some larger problems in airline companies and railway companies. Unfortunately we could not find similar benchmark problems from literature to compare our results and the results presented here are result of solving real life problems from consultants of XIMES Company.

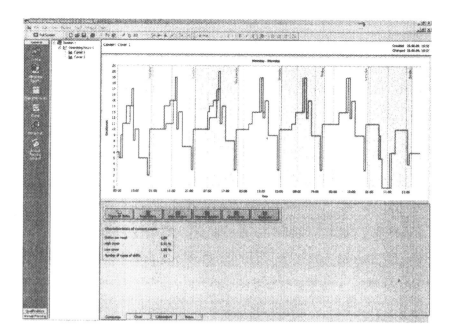

Figure 1: Screenshot of Operating Hours Assistant

We now describe the process of the generation of shifts with breaks in OPA for a specific problem. In Figure 1 the screenshot of the software (OPA) is given. The generation of solution requires several steps to be defined from decision maker.

4.1 Definition of temporal requirements

The first step in designing shifts is to define the temporal requirements (see Figure 2). Typically, the temporal requirements would be given for a week, but they can also be given for one day or less then seven days. In our case, when the temporal requirements are given for a week, the cyclic structure has to be considered (e.g., the night shift that begins on Sunday at 23:00 is 8 hours long and impacts the first day of the next week). For the problem we consider here the temporal requirements defined for one week. Figure 2 shows part of the requirements input screen.

4.2 Constraints regarding shift types

Shift types determine the possible start and length of the shifts. In this case (see Figure 3), five shift types are defined, morning shift, day shift, evening shift, night shift, and post shift. Shifts generated by algorithms should fulfill

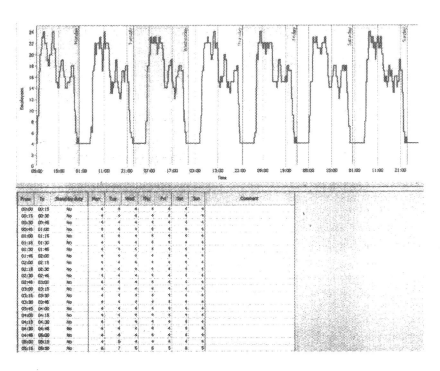

Figure 2: Definition of temporal requirements in Operating Hours Assistant

Types Of Shifts

Abbr.	Name	Start			Length inclusive breaks			Standby duty	Travel to work	Unpaid breaks in minutes	
		Optimum	Earliest	Latest	Optimum	Minimum	Maximum			No time assigned	Time assigned
M	Morning shift	06:00	05:00	07:45	8:30	7:30	9:30	No	Yes	1 break(s)	
D	Day shift	10:00	08:00	11:45	8:30	7:30	9:30	No	Yes	1 break(s)	
A	Afternoon shift	14:00	12:00	15:45	8:30	7:30	9:30	No	Yes	1 break(s)	
P	Post shift	17:00	16:00	19:45	8:30	7:30	9:30	No	Yes	1 break(s)	
N	Night shift	22:00	20:00	22:30	8:00	7:30	8:30	No	Yes	1 break(s)	

Figure 3: Definition of shift types in Operating Hours Assistant

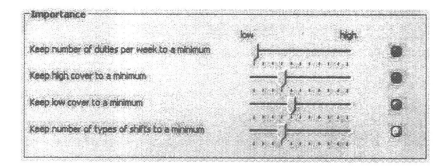

Figure 4: Definition of weights about the criteria in Operating Hours Assistant

the criteria required by the shift types. For example, morning shift can start between 5:00-7:40 and their length should be from 7,5 - 9,5 hours.

4.3 Weights of criteria

The solution to the shift design problem is evaluated with a scalar function, which combines four weighted criteria: excess in minutes, shortage in minutes, number of shifts and distance from average number of duties per week. OPA offers the possibility to change the importance of these criteria (Figure 4). The decision maker can include his preferences easily. For this case the following weights are selected from decision maker for the criteria: $overcoverWieght = 0.6$, $undercoverWeight = 0.8$, $NumberOfShiftWeight = 36$, $distanceFromAverageNumberOfDutiesPerWeek = 0$

4.4 Definition of break types

The last phase in problem definition is to define break types for each shift. In Figure 3 each shift type has exactly one break type. Break types determine the possible legal region of the start of a break and its length. In this case for each shift type has the same break type (see Figure 5).

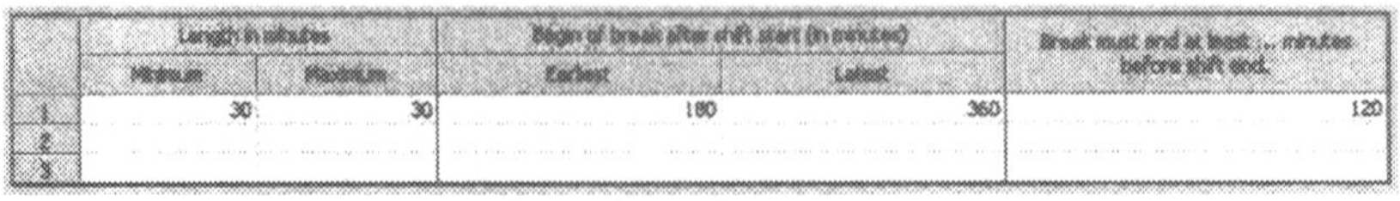

	Length in minutes		Begin of break after shift start (in minutes)		Break must end at least ... minutes before shift end.
	Minimum	Maximum	Earliest	Latest	
1	30	30	180	360	120
2					
3					

Figure 5: Definition of break types in Operating Hours Assistant

4.5   Generation of shifts

After the constraints have been defined, the algorithm for the generation of shifts can be called. As described in this paper the generation of shifts with breaks is done in two phases. In the first phase the algorithm for finding of a solution for shifts without breaks is executed. This algorithm iteratively improves the initial solution. User get a visual representation of the solution found so far and can thereby watch improvements. The algorithm can be stopped at any time and can be started all over again from any solution. In case the decision maker is not satisfied with a preliminary solution, the weights can be changed and attempts could be made to improve the current solution. After the shifts without breaks are generated the method proposed in this paper is applied to generate breaks for each shift and each employee.

For the given requirements, constraints and weights, algorithm which combine basic tabu search and guided search and starts with a good initial generates the solution with shifts without breaks which has the following features: $overcover = 8.04\%$, $undercover = 0\%$, $NumberOfShift = 21$, $AverageNumberOfDutiesPerWeek = 4.9$.

The algorithm for the generation of breaks which is applied after this phase generates all breaks for each employee and shift and could improve significantly the quality of the solution consideration weighted sum of overcover and undercover. The solution found after two phases has these features: $overcover = 3.53\%$, $undercover = 2.36\%$, $NumberOfShift = 21$, $AverageNumberOfDutiesPerWeek = 5.23$.

In in Figure 6 the solution which contains 21 shifts for this problem found by OPA is presented. The last column in this Figure indicates the number of breaks for each shift. For example the shift M6 has 14 breaks which are represented in Figure 7

5   CONCLUSION

In this paper a system for the generation of shifts with breaks was presented. A method for the generation of breaks was discussed in detail. The presented method is based on the greedy assignment of breaks in legal positions in shifts and improvement of solution by local changes of length and position of breaks. The method was shown to give good results in practice. The use of this application at a large European airport was presented. The system can produce better solutions than experienced professional planners in shift scheduling although it

Abbr.	Full name	Start	End	Unpaid breaks in Time assigned	WH in h	OH in h	Duties Mon	Tue	Wed	Thu	Fri	Sat	Sun	Sum
M1	Morning shift	06:15	13:45	...	7:00	7:30	9	6	6	6	10	9	10	56
M2	Morning shift	07:45	17:00	...	8:45	9:15	1	1		1	1			4
M3	Morning shift	06:00	15:00	...	8:30	9:00	4	5	2	4	5	4	4	28
M4	Morning shift	07:00	14:30	...	7:00	7:30	3	4	3	3	3	3	3	22
M5	Morning shift	05:00	12:45	...	7:15	7:45	1	1	1	1				4
M6	Morning shift	05:15	12:45	...	7:00	7:30	2	1	3	1	2	2	3	14
M7	Morning shift	05:30	13:30	...	7:30	8:00	3			3	2			8
M8	Morning shift	05:15	13:15	...	7:30	8:00		1	1	1		1	1	5
M9	Morning shift	06:00	13:30	...	7:00	7:30	1	4	7	3	3	2	3	23
D1	Day shift	11:15	18:45	...	7:00	7:30		1	2	1				4
A1	Afternoon shift	13:30	21:45	...	7:45	8:15	1		2			1		4
A2	Afternoon shift	13:30	22:15	...	8:15	8:45			2				4	6
A3	Afternoon shift	15:45	00:00	...	7:45	8:15	1	1			1		1	4
A4	Afternoon shift	15:15	23:00	...	7:15	7:45						1		1
A5	Afternoon shift	13:45	21:30	...	7:15	7:45	2	3	1		4	3	2	15
A6	Afternoon shift	13:45	22:00	...	7:45	8:15	4	2	4	5	2	4	4	25
A7	Afternoon shift	15:00	22:30	...	7:00	7:30	7	7	4	5	7	5	4	39
A8	Afternoon shift	15:30	23:00	...	7:00	7:30	1	1	2	3	1	2	1	11
A9	Afternoon shift	14:30	22:15	...	7:15	7:45	2	3	4	3	3	2	2	19
P1	Post shift	19:45	05:00	...	8:45	9:15		1	1				1	3
N1	Night shift	22:15	06:15	...	7:30	8:00	4	3	3	4	4	4	3	25

Figure 6: Solution generated by OPA

Assigned time of break for shift: M6 Morning shift (05:15 - 12:45)

Attention: If a person has several breaks per shift, these may not overlap!

Shift starts on weekday	Person	Break 1 Start	Length in minutes	Break 2 Start	Length in minutes	Break 3 Start	Length in minutes
Monday	1.	08:45	30				
	2.	09:45	30				
Tuesday	1.	08:15	30				
Wednesday	1.	08:15	30				
	2.	08:30	30				
	3.	10:00	30				
Thursday	1.	08:15	30				
Friday	1.	08:30	30				
	2.	08:45	30				
Saturday	1.	08:45	30				
	2.	09:45	30				
Sunday	1.	08:15	30				
	2.	08:15	30				
	3.	08:30	30				

Figure 7: Breaks generated for shift M6

is based on a simple algorithm. It makes possible the generation of a good solutions in a relatively short time, thereby reducing costs and finding better solutions for problems that appear in practice. For the future work it would be interesting to further analyze whether generating shifts and breaks during the local search would give better results than solving this problem in two phases, although in our opinion this would increase the time to reach solutions because the number of neighborhood solutions during each iteration would be tremendously increased. Further, it would be interesting to analyze the behavior of other algorithms (e.g., tabu search) when the repair steps are applied in breaks in the last phase.

Acknowledgment

This work was supported by FWF (Austrian Science Fund) Project No. **Z29-N04**.

References

[1] Turgut Aykin. A comparative evaluation of modeling approaches to the labor shift scheduling problem. *European Journal of Operational Research*, 125:381 –397, 2000.

[2] Jacobs L.W. Bechtold, S.E. Implicit modeling of flexible break assignments in optimal shift scheduling. *Management Science*, 36(11):1339 –1351, 1990.

[3] G.B. Danzig. A comment on eddie's traffic delays at toll booths. *Operations Research*, 2:339 –341, 1954.

[4] Johannes Gärtner, Nysret Musliu, and Wolfgang Slany. Rota: A research project on algorithms for workforce scheduling and shift design optimisation. *Artificial Intelligence Communications*, 14(2):83–92, 2001.

[5] Luca Di Gaspero, Johannes Gärtner, Guy Kortsarz, Nysret Musliu, Andrea Schaerf, and Wolfgang Slany. The minimum shift design problem: Theory and practice. In *11th Annual European Symposium on Algorithms, Budapest*, 2003.

[6] Nysret Musliu, Andrea Schaerf, and Wolfgang Slany. Local search for shift design. *European Journal of Operational Research*, 153(1):51–64, 2004.

[7] G. Thompson. Improved implicit modeling of the labor shift scheduling problem. *Management Science*, 41(4):595–607, 1995.

A Topological Model Based on Railway Capacity to Manage Periodic Train Scheduling*

M.A. Salido[1], F. Barber[2], M. Abril[2], P. Tormos[3], A. Lova[3], L. Ingolotti[2]

DCCIA[1], Universidad de Alicante, Spain

DSIC[2], DEIOAC[3], Universidad Politécnica de Valencia, Spain

{msalido, fbarber, mabril, lingolotti}@dsic.upv.es

{ptormos, allova}@eio.upv.es

Abstract

Railway capacity has been a significant issue in the railway industry. Over the last few years, numerous approaches and tools have been developed to compute railway capacity. In this paper, we compute railway capacity to design a topological model for solving periodic train scheduling, developed in collaboration with the National Network of Spanish Railways (RENFE). This topological technique transforms the railway optimization problem in subproblems such that a traffic pattern is generated for each subproblem. These traffic patterns will be periodically repeated to compose the entire running map. The results show that this technique improve the results obtained by well known tools as LINGO and ILOG Concert Technology (CPLEX).

1   Introduction

Rail transport has played a major role in the economic development of the last two centuries. It represented a major improvement in land transport technology and has obviously introduced important changes in the movement of freight and passengers. Over the last few years, railway traffic has increased considerably, which has created the need to optimize the use of railway infrastructures. This is, however, a very difficult task. Thanks to developments in computer science and advances in the fields of optimization and intelligent resource management, railway managers can optimize the use of available infrastructures and obtain useful conclusions about their topology.

The overall goal of a long-term collaboration between our group at the Polytechnic University of Valencia (UPV) and the National Network of Spanish Railways (RENFE) is to offer assistance to help in the planning of train scheduling, to obtain conclusions about the maximum capacity of the network, to identify bottlenecks, to determine the consequences of changes, to provide support in the resolution of incidents, to provide alternative planning and real

---

*This work has been partially supported by the project DPI2001-2094-C03-03 from the Spanish Government and the project GV04B/516 from the Generalidad Valenciana.

traffic control, etc. Besides of mathematical processes, a high level of interaction with railway experts is required to be able to take advantage of their
experience.

Railway capacity has been a significant issue in the railway industry. Many
approaches and tools have been developed to compute railway capacity. However, capacity is a complex and loosely defined term that has numerous meanings. In general, within a rail concept, capacity can be described as "a measure
of the ability to move a specific amount of traffic over a defined rail line with a
given set of resources under a specific service plan" [7]. This could mean anything from the number of tons moved, speed of trains, on-time-performance,
available track maintenance time, service reliability, or maximum number of
trains per day that the subdivision can handle. Kreuger classified the capacity
is different kinds: theoretical capacity, practical capacity, used capacity and
available capacity.

Different models and mathematical formulations for train scheduling have
been created by researchers [9], [3], [8], [5], [4], [2], etc. Several European
companies are also working on similar systems. These systems include complex
stations, rescheduling due to incidents, rail network capacities, etc. These are
complex problems for which work in network topology and heuristic-dependent
models can offer adequate solutions.

In this paper, we formalize railway capacity (theoretical capacity) to design
a topological model for solving periodic train scheduling. This technique has
been inserted in our system [1] and it is committed to solve this problem in
order to obtain as good and feasible running map as possible. The system is
able to plot the obtained running map. A running map contains information
regarding railway topology (stations, tracks, distances between stations, traffic
control features, etc.) and the schedules of the trains that use this topology (arrival and departure times of trains at each station, frequency, stops, junctions,
crossing, etc,) (section 2). In our system, the railway running map problem
is formulated as a Constraint Optimization Problem (COP). Variables are fre-
quencies, arrival and departure times of trains at stations. Constraints are
composed by user requirements and the intrinsical constraints (railway infrastructures, rules for traffic coordination, etc.). These constraints are composed
by the parameters defined using user interfaces and database accesses. The
objective function is to minimize the journey time of all trains. The problem
formulation is (traditionally) translated into a formal mathematical model to
be solved for optimality by means of mixed integer programming techniques. In
our framework, the formal mathematical model is partitioned in two different
subproblems: integer programming problem composed by the constraints with
integer variables and linearized problem in which integer variables have been
instantiated. Therefore, the problem constraints are classified such that most
restricted constraints are studied first [10]. The most restricted constraints
are considered to be composed of integer variables. In this way, our system
studies first the integer programming problem and then it solves the linearized
problem. The integer programming problem will be partitioned in a set of
subproblems such that the solution of each subproblem will generate a traffic

pattern. The partition is carried out through the stations that take part in the running map. Each block of the partition is composed by contiguous stations, so that each traffic pattern represents the running map corresponding to each block of constraints. In Figure 1, a possible block of the partition may be composed by the first four stations: *Malaga Cent, Malaga Renfe, Los Prados* and *Aeropuerto*. Each traffic pattern will be periodically repeated to composed the entire running-map.

2 Problem Topology

A sample of a running map is shown in Figure 1, where several train crossings can be observed. On the left side of Figure 1, the names of the stations are presented and the vertical line represents the number of tracks between stations (one-way or two-way). The objective of the system is to obtain a correct and optimized running map taking into account: (i) the railway infrastructure topology, (ii) user requirements (parameters of trains to be scheduled), (iii) traffic rules, (iv) previously scheduled traffic on the same railway network, and (v) criteria for optimization.

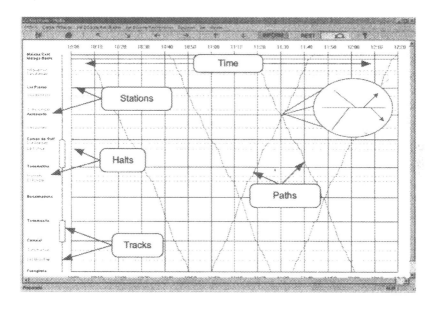

Figure 1: A sample of a running map

On a rail network, the user needs to schedule the paths of n trains going in one direction and m trains going in the opposite direction, trains of a given type and at a desired scheduling frequency.

The type of trains to be scheduled determines the time assigned for travel between two locations on the path. The path selected by the user for a train trip determines which stations are used and the stop time required at each station for commercial purposes. In order to perform crossing in a section with a one-way track, one of the trains should wait in a station. This is called a *technical stop*. One of the trains is detoured from the main track so that the other train can cross or continue. (Figure 2).

For periodic train scheduling, we assume that all the trains in the same direction are of the same type and they stop in the same stations.

2.1 Railway Traffic Rules, topological and requirement constraints

A valid running map must satisfy and optimize the set of existing constraints in the periodic problem. Some of the main constraints to be considered are:

1. **Traffic rules** guarantee crossing operations. The main rules to take into account are:

   - *Crossing constraint*: Any two trains and going in opposite directions must not simultaneously use the same one-way track. The crossing of two trains can be performed only on two-way tracks and at stations, where one of the two trains has been detoured from the main track (Figure 2). Several crossings are shown in Figure 1.

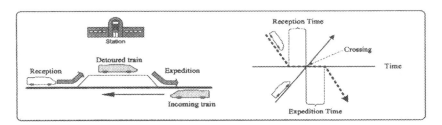

Figure 2: Constraints related to crossing in stations

   - *Expedition time constraint.* There exists a given time to put a detoured train back on the main track and exit from a station.

   - *Reception time constraint.* There exists a given time to detour a train from the main track so that crossing or overtaking can be performed.

2. **User Requirements**: Constrains due to user requirements are:

   - *Type of train and Number of trains* going in each direction to be scheduled and *travel time* between locations.

   - *Path of trains*: Locations used and *stop time* for commercial purposed in each direction.

- *Scheduling frequency.* The frequency requirements of the departure of trains in both directions. This constraint is very restrictive, because, when crossing is performed, trains must wait for a certain time interval at stations. This interval must be propagated to all trains going in the same direction in order to maintain the established scheduling frequency.

In accordance with user requirements, the system should obtain the best solutions available so that all constraints are satisfied. Several criteria can exist to qualify the optimality of solutions: minimize duration and/or number of technical stops, minimize the total time of train trips (span) of the total schedule, giving priority to certain trains, etc.

2.2   General System Architecture

The general outline of our system is presented in Figure 3. It shows several steps, some of which require the direct interaction with the human user to insert requirement parameters, parameterize the constraint solver for optimization, or modify a given schedule. First of all, the user should require the parameters of the railway network and the train type from the central database (Figure 3).

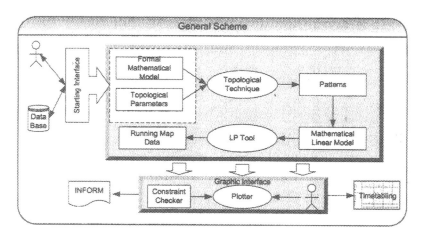

Figure 3: General scheme of our tool.

This database stores the set of locations, lines, tracks, trains, etc. Normally, this information does not change, but authorized users may desire to change this information. With the data acquired from the database, the system generates the formal mathematical model. This model is composed by a large number of mixed-integer constraints. To translate the mixed-integer problem into a linear problem, a topological technique is carried out to assign value to each integer variable. This technique carries out a partition of the stations such that each block of stations represents a subproblem and a traffic pattern (solution) must be generated for each subproblem. This traffic pattern is generated based on the problem topology such as the number of stations, the train frequency, the type of stations, and mainly the distance among the stations. Once the traffic patterns are generated, the integer variables are instantiated and the linearized problem is straightforward solved returning the running map data. If the mathematical model is not feasible, the user must modify the parameters, mainly the most restrictive ones. If the running map is consistent, the graphic interface plots the scheduling. Afterwards, the user can graphically interact with the scheduling to modify the arrival or departure times. Each interaction is automatically checked by the constraint checker in order to guarantee the consistency of changes. The user can finally print out the scheduling, to obtain reports with the arrival and departure times of each train in each location, or graphically observe the complete scheduling topology.

3 Railway Capacity

Railway capacity is a quite old argument. How can a railway section be full, if at every cross section only once in 10 minutes or so a train passes? Most of the time there is nothing to see [11]. Certainly, there exist many definitions of railway capacity, but there does not yet exist an accepted definition of capacity on railway networks. So that, we will adopt the following definition of railway capacity.

Definition. Railway capacity is the maximum number of trains which can be scheduled in the railway in a fixed period of time.

Based on this definition, railway capacity will be subjected to a topological restrictions of the railway (distance between trains, number of lines, speed of trains, etc). For instance, if all sections have two-ways tracks, railway capacity will be higher than in sections with only one-way tracks. On the opposite, if there is two very distant cities joined by a one-way track, the railway capacity will be conditioned by this track, because once a train departures from one station to the other, no train can departure from this last station since the former train arrives. These tracks are bottlenecks and they condition the railway capacity. This example answers the question below (for many minutes there is no train to see).

In this section, we formalize the distance that trains must maintain to guarantee a feasible schedule. This distance will determine railway capacity. So, our aim is to geometrically study each train with tracks between stations.

We assign to each type of train and each track an angle that represent the speed of this train in this track. As we maintain in our database the distance of each track (d) and the journey time for each train-track (t), the angle α can be straightforward deduced (Figure 4).

In this way, we define the angle α as arc tangent of distance (in meters) divided by time (in seconds). This angle is ranged between 0 and 90 as intuitively can be seen in the running-map. Thus an angle $\alpha \to 0$ means that the train has traveled a very short distance in a long time. Alternatively, an angle

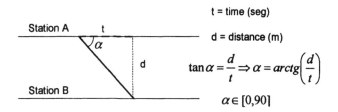

Figure 4: Angle per train and track.

$\alpha \to 90$ means that the train has traveled a very long distance in a short time.

Once, we have ranged the speed in the interval $[0, 90]$, we will study railway capacity by means of the minimum security distance for each track. We will focus on periodic trains and one-way tracks. Thus, all trains in each direction are of the same type.

For each track of distance "d" between two contiguous stations and each pair of trains in opposite direction, the total time (tt) of both journeys (up direction and down direction) is $tt = h + t1 + t2 = h + d \cdot (\cot\alpha + \cot\beta)$, where $h = mrt + met$ is the sum of the *minimum reception time* (mrt) of the train that arrives plus the *minimum expedition time* (met) of the train that departures. These values (t1 and t2) are trigonometrically obtained as can be seen in Figure 5.

$$\sin\alpha = \frac{d}{Ta}; Ta = \frac{d}{\sin\alpha}$$
$$\cos\alpha = \frac{d2}{Ta}; t2 = \cos\alpha \cdot Ta \quad \Big\} \to t2 = \frac{d \cdot \cos\alpha}{\sin\alpha} = d \cdot ctg\alpha$$

$$\sin\beta = \frac{d}{Tb}; Tb = \frac{d}{\sin\beta}$$
$$\cos\beta = \frac{d}{Tb}; t1 = \cos\beta \cdot Tb \quad \Big\} \to t1 = \frac{d \cdot \cos\beta}{\sin\beta} = d \cdot ctg\beta$$

$$tt = h + d \cdot ctg\alpha + d \cdot ctg\beta = (ctg\alpha + ctg\beta) \cdot d$$

Figure 5: Minimum security distance of a track.

Applying this formula to each of the k tracks of the network, the railway capacity (denoted by C) for a time period tp is:

$$C = 2 \cdot \left\lfloor \frac{tp}{Max\{h_i + d_i \cdot (\cot\alpha_i + \cot\beta_i)\}_{i=1\ldots k}} \right\rfloor \tag{1}$$

It must be taken into account that the bottleneck of the railway will occur in the station that satisfies $Max\{h_i + d_i \cdot (\cot\alpha_i + \cot\beta_i)\}_{i=1\ldots k}$. So that, the minimal frequency must be greater than the bottleneck.

Theorem. Given a railway R with one-way tracks with capacity C in a period tp, no additional train can be scheduled.

Proof. (Proof by Contradiction.) Assume to the contrary that there is a new train T that can be scheduled in R. Given the capacity C and the period tp, we can obtain the track j with maximum total time. Due to track j is a one-way track and train T is scheduled in this track, then to avoid crossing this train can only arrive or departure from critical station (all trains join) in the temporal interval h, that is, between the arrival of the predecessor train and the departure of the successor train. In this case $tt_k = h_k + t1 + t2$, where h_k is the sum of mrt plus met plus the necessary time for train T to *cross the station* (cs). Obviously $cs > 0$, so that $h_k = mrt + met + cs$. However, we define $h_k = mrt + met \rightarrow cs = 0$. # contradiction. So, any new train can be scheduled in railway R. □

4 Topological Constraint Optimization Technique

The railway optimization problem is considered to be more complex than job-shop scheduling [6], [12]. Here, two trains, traveling in opposite directions use tracks between two locations for different durations, and these durations are causally dependent on how the scheduling itself is done (ie: order of tasks), due to the stopping, and starting time for trains in a non-required technical stop, expedition, reception times, etc. Some processes (detour from the main railway) may or may not be required for each train at each location. In our system, the problem is modeled as a COP, where finite domain variables represent frequency and arrival and departure times of trains of locations. Relations on these variables permit the management of all the constraints due to the user requirements, topological constraints, traffic rules, commercial stops, technical operations, maximum slacks, etc. Hundred of trains, of different types, in different directions, along paths of dozens of stations have to be coordinated. Thus, many variables, and many and very complex constraints arise. The problem turns into a mixed-integer programming problem, in which thousands of inequalities have to be satisfied and a high number of variables take only integer values. As is well known, this type of model is far more difficult to solve than linear programming models. So, our objective is to solve this problem previously assigning values to integer variables such that the mixed-integer programming problem is transformed into a linear programming problem. Then, the linearized problem is easily solved. In this way, the topological constraint optimization technique is committed to this goal.

The topological constraint optimization technique generates traffic patterns based on our definition of railway capacity.

For example, if two stations are so far away so that a train takes more than ten minutes in travelling this itinerary, there exist a physical constraint (bottleneck), because it is not possible to assign a five minutes frequency due to trains in opposed directions must be crossed between both stations. As we pointed out in section 3, these type of tracks determine the railway capacity. Figure 6 shows this feature. Thus, the frequency must be greater than the minimal allowed frequency between both stations.

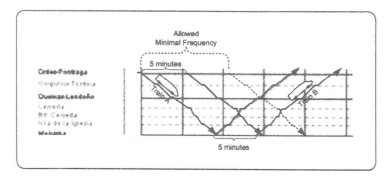

Figure 6: Example of bottleneck.

4.1 Topological Technique

The main idea of this technique is to generate a traffic pattern based on our definition of railway capacity. Each traffic pattern is generated for each set of stations such that the union of these traffic patterns determine the journey of each train. Figure 7 shows a possible set of stations (block).

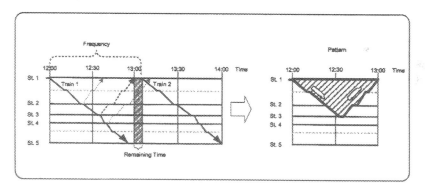

Figure 7: First traffic pattern generation.

The block of stations will be selected taking into account the speed of the trains, the distance among stations and mainly the frequency inserted into the problem. Each traffic pattern covers the block of stations necessary for a train to go from the first station of the block to the last station of the block and return from the last station to the first one (round trip). This round trip must arrive to the first station (St.1) as close but before to the following train departure (Train 2) as possible. Thus, our objective is to minimize the remaining time between the frequency and the round trips. Each possible round trip will involve a different set of constraints. The round trip that minimize the remaining time will be selected as the *pattern*. This traffic pattern will be composed by a higher number of stations than the rest of possible round trips.

Once the first traffic pattern has been generated, the block of stations involved in this traffic pattern are temporally removed in order to study the following pattern with the remaining stations. Figure 8 shows the generation of the second pattern using the same strategy.

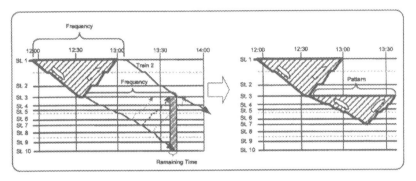

Figure 8: Second Pattern generation.

Therefore, when the second traffic pattern is generated, the topological technique studies the following traffic pattern until there is no station left. In Figure 9, we can observe an example of running map with three complete traffic patterns and some stations without traffic pattern. However, it is usual that there are some stations left. These stations are not involved in any traffic pattern. We must take into account that the best traffic pattern in a block of stations implies to start the following block of stations in the last station of the previous block. We must check all traffic patterns together in order to obtain the journey. Moreover, the first combination of traffic patterns may not be the best solutions due to existence of some combinations of traffic patterns. This combination depends on the number of stations that are not involved in a traffic pattern.

Figure 9 shows an example in which three stations are not involved in any traffic pattern. So, some combinations are possible and they are restricted to the set of stations involved in the first traffic pattern. Thus, these three stations can be sorted between the first and the last traffic pattern. In this way, the first traffic pattern may start at the second or third station and the last traffic pattern may finish in the penultimate or last but two station. However, due to efficient use of resources, or depending on the importance of the station, it is more appropriate the first traffic pattern (last traffic pattern) starts (finishes) at the first (last) station.

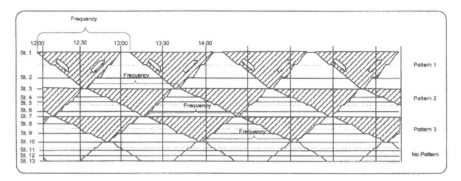

Figure 9: Periodic Pattern generation.

5 Evaluation

The application and performance of this system depends on several factors: Railway topology (locations, distances, tracks, etc.), number and type of trains (speeds, starting and stopping times, etc.), frequency ranges, initial departure interval times, etc.

In this section, we compare the performance of our topological technique with some well-known COP solvers: CPLEX and LINGO, because they are the most appropriate tools for solving these types of problems. However, the system carried out important preprocessing heuristics [1] before executing these well-known COP solvers in order to significantly reduce the size of this type of problems.

This empirical evaluation was carried out integrating both different types of problems: benchmark (real) problems and random problems. Thus, we defined random instances over a real railway infrastructure that joins two important Spanish cities (La Coruña and Vigo). The journey between these two cities is currently divided by 40 dependencies between stations (23) and halts (17).

In our empirical evaluation, each set of random instances was defined by the 3-tuple $< n, s, f >$, where n was the number of trains in each direction, s the number of stations/halts and f the frequency. The problems were randomly generated by modifying these parameters. Thus, each of the tables shown sets two of the parameters and varies the other one in order to evaluate the algorithm performance when this parameter increases.

In Table 1, we present the running time and the journey time in problems where the number of trains was increased from 5 to 50 and the number of stations/halts and the frequency were set at 40 and 90, respectively: $< n, 40, 90 >$. The results shows that CPLEX obtained better running time and journey time than LINGO. However, it can be observed that the running time is lower using the topological technique than the other two COP tools. Furthermore, our technique always obtained the same journey time (lower than CPLEX and LINGO) due to the fact that it generates the corresponding traffic patterns and it is independent of the number of trains. Figure 10 shows the system interface executing our technique with the instance $< 10, 40, 90 >$. The first window shows the user parameters, the second window presents the best solution obtained in this moment, the third window presents data about the best solution found, and finally the last window show the obtained running map.

Table 1: Running time and journey time in problems with different trains.

$<n,40,90>$	CPLEX		LINGO		TOPOLOGICAL	
Trains	runtime	journey time	runtime	journey time	runtime	journey time
5	5"	2:29:33	8"	2:30:54	3"	2:22:08
10	8"	2:26:04	17"	2:31:37	4"	2:22:08
15	13"	2:26:18	24"	2:31:51	5"	2:22:08
20	16"	2:26:25	35"	2:31:58	5"	2:22:08
50	55"	2:31:09	1302"	2:32:11	10"	2:22:08

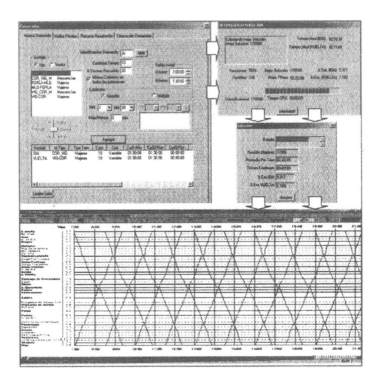

Figure 10: System Interface.

Table 2 shows the running time and the journey time in problems where the number of stations was increased from 10 to 60 and the number of trains and the frequency were set at 10 and 90, respectively: $< 10, s, 90 >$. In this case, only stations were included to analyze the behavior of the techniques. It can be observed that the running time was lower using our technique in all instances. The journey time was also improved using our topological technique. It is important to realize the difference between the instance $< 10, 40, 90 >$ of the Table 1 and the instance $< 10, 40, 90 >$ of the Table 2. They represents the same instance, but in Table 2 we only used stations (no halts), so that the number of possible crossing between trains is much more larger. This item reduced the journey time from 2:22:08 to 2:20:22, but the number of combination increased the running time from 4" to 7". Furthermore, CPLEX and LINGO maintained similar behaviors.

Table 2: Running time and journey time in problems with different number of stations.

<10,s,90>	CPLEX		LINGO		TOPOLOGICAL	
Stations	runtime	journey time	runtime	journey time	runtime	journey time
10	2"	0:58:36	4"	0:58:06	1"	0:57:36
20	3"	1:04:11	20"	1:04:11	2"	1:04:11
30	15"	1:45:08	42"	1:45:38	4"	1:45:08
40	56"	2:23:16	28"	2:24:36	7"	2:20:22
60	340"	3:44:28	326"	3:44:22	40"	3:32:15

In Table 3, we present the running time and the journey time in problems where the frequency was increased from 60 to 140 and the number of trains and the number of stations were set at 20 and 40, respectively: $< 20, 40, f >$. It can be observed that the frequency the topological technique improved the journey time when the frequency increased. As in previous results, the running time of the topological technique was lower than CPLEX and LINGO.

Table 3: Running time and journey time in problems with different cadencies.

<20,40,f>	CPLEX		LINGO		TOPOLOGICAL	
Frequency	runtime	journey time	runtime	journey time	runtime	journey time
60	>43200"	-	>43200"	-	36"	2:32:11
90	17"	2:26:25	32"	2:31:58	5"	2:22:08
100	18"	2:23:10	34"	2:22:55	3"	2:19:09
120	16"	2:16:17	27"	2:18:47	4"	2:16:00
140	17"	2:20:18	27"	2:16:19	4"	2:17:03

6   Conclusions

We have formalized railway capacity to design a topological model for solving periodic train scheduling in collaboration with the National Network of Spanish Railways (RENFE). This technique has been inserted into the system to solve more efficiently periodic timetables. This system, at a current stage of integration, supposes the application of methodologies of Artificial Intelligence in a problem of great interest and will assist railways managers in optimizing the use of railway infrastructures and will help them in the resolution of complex scheduling problems.

References

[1] Barber, F., Salido, M.A., Ingolotti, L., Abril, M., Lova, A., Tormos, P. *An Interactive Train Scheduling Tool for Solving and Plotting Running Maps*, Current Topics in Artificial Intelligence LNAI 3040, 646-655 (2004).

[2] Bussiecky, M.R., Winter, T., Zimmermann, U.T. *Discrete optimization in public rail transport*, Mathematical Programming 79(3), (1997), 415-444.

[3] Caprara, A., Fischetti, M., Guida, P., Monaci, M., Sacco, G., Toth, P. *Solution of Real-World Train Timetabling Problems*, 34th Annual Hawaii International Conference on System Sciences **3** (2001).

[4] Chiu, C.K., Chou, C.M., Lee, J.H.M., Leung, H.F., and Leung, Y.W., *A Constraint-Based Interactive Train Rescheduling Tool*, Constraints **7** (2002), 167–198.

[5] Kaas, A.H., *Methods to Calculate Capacity of Railways*, Ph. Dissertation (1998).

[6] Kreuger, P.; Carlsson, M.; Olsson, J.; Sjoland, T.; Astrom, E. *The TUFF train scheduler: Two duration trip scheduling on multi directional track networks*. In Proc. of the workshop on Tools and Environments for (Constraint) Logic Programming, (1997).

[7] Krueger, H. *Parametric Modelling in Rail Capacity Planning*. Canadian National Railway, (1998).

[8] Lindner, T., *Train schedule optimization in public rail transport*, Ph. Dissertation, Technische Universitat Braunschweig, Germany, (2000).

[9] Oliveira, E., Smith, B.M., *A Job-Shop Scheduling Model for the Single-Track Railway Scheduling Problem*, Research Report 2000.21, University of Leeds, (2000).

[10] Salido, M.A., Barber, F., *A Constraint Ordering Heuristic for Scheduling Problem*, 1st Multidisciplinary International Conference on Scheduling: Theory and Applications (MISTA 2003), (2) 476-491, (2003).

[11] Weits, E., *Railway Capacity and Timetable Complexity*, 7th International Workshop on Project Management and Scheduling, Euro (2000).

[12] Zuidwijk, R.A., Kroon, L.G., *Integer Constraints for Train Series Connections*, Erasmus Research Institute of Management (ERIM), Discussion Paper. (2002).

Collaborative Search: Deployment Experiences

Jill Freyne and Barry Smyth

Smart Media Institute, Department of Computer Science,
University College Dublin, Ireland.

Abstract

Collaborative search is an approach to Web search that is designed to deal with the type of vague queries that are commonplace on the Web. It leverages the search behaviour of communities of like-minded users to re-rank results in a way that reflects community preferences. This paper builds on our previous work which described the core technology and offered preliminary evaluation results. In this paper we describe the deployment of collaborative search technology as the I-SPY search engine and elaborate on these deployment experiences, focusing in particular on more comprehensive evaluation results that demonstrate the value of collaborative search in live-user trials.

1 Introduction

Modern search engines continue to struggle with the challenges presented by Web search: vague queries, impatient users and an enormous, and rapidly expanding, collection of unmoderated, heterogeneous documents all make for an extremely hostile search environment. In our research we argue that conventional approaches to Web search—those that adopt a traditional, document-centric, information retrieval perspective—are limited by their refusal to consider the past search behaviour of users during future search sessions. In particular, we argue that in many circumstances the search behaviour of users is repetitive and regular; the same sort of queries tend to recur and the same type of results are often selected. We have previously described an approach called *collaborative search* which is designed to take advantage of this repetition and regularity, by tracking the search behaviour of communities of like-minded users in order to promote results that they have been found to be interesting and relevant in the past [9, 10, 5].

In our previous work we focused on the underlying technology and described an early prototype implementation called I-SPY, plus some preliminary evaluation results based largely on the assumed search behaviour of artificial users. The main purpose of this paper is two-fold:

1. We present the results of a comprehensive live-user trial on a focused search task in order to complement previous evaluations;

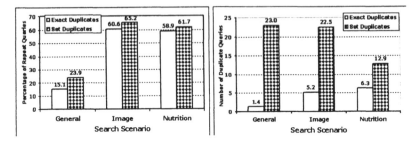

Figure 1: (a) The percentage of queries that are duplicates in the General, Image and Nutrition query logs.(b) The average degree of duplication for each duplicate query in the General, Image and Nutrition query logs.

2. We highlight recent developments that have arisen as a direct result of the I-SPY deployment and feedback from its users;

The remainder of this paper is organised as follows. In the next section we motivate our approach by highlighting new results concerning query repetition in Web search. Section 3 reviews the collaborative search approach, Section 4 describes the latest version of the I-SPY system and Section 5 provides a detailed account of our live-user study. Finally, before concluding, we summarise a number of important lessons that we have learned during this deployment including our plans for future enhancements.

2 Repetition & Regularity in Web Search

There are two key ideas about Web search that inform our research and motivate our collaborative search strategy: *query repetition* and *selection regularity*. First we assume that the world of Web search is a repetitive place: similar queries tend to recur. Second, we assume that the world of Web search is a regular place: searchers tend to select similar results for similar queries. If these assumptions hold we believe that significant performance benefits can be realised by reusing past search histories.

In the past, a number of commentators have questioned the validity of these ideas, citing low levels of query repetition in particular as an argument against collaborative search. In this section we will provide evidence to suggest that the first of these assumptions does hold to lesser or greater extent across a variety of Web search scenarios, and later on we will show, through our evaluation results, that the second assumption also holds in many of these scenarios.

In order to assess the degree of repetition among Web search queries we will make use of 3 different query logs for different types of search task— 6535 general Web search queries (from Excite), 33478 image search queries (Image), and 16008 queries from specialised search logs relation to nutrition issues (Nutrition)—[6, 8, 11].

For each of these logs we computed the percentage of queries for which there is a duplicate. We are interested in two types of duplicate: an *exact duplicate* means that the same query terms are used in the same order; a *set duplicate* means that the same query terms are used regardless of order. The results are shown in Figure 1(a). They indicate that in general Web search exact duplicate queries are relatively rare, accounting for just over 15% of the general Excite queries; although nearly 24% of queries have set duplicates. However, in the more specialised search scenarios, represented by Image and Nutrition, duplicate queries are far more common. In both of these logs exact duplicate queries account for approximately 60% of the queries and set duplicates are slightly higher.

Of course the fact that a given query is duplicated does not tell us anything about how many duplicates exist; this is important in collaborative search as more duplicate search sessions means there is a greater amount of evidence available to make informed relevancy decisions when it comes to re-ranking search results for a particular community of users. Figure 1(b) shows the degree of duplication in terms of the average number of duplicates that exist for each duplicated query. Again we distinguish between exact duplicates and set duplicates. The results are again promising. The degree of exact duplication tends to be quite low, especially in general search, but much greater duplication is found when we ignore query-term ordering. For example, even in general search, for the 24% of queries that are (set) duplicates, we find that each of these queries can be associated with another 23 duplicate queries. Similar results are found in Image search, although this time the basic duplication level is of course much higher, at about 60%, In Nutrition we find that on average the duplicate queries can be associated with about 13 other queries.

These high repetition rates in specialised domains provide a firm foundation for the collaborative search approach. After all, its community-based focus is designed to create specialised search domains for communities of like-minded individuals.

3   A Review of Collaborative Search

Collaborative search is motivated by two key ideas. First, specialised search engines attract communities of users with similar information needs and so serve as a useful way to limit variations in search context. For example, a search field on an AI Web site is likely to attract queries with a computer-related theme, and queries such as '*cbr*' are more likely to relate to Case-Based Reasoning than to the Central Bank of Russia. Second, by monitoring user selections for a query it is possible to build a model of query-page relevance based on the probability that a given page p_j will be selected by a user when returned as a result for query q_i.

The collaborative search approach combines both of these ideas in the form of a meta-search engine that analyses the patterns of queries, results and user selections from a given search interface. The basic architecture is presented in

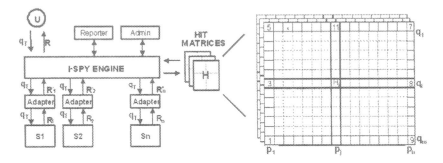

Figure 2: The collaborative search architecture combines meta-search with a facility for storing the search histories of individual communities of searchers.

Figure 2. It presents a meta-search framework in which each target query, q_T, is submitted to base-level search engines $(S_1 - S_n)$ after adapting q_T for each S_i using the appropriate adapter. Similarly, the result set, R_i, returned by a particular S_i is adapted to produce R_i', which can then be combined and re-ranked, just like a traditional meta-search engine. Its key innovation involves the capture of search histories and their use in ranking metrics that reflect user behaviour.

The unique feature of collaborative search is its ability to personalize search results for a particular community of users without relying on content-analysis techniques (e.g.[3, 7]). It achieves this by maintaining records of queries and page selections stored in a so-called *hit matrix* (see Figure 2). Each element of the hit matrix, H_{ij}, contains a value v (that is, $H_{ij} = v$) to indicate that v_{ij} users have found page p_j relevant for query q_i. In other words, each time a user selects a page p_j for a query term q_i, the hit matrix is updated accordingly.

$$Relevance(p_j, q_i) = \frac{H_{ij}}{\sum_{\forall j} H_{ij}} \tag{1}$$

Collaborative search exploits the hit matrix as a *direct* source of relevancy information. After all, its entries reflect concrete relevancy judgments by users with respect to query-page mappings; it tells us that v users selected page p_j when it is retrieved for query q_i. This information is used to estimate the relevance of a page p_j to query q_i as in Equation 1. The collaborative search architecture is described in more detail in last years proceedings [10].

4   I-SPY

I-SPY is our implementation of collaborative search. Over the past 18 months it has been deployed on the Web in University College Dublin, where it has primarily been accessed by staff and students of the Department of Computer Science. The current deployment utilises 6 underlying search engines — Google,

Figure 3: Creating an 'AI Conferences' Community.

WiseNut, Ask, HotBot, AlltheWeb, Teoma and Yahoo — and implements a version of collaborative search that relies on exact query matching as described above. In this section we will outline I-SPY's main functionality, focusing on its community creation and personalization features.

4.1 Creating a Community

Fundamentally, I-SPY is designed to operate as a community-based search engine. Its ability to improve the result rankings of the underlying search engines depends on there being a pattern in the queries submitted by searchers and the results that they select. To facilitate this I-SPY makes it easy for users or groups to create their own search service by filling out a simple form. The result is that I-SPY will create a separate hit-table for this community and provides the user with a URL where their particular I-SPY service can be accessed. In addition, a simple piece of javascript code can be provided to allow users to place an I-SPY search box on their own Web site, such that queries through this search box are directed through their community hit-matrix.

For example, Figure 3 shows a screen-shot of this form during the creation of a search service designed to focus on AI conferences. This service can be offered through search boxes on a range of AI related Web sites, for example, as a specialised conference search facility. If properly labelled then it should attract queries that are associated with AI related conferences and the results selected should be conference related results. For example, we might expect that the query *Cambridge* should return a list of conferences that are due to be

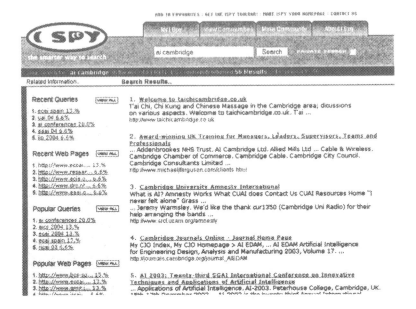

Figure 4: Results for "ai cambridge" shortly after the creation of the 'AI Conferences' community.

held in Cambridge this year. Even though the query is extremely vague, over time some users who have used it will have taken the time to select results that relate to Cambridge conferences rather than other features of Cambridge.

Additional community based features include the presentation of recent and successful queries(ones that have resulted in pages being selected) that have been submitted by community members, alongside recent and popular page selections; see Figure 5.

4.2 Example Session

Figures 4 and 5 show two screen-shots from the AI-Conference community in I-SPY to demonstrate the type of result re-ranking that I-SPY supports. Figure 4 shows the result page for the query "ai Cambridge" shortly after the community has been created. The user in question is looking for information relating to this year's AI-2004 conference but since their query is vague, the default results are not very relevant; in fact, only the 5th result is close—it relates to last year's AI-2003 conference—while the others relate to AI related books published by Cambridge University Press and Amnesty International in Cambridge University. Indeed the main page for AI-2004 does not even appear in the first 20 results returned for this query.

In contrast, Figure 5 shows the results for the same query after the com-

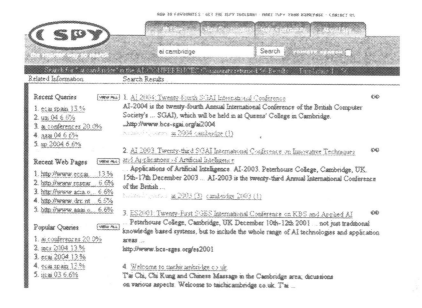

Figure 5: Results for "ai cambridge" for 'AI Conferences' community after an extended period of usage.

munity had been in use for some time. Now the first few results are different. Previous searches for this query have resulted in the selection of a range of pages that are more relevant to this community's focus — AI conferences — and in particular AI 2003 and 2004 home-pages are promoted (indicated by the I-SPY 'eyes') along with the ES 2001 home-page.

5   Live-User Evaluation

To test I-SPY's ability to adapt to a community of searchers we 'encouraged' 92 computer science students from the Department of Computer Science at University College Dublin to take part in an AI quiz. They were asked to answer a set of 25 AI-related general knowledge questions each requiring the student to find out a particular fact (time, place, person's name, system name etc.); see Table 1 for a number of sample questions.

Each student received a randomised list of these 25 questions – that is, all 25 questions in a random order – and they were asked to use the I-SPY search engine to locate their answers; the students were actively monitored to ensure that they used I-SPY only. They were instructed to attempt as many questions as possible within the allotted time and they were asked to record their answers and the URL where their answers were found on their question sheets. I-SPY was set up with an empty hit-matrix to draw on results from 4 underlying search

Table 1: Sample questions used in the live-user trial.

What game did Arthur Samuels help computers to play?
Who was Shakey?
How many bits are in a nibble?

engines (Google, Hotbot, Wisenut and AllTheWeb).

5.1 Methodology

The students were randomly divided into two groups. Group 1 contained 45 students and group 2 contained the remaining 47. Group 1 served as the *training group* for I-SPY in the sense that their search histories were used to populate the I-SPY hit-matrix but no re-ranking occurred for their search results; this group also served as a control against which to judge the search behaviour of the second group of users. The second group served as the *test group*. They benefited from I-SPY's re-ranking based on their own incremental usage and the hit matrix produced by the first group. The results presented relate to a 45-minute test-time for each group.

5.2 Test Scores

We are particularly interested in a number of key issues related to the effectiveness of I-SPY's collaborative search functionality. First and foremost, is there any evidence that collaborative search benefits users when it comes to helping them to more efficiently locate relevant information? In other words is there any difference between the groups in terms of the number of questions attempted or correctly answered?

Figure 6(a) presents the mean number of questions attempted for the 45 group 1 users and the 47 group 2 users. There appears to be an obvious advantage for the group 2 users who answered 40% more questions on average when compared to group 1 (9.9 vs. 13.9 for group 1 and group 2, respectively);this difference is statistically reliable at $p < 0.01$ with $n(89) = -5.39$. Perhaps more importantly, in comparison to group 1, group 2 users answered 52% more of these questions correctly (see Figure 6(b)); again this difference is statistically reliable at $p < 0.01$ with $n(67) = -5.84$. Indeed, the average group 2 user answered more questions correctly than the average group 1 user even attempted; 11.5 average questions correct per user in group 2 versus only 9.9 questions attempted in group 1.

The detail behind these mean figures is presented in histogram form in Figures 7(a) and 7(b) where we look at the number of individual students who attempted (Figure 7(a)) or correctly answered (Figure 7(b)) up to a given number of questions. Once again the difference between the user groups becomes clear. For example, the group 1 users attempted between 3 and 15 questions, answering between 1 and 13 of these questions correctly. This is in contrast to

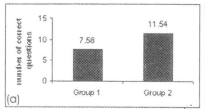 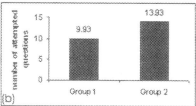

Figure 6: (a) Mean number of questions attempted per user. (b) Mean number of questions answered correctly per user.

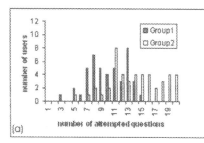 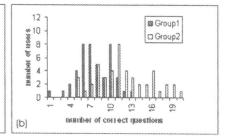

Figure 7: (a) Number of questions attempted. (b) Number of questions correctly answered.

the group 2 users who attempted between 5 and 20 questions and answered a similar range of questions correctly.

To place these differences in context, Figure 8 plots the percentage of students in each group that managed to answer a given test score, measured as the percentage of questions answered correctly. We have also highlighted key scoring thresholds that correspond to passing (40%), honours (55%) and distinction (70%) grades. The results reveal the significance of the differences between the two user groups from a grading perspective. More than twice as many group 2 students (70% of the group or 33 students) achieved a passing grade than the group 1 students (30% or 13 students). Moreover 56%, or 14 of the group 2 students achieved an honours grade and yet none of the group 1 students managed to score beyond 52% (13 out of the 25 questions). Finally, 5 of the group 2 students achieved distinctions. The point here appears to be clear: I-SPY's collaborative search technique has helped students to answer questions more efficiently and more successfully. In the remaining sections we will attempt to better understand the reasons behind this advantage by looking for biases within the user groups and by comparing their granular search behaviors at a result selection level.

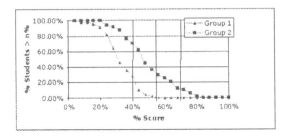

Figure 8: Percentage of students in each group that managed to achieve a given test score

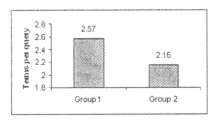

Figure 9: Average number of terms per query.

5.3 Group Differences

Of course one reason for the search differences between the user groups might simply be explained by some bias in the way that the groups were formed or the test conducted, so that group 2 users were advantaged. Although the test conditions were carefully controlled and the student selection process was random we did attempt to shed light on such issues by examining the type of queries used by the different user groups; perhaps the group 2 users were capable of formulating more effective queries than the group 1 users?

Firstly, it is worth highlighting that more than 70% of the unique queries used by the group 1 users were also used by the group 2 users and these repeated queries were used by approximately 65% of the users. This high repeat rate would suggest a close correspondence between the query capabilities of each group. However, it is also worth pointing out that when we compared the average query length (terms per query) for each group of users we found group 2 users to be using slightly shorter queries (see Figure 9); group 1 users used 2.57 terms per query on average compared to 2.16 terms per group 2 query. In other words, aside from repeating queries, the group 2 users appear to provide queries that have fewer terms and that as such, and all other things being equal, are likely to be more vague than the queries provided by group 1 users. If anything this suggest that the group 1 users might be slightly advantaged.

Finally, given that I-SPY has no ability to re-rank the results that are returned for non-repeating queries we would expect no real difference in the selection behaviour of the users for such queries if both groups are truly similar. When we examined the average position of the results selected for these non-repeating queries we found that the group 1 users had an average result selection position of 2.98 compared to 3.12 for the group 2 users. Once again, this minor difference appears to operate in the favour of the group 1 users and is consistent with the fact that these users do seem to be using slightly longer, and possibly more precise, queries; more precise queries should see relevant results with lower positional values.

From this analysis it appears to be valid to conclude that there is no significant bias operating in favour of the group 2 users that might go to explain the significant improvements in their search performance. If anything there is some evidence that perhaps the group 1 users were at a slight advantage when it came to their query construction abilities, making the positive I-SPY results for the group 2 users even more significant.

5.4   Result Selections

We contend that the success of the group 2 users is not due to any inherent bias regarding their searching abilities, but rather that it is a direct result of I-SPY's re-ranking process. In short, I-SPY is frequently able to promote previous user result selections to the group 2 users. These selections will appear higher up in the result lists and, assuming they appear to be just as relevant to the group 2 users as they did to the group 1 users, we should find that the group 2 users respond by selecting more results from higher positions within the result lists. In doing so, the group 2 users are likely to follow fewer false-leads, because popular selections will be promoted higher than spurious selections that are more likely to be false-lead. This should help the group two users to locate relevant results more quickly and more frequently and would explain their ability to attempt more questions, than the group 1 users, and their ability to answer more of these questions correctly.

Figure 10(a) confirms this hypothesis with a graph showing the number of results followed from different result positions for the two user groups. As predicted there is a clear difference, with group 2 users following more results from position 1 and 2 than the group 1 users. For instance, group 2 users select twice as many results in position 1 than the group 1 users, presumably reflecting the fact that, for group 2 users, twice as many position results are relevant, because many of these results have been promoted due to I-SPY's re-ranking. Overall, 84% of the results selected by group 2 users fall in the 1-3 position range. In contrast to reach this figure for group 1 we must consider a result range that goes as far as position 8. This argument is further supported by the average position of selected results (Figure 10(b)). The group 2 users selected results with an average position of 2.24 whereas the group 1 users selected results with an average position of 4.26; a 42% reduction in the position of selected results for group 2 users when compared to group 1 users; this difference is statistically

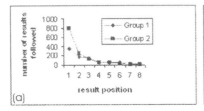 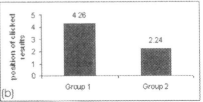

Figure 10: (a) Results followed per result-list position. (b) Average positions of selected results.

significant at $p < 0.01$.

5.5 Summary

The primary aim of this experiment was to demonstrate the effectiveness of I-SPY under realistic search conditions; results of more limited live user trials as well as comprehensive artificial user evaluations have previously been reported and demonstrated similar positive benefits [9, 10, 5]. We believe that the results show a clear and significant advantage for the I-SPY users when compared to the control group. The group 2 users are capable of answering more questions correctly by examining fewer search results; a powerful demonstration of I-SPY's enhanced search performance in the absence of any alternative explanation by way of any strong bias in the search skills of one of the user groups.

6 Lessons Learned

The deployment of I-SPY within University College Dublin has provided a relatively controlled environment to test the scalability and robustness of I-SPY and its collaborative search architecture. In addition the comments and feedback from interested users have served as the catalyst for a range of new developments.

6.1 Exploiting Query Similarity

The current version of I-SPY is limited by its reliance on exact matches between current and past queries. This limits I-SPY in two ways. First, it means that non-duplicate queries cannot be addressed by I-SPY; as discussed in Section 2 this accounts for about 40% of queries in specialised searches. Second, even when duplicates are available for a query, the number of reusable sessions is limited; in Section 2 we saw that the average duplicate query was associated with between 5 and 20 past search session. Recently we have tackled this issue by proposing a way to reuse the search sessions associated with similar queries as well as duplicate queries by discounting their influence on relevance. Evaluation results indicate that this approach can significantly improve the range of queries that I-SPY can deal with ($> 80\%$) and the average number of reusable sessions (> 100) in the search logs tested. Moreover, the new approach improves significantly on the precision and recall characteristics of I-SPY; see [1] for further information.

6.2 Query Recommendation

We have described how I-SPY uses usage data to compute query-page relevance values. We have also developed a way of using the same data to make high-quality query recommendations. The basic idea is to recommend alternative queries alongside relevant pages. The recommended queries are chosen for a given page because they have previously caused the selection of a page, as opposed to simple overlaps with the current query. Moreover, the queries can be ordered according to their relevance to the page by using I-SPY's normal relevance metric. For example, in Figure 5 the top 2 results are associated with a number of recommended (or related) queries. In [2] we have described this query recommendation technique in detail and presented evaluation results to show that it is capable of recommending genuinely useful queries that, if chosen, are likely to result in the retrieval of pages that are relevant to the searcher's needs.

6.3 Result Diversity

Most search engines place significant emphases on query-page similarity when it comes to retrieving and ranking search results. This often leads to a lack of diversity within the top ranking results, with the best results being very similar to each other. In [4] we argue that this limits how well the top ranking results cover the information space and we propose a method for increasing result diversity while at the same time preserving query similarity. In the future we plan to incorporate this diversity-enhancing method into I-SPY to improve its result coverage.

7 Conclusions

In [10] we described the collaborative approach to search, which leverages the usage histories of communities of searchers to improve the ranking of standard search-engine result lists. In that paper we presented preliminary evaluation work based on a limited cohort of users. In this paper we have taken the opportunity to present the results of a more comprehensive live-user trial based on a full deployment of the I-SPY technology. The results are again promising, with I-SPY searchers benefiting significantly from the search histories of their peers. We have also outlined a number of recent extensions to the collaborative search idea which are to be deployed in the near future.

References

[1] E. Balfe and B. Smyth. Case-Based Collaborative Web Search. In *Proceedings of 16th European Conference on Case-Based Reasoning*, 2004.

[2] E. Balfe and B. Smyth. Collaborative Query Recommendation for Web Search. In *Proceedings of 16th European Conference on Artificial Intelligence*. IOS Press, 2004.

[3] K. Bradley, R. Rafter, and B. Smyth. Case-based User Profiling for Content Personalization. In O. Stock P. Brusilovsky and C. Strapparava, editors, *Proceedings of the International Conference on Adaptive Hypermedia and Adaptive Web-based Systems*, pages 62–72. Springer-Verlag, 2000.

[4] M. Coyle and B. Smyth. On the Importance of Being Diverse: An Analysis of Similarity and Diversity in Web Search. In *Proceedings of 2nd International Conference on Intelligent Information Processing*, 2004.

[5] J. Freyne, B. Smyth, M. Coyle, E. Balfe, and P. Briggs. Further Experiments on Collaborative Ranking in Community-Based Web Search. *Artificial Intelligence Review: An International Science and Engineering Journal*, 21 (3-4):229–252, June 2004.

[6] Bernard J. Jansen, Amanda Spink, Judy Bateman, and Tefko Saracevic. Real Life Information Retrieval: A Study of User Queries on the Web. *SIGIR Forum*, 32(1):5–17, 1998.

[7] S. Lawrence and C. Lee Giles. Context and Page Analysis for Improved Web Search. *IEEE Internet Computing*, July-August:38–46, 1998.

[8] Seda Ozmutlu, Amanda Spink, and Huseyin C. Ozmutlu. Multimedia web searching trends: 1997-2001. *Inf. Process. Manage.*, 39(4):611–621, 2003.

[9] B. Smyth, E. Balfe, P. Briggs, M. Coyle, and J. Freyne. Collaborative Web Search. In *Proceedings of the 18th International Joint Conference on Artificial Intelligence, IJCAI-03*, pages 1417–1419. Morgan Kaufmann, 2003. Acapulco, Mexico.

[10] B. Smyth, J. Freyne, M. Coyle, P. Briggs, and E. Balfe. I-SPY: Anonymous, Community-Based Personalization by Collaborative Web Search. In *Proceedings of the 23rd SGAI International Conference on Innovative Techniques and Applications of Artificial Intelligence*, pages 367–380. Springer, 2003. Cambridge, UK.

[11] A. Spink and J. Bateman. Searching Heterogeneous Collections of the Web: Behaviour of Excite Users. *Information Research*, 4(2), 1998.

SESSION 3:

DIAGNOSIS AND MONITORING

A Model-Based Approach to Robot Fault Diagnosis

Honghai Liu and George M. Coghill

Department of Computing Science, University of Aberdeen

AB24 3UE Aberdeen UK

Abstract

This paper presents a model-based approach to online robotic fault diagnosis: First Priority Diagnostic Engine (FPDE). The first principle of FPDE is that a robot is assumed to work well as long as its key variables are within acceptable range. FPDE consists of four modules: the bounds generator, interval filter, component-based fault reasoning (core of FPDE) and fault reaction. The bounds generator calculates bounds of robot parameters based on interval computation and manufacturing standards. The interval filter provides characteristic values in each predetermined interval to denote corresponding faults. The core of FPDE carries out a two-stage diagnostic process: first it detects whether a robot is faulty by checking the relevant parameters of its end-effector, if a fault is detected it then narrows down the fault at component level. FPDE can identify single and multiple faults by the introduction of characteristic values. Fault reaction provides an interface to invoke emergency operation or tolerant control, even possibly system reconfiguration. The paper ends with a presentation of simulation results and discussion of a case study.

1 Introduction

Research on robotic diagnosis and fault tolerance is a considerable challenge for both artificial intelligence and robotics communities [18, 12].

Many contributions have been made to this topic in the past two decades [6, 2, 9]. Visinsky *et al* [17] provided a layered fault tolerance framework, for remote robots, consisting of servo, interface and supervisor layers. The layers form a hierarchy of fault tolerance which provide different levels of detection and tolerance capabilities for structurally diverse robots. Schroder [14] proposed a qualitative approach to fault diagnosis of dynamical systems, mainly process control systems. However, most of current fault diagnosis approaches focus on one of robot fault categories, hardware failure, or faults caused by modelling errors or uncertainty.

This paper proposes the first priority diagnostic engine *FPDE* to diagnose robot faults from the viewpoint of composite data streams of robotic key variables. The *FPDE* approach recategorized robot faults into sensor fault, robotic behaviour fault and modelling error. Sensor faults can be diagnosed by low-level sensor diagnosis. A robotic behaviour fault is composed of orientation faults and translational faults. The behaviour fault could be caused by hardware failures, e.g. gearbox fault excluding sensory fault and uncertainty factors.

Uncertainty motion collision can lead to orientation fault and/or translational fault. The FPDE first diagnoses predetermined key priority variables only (e.g. position of an end-effector), a robot is assumed to have no fault if the key priority variables are within acceptable bounds; otherwise it goes to diagnose its variables at a lower level. The interval filter is introduced to deal with noise from measurements. The FPDE deals with large degree of noise produced from payload change, by simply ignoring false faults in the time interval of gripper action. Once a fault is detected, characteristic values automatically isolate the fault position. The characteristic mapping presents the relation between the inputs and outputs of a physical system using characteristic values, which are characteristic quantities extracted from quantitative intervals of a domain in order to describe their corresponding qualitative information, for fault diagnosis purposes, Hence, the FPDE can be applied to general dynamical systems independent of their control systems design. This approach can diagnose both sensor-based parameters and nonsensor-based.

In next section we present the problem formulation of robotic fault diagnosis and a robotic diagnosis system. In Section 3 we describe the FPDE approach, and in Section 4 we give a case study based on the simplified robot arm of Beagle 2 Lander, finally conclusions are presented.

2   Problem Formulation and Solution

This section introduces an interval-computation based description for robotic faults, and proposes a model-based reasoning solution to the problem.

2.1   Robotic Fault Description

Generally speaking, there are two types of parameter in robotic diagnosis, sensor-based parameters and nonsensor-based parameters. The latter usually can be mathematically described by the former. Let us use capital letters (e.g., Θ_i) to describe variables that are not necessarily uniquely determined by our knowledge, i.e., that can be values from an interval. In these terms, if a measurement leads us to a conclusion that the value of this variable belongs to an interval $[\theta_i^-, \theta_i^+]$, then we can express this knowledge as: $(\theta_i^- \leq \Theta_i \leq \theta_i^+)$. It means there is no fault for variable Θ_i, otherwise there is fault detected. In these terms, the basic problem of fault diagnosis for a n-link robot can be reformulated into the following two steps:

- For sensor-based parameters (e.g., Θ_i), to check whether the following formula is true provided Θ_i.

$$\forall \Theta_i, \exists (\theta_i^- \leq \Theta_i \leq \theta_i^+) \tag{1}$$

- For nonsensor-based parameters (e.g., Y_i), to check whether the following formula is true provided θ_i^-, θ_i^+ and y_j^-, y_j^+.

$$\forall \Theta_i \in \left(\theta_i^- \leq \Theta_i \leq \theta_i^+\right),$$
$$\exists \left(y_m^- \leq f_m \left(\Theta_1, \cdots, \Theta_n\right) \leq y_m^+\right) \tag{2}$$

Where $i = 1, 2, \cdots, n$ stand for n sensor-based parameters, e.g. orientation angles from robotic sensors, $j = 1, 2, \cdots, m$ stand for m nonsensor-based parameters, e.g. position of an end-effector.

Actually by checking the validity of these formulas, we can check whether both sensor-based and nonsensor-based parameters are within their bounds. If all parameters meet the above bounds requirement, it means that the n-link robot works in acceptable condition, otherwise a fault has been detected, based on which further diagnosis should be carried on.

2.2 Robot Diagnosis System

A robot diagnosis system shown in figure 1 is proposed as a solution to the problem of robotic faults. The structure consists of three sections: the robotic system, motion planner and robotic fault reasoning: the *FPDE*. The robotic system could be a kinematics-based or dynamics-based system, which usually includes physical robots, sensors and motion control unit. The motion planner is used to plan robot motion to meet the task requirements. It generates the desired data (e.g. Θ_d, $\dot{\Theta}_d$ and τ) for both motion control unit and fault diagnosis. The motion planner is usually packaged with the robot by the robot provider or developed by the robotic application developer. It is the main reason why we separate fault diagnostic program as a independent package from the motion planner.

The robotic fault reasons the *FPDE* basically generates the desired bounds (e.g. Θ_b, $\dot{\Theta}_b$) of robot parameters, and compares them with sensor data (e.g. Θ_s, $\dot{\Theta}_s$) based on both robotic kinematics or dynamics and interval computation [3]. The outputs of the *FPDE* are fault report and fault reaction. The former lists fault predictions, fault and possible failures caused by the fault, the latter performs robotic emergency service or even reconfiguration of the robotic system.

3 Robotic Fault Reasoning

Generally speaking, robotic faults include hardware failures, modelling errors and uncertainty issues. The sensor failures could happen to optical encoders, tachometers and relevant electrical circuits. The modelling errors are caused mainly by choosing an unsuitable model, for example, a kinematic model being used for robot in a high speed situation. The uncertainty factors usually are from external collisions.

The proposed *FPDE* approach recategorized robotic fault into sensor fault, robotic behaviour fault and modelling errors. A robotic behaviour fault is composed of orientation faults and translational faults. The behaviour fault could

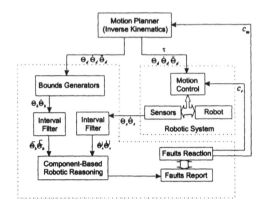

Figure 1: The *FPDE* Robotic Fault Reasoning

be caused by hardware failures, e.g. gearbox fault excluding sensory fault and uncertainty factors. Uncertainty motion collision can lead to orientation fault and/or translational fault. The operational relation of the *FPDE* in robotic fault diagnosis is illustrated in figure 2. The sensor detection running first in a diagnostic cycle is necessary to ensure that the *FPDE* has a correct scenario.

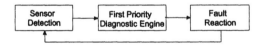

Figure 2: Operational relation in robotic diagnostic system

The *FPDE* approach to robotic fault diagnosis is carried out at the component level of a robot. A robotic component herein denotes a robotic arm segment (e.g. a link) or a robotic joint (e.g. a motor). The first principle for the *FPDE* is that a robot operates in acceptable condition if and only if the robotic parameters of its end-effector meet the requirement set by its motion planner. To deal with this, the *FPDE* is developed into four sections: the bounds generator, interval filter, component-based robotic reasoning (core of the *FPDE*) and fault reaction.

3.1 Robotic Bounds Generation

Different models affect fault diagnosis of a robot in some certain extent [17]. The bounds generator in figure 1 is proposed to generate corresponding bounds of the robot parameters depending on different models. In accordance with the diagnostic model of dynamic systems [5], it generates bounds for the end-effector of a robot in the fault detection stage and for each link and joint in the fault isolation stage. In the case of kinematic models [4], the bounds of the robotic joints, $[\theta_i^-, \theta_i^+]$, are easily calculated due to the fact that 90% of their bounds can be determined by the mechanical characteristics of motors [16],

Θ_f, and manufacture accuracy of industry, Θ_m. The manufacture accuracy is required to be not more than 5%. Hence the interval of Θ can be set as follows,

$$\Theta = Max((\theta_f^- \leq \Theta_f \leq \theta_f^+), (\theta_m^+ \leq \Theta_m \leq \theta_m^+)) \tag{3}$$

Where $\Theta_f = \frac{10}{9}\Theta_{offset}$, $\Theta_m = 5\%\hat{\Theta}_s$. The Θ is the vector consisting of maximum value of Θ_f, and Θ_m in each time interval. The Θ_{offset} is robotic repeatability required legally in robot datasheet.

The bounds of robotic parameters of an end-effector (e.g., $[y^-, y^+]$) usually are given by empirical approaches or experimental methods in practice.

3.2 Interval Filter

Many theoretical and practical contributions to filter development have been made in both control and AI communities such as Kalman filter and extended Kalman filters [8],[11], and non-Kalman filters [10], [7]. In general a filter is a device or an algorithm that removes something from whatever passes through it. Filters and filter-related methods extract similarity or characteristics of data from channels to meet system requirement [15], [13].

The interval filter is designed to detect faults and extract characteristic values of robot parameters in each predetermined time interval s. Probability theory is used to detect faults from data with noise. It is a practical problem for diagnosis task to deal with measurements with, sometimes, huge noise. The selection of characteristic values is application-dependent. The characteristic values, defined as the maxima in each interval, are extracted from time intervals of robotic motion to describe their corresponding fault information with high possibility. That is, the fault of a dynamic system is qualitatively described by discrete quantitative values in terms of predefined intervals. A probability function in the time interval j is introduced in the following,

$$\Pr(p_j) = \frac{\sum_{i=1}^{s} \omega_i}{s - \sum_{i=1}^{s} \omega_i}$$

Where

$$\begin{cases} \omega_i = 1 & \omega_i \in ((e^- \leq E \leq e^+) \wedge (e^- \leq 0 \wedge 0 \leq e^+)) \\ \omega_i = 0 & otherwise \end{cases}$$

The $\sum_{i=1}^{s} \omega_i$ is the number of sampling data within their bounds. Fault detection is based on the fact whether the ratio is less than a constant threshold λ. The threshold for different sensors can be set based on empirical approaches and sensor datasheet. The difference, E, between data from the bounds generator and from robot sensors is defined as $e^- = \Theta^+ - \Theta_s$ and $e^+ = \Theta_s - \Theta^-$, for a kinematic model; $e^- = \tilde{\Theta}^+ - \Theta_s$ and $e^+ = \Theta_s - \tilde{\Theta}^-$, for a dynamic model.

For example, the position of an end-effector at a time instant can be described by the interval filter as given by the following equation,

$$\hat{X}(t) = \sum_{i=1}^{n} \hat{l}_i \cos \hat{\Theta}_i(t)$$

$$\hat{Y}(t) = \sum_{i=1}^{n} \hat{l}_i \sin \hat{\Theta}_i(t)$$

$$(4)$$

Where $\hat{X} \in [x^-, x^+]$ and $\hat{Y} \in [y^-, y^+]$ Equations 4 and 5 are applied, the $\hat{X}$ and $\hat{Y}$ can be estimated by their characteristic values in the time interval. The characteristic function designed to generate characteristic values is a key problem. In this paper the characteristic function is designed by the fact: characteristic values are those whose distances are maxima from corresponding bounds. Therefore, qualitative information in predetermined time interval is denoted by their corresponding characteristic values. The qualitative parameter of an end-effector in the ith time interval can be derived as follows,

$$f_{cp}\left(\hat{\Theta}_1(t) \wedge \cdots \wedge \hat{\Theta}_n(t)\right) \to \hat{X}(i)$$

$$f_{cp}\left(\hat{\Theta}_1(t) \wedge \cdots \wedge \hat{\Theta}_n(t)\right) \to \hat{Y}(i)$$

$$(5)$$

The qualitative state of $\hat{X}(i)$ and $\hat{Y}(i)$ depend on the output of the characteristic functions by checking whether equation 6 is true. Similarly, the above can apply to velocity of the end-effector as given as follows,

$$\dot{\hat{X}}(t) = -\sum_{i=1}^{n} \hat{l}_i \dot{\hat{\Theta}}_i \sin \hat{\Theta}_i(t)$$

$$\dot{\hat{Y}}(t) = \sum_{i=1}^{n} \hat{l}_i \dot{\hat{\Theta}}_i \cos \hat{\Theta}_i(t)$$

$$(6)$$

Where $\dot{\hat{X}} \in (\dot{x}^-, \dot{x}^+)$ and $\dot{\hat{Y}} \in (\dot{y}^-, \dot{y}^+)$

$$f_{cv}\left(\hat{\Theta}_1(t) \wedge \cdots \wedge \hat{\Theta}_n(t)\right) \to \dot{\hat{X}}(i)$$

$$f_{cv}\left(\hat{\Theta}_1(t) \wedge \cdots \wedge \hat{\Theta}_n(t)\right) \to \dot{\hat{Y}}(i)$$

$$(7)$$

3.3 Component-Based Robotic Reasoning

The first principle of component-based robotic reasoning, core of the *FPDE*, is that a robot is not faulty as long as its first-priority parameter is in the acceptable bounds. For a robot, the first-priority parameters are those of its end-effector. The *FPDE* can narrow down a fault at robotic component level. (e.g., links or motors). The algorithm can detect both single fault and multiple faults in a robotic system.

The algorithm *FPDE* is described in the following,

FPDE Algorithm

1. Install T_d, $\dot{T}_d$ as input, $\lambda = \lambda_v = \lambda_p = 1$.

2. a PID-based motion planner generates desired joint information, Θ_d, $\dot{\Theta}_d$.

3. Bound generators.

   (a) IF(Kinematic Model), set $k=5\%$

      i. Desired bounds of the end-effector, $[T_d^-, T_d^+]$, $[\dot{T}_d^-, \dot{T}_d^+]$
         $T_d^\pm = T_d(1 \pm k)$, $\dot{T}_d^\pm = \dot{T}_d(1 \pm k)$

      ii. Desired joint bounds, $[\Theta_d^-, \Theta_d^+]$, $[\dot{\Theta}_d^-, \dot{\Theta}_d^+]$
         $\Theta_d{}^\pm = Max(\Theta_d(1 \pm k) \wedge \Theta_{offset})$,
         $\dot{\Theta}_d^\pm = \dot{\Theta}_d(1 \pm k)$.

   (b) IF(Dynamic Model)

      i. $T_d^\pm = \tilde{T}_d^\pm$, $\dot{T}_d^\pm = \dot{\tilde{T}}_d{}^\pm$

      ii. $\Theta_d^\pm = \tilde{\Theta}_d^\pm$, $\dot{\Theta}_d^\pm = \dot{\tilde{\Theta}}_d{}^\pm$

4. Interval filter for sensory data.

   (a) Characteristic values for the position of the end-effector,
      $T_{cp} = f_{cp}(t, \lambda, T_s)$, where T_s is from equations 4, 5.

   (b) Characteristic values for the speed of the end-effector,
      $\dot{T}_{cv} = f_{cv}(t, \lambda, \dot{T}_s)$, where $\dot{T}_s$ is from equations 4, 7.

5. Component-based fault reasoning.

   (a) Reasoning about orientation faults.

      i. $\Theta u = \Theta_s - \Theta_d^+$,
         $\Theta d = \Theta_s - \Theta_d^-$.

      ii. IF $(\Theta u \geq 0 \ or \ \Theta d \leq 0)$
         THEN Calculate $Max(\lambda_p, \hat{\Theta}u)$ and $Max(\lambda_p, \hat{\Theta}d)$.

      iii. Generate orientation faults, $OF_p(t_p, \lambda_p, \hat{\Theta}_u, \hat{\Theta}_d)$

      iv. $\dot{\Theta}u = \dot{\Theta}_s - \dot{\Theta}_d^+$,
         $\dot{\Theta}d = \dot{\Theta}_s - \dot{\Theta}_d^-$.

      v. IF $(\dot{\Theta}u \geq 0 \ or \ \dot{\Theta}d \leq 0)$
         THEN Calculate $Max(\lambda_v, \hat{\dot{\Theta}}u)$ and $Max(\lambda, \hat{\dot{\Theta}}d)$.

      vi. Generate orientation faults, $OF_v(t_v, \lambda_v, \hat{\dot{\Theta}}u, \hat{\dot{\Theta}}d)$

   (b) Reasoning about translational faults.

      i. $l_d(i)^\pm = l_d(i)(1 \pm k)$

      ii. For i=1 To Length(Θ_d)
         For j=1 To length(Θ_s)
         IF (j Not Equal To i) Then $l_s(j) = l_d(j)$
         $\hat{l}_s(i)$ can be achieved by equations 4, 5 and 7.
         IF $(\hat{l}_s(i) \in [l_d(i)^-, l_d(i)^+])$ THEN No transitional faults
         ELSE set $\hat{l}_u$, $\hat{l}_d$.

      iii. Generate transitional faults, TF(t_l, λ, $\hat{l}_u$, $\hat{l}_d$).

   (c) Modelling faults.

6. Return NO FAULTS.

The *FPDE* incorporates functions from the bounds generator, interval filter and component-based reasoning. The bounds generator generates bounds for the Cartesian trajectory, joint trajectory and the other relevant parameters. The bounds generator is based on industrial experience to ensure that relevant accuracy is not more than 5 percent, and it is within its physical requirement such as repeatability of motors. The interval filter generates characteristic values to compare with sensory data in a predetermined time interval. The characteristic function is designed to meet the corresponding application requirement. For robotic fault diagnosis, the characteristic function is to calculate maximum robot parameters of its end-effector deviating from their bounds. The advantage of the interval filter is that it converts quantitative information into qualitative information based on numerical data. It provides a solution to clear the ambiguity of conversion between quantitative and qualitative information. That is, the mapping between quantitative and qualitative information can be set by some certain characteristic numerical values. It should be noted that the characteristic function used to generate characteristic values has to be carefully designed in order to meet certain requirement of its corresponding qualitative meaning.

Compared with the other robot and mechanism diagnostic approaches (e.g. [17]), the *FPDE* recategorizes fault into behaviour fault and modelling faults. The behaviour fault is composed of orientation fault and translational fault. The former usually is caused by physical failures of motors and links and uncertainty collision, or link overflection; the latter is mainly caused by link overflection. The orientation fault is detected based on upper bound deviations and lower bound deviations as described in the following:

$$If\,(\Theta u \geq 0\,or\,\Theta d \leq 0)\,Then\,Max(\lambda_p,\,\hat{\Theta}u)\,or\,Max(\lambda_p,\,\hat{\Theta}d),$$

$$If\,(\dot{\Theta}u \geq 0\,or\,\dot{\Theta}d \leq 0)\,Then\,Max(\lambda_v,\,\hat{\dot{\Theta}}u)\,or\,Max(\lambda_v,\,\hat{\dot{\Theta}}d).$$

Results from the mapping of characteristic values present sufficient information to detect fault and isolate their faulty location. For example, the function of the orientation fault, $OF_v(t_v,\,\lambda,\,\hat{\Theta}u,\,\hat{\Theta}d)$, gives the estimated upper bound deviation, estimated lower bound deviation and their corresponding time instant. Faults can be isolated in their corresponding time intervals, multiple faults can be identified by the characteristic values. The introduction of characteristic values not only helps to clear the ambiguity of conversion between quantitative and qualitative information, but also to detect multiple faults in a time interval.

An orientation fault can be detected and isolated with the aid of robotic sensors in the *FPDE*. Transitional fault can be trickily diagnosed even without information from sensors. As we know there are usually no sensors for industrial robot link. The *FPDE* assumes that sensor data from motors is believable, and all link parameters except the test link, are replaced by the desired data, the faulty situation of the test link can be checked to see whether it meets link bounds in equations 5 and $(e^- \leq E \leq e^+) \wedge (e^- \leq 0 \wedge 0 \leq e^+)$, Where $e^- = l^+ - l_s$ and $e^+ = l_s - l^-$.

Joint	Joint 1	Joint 2	Joint 3
Offset	1.10422deg	0.637987deg	−0.756872deg

Table 1: Joint repeatability parameters

Modelling errors are unavoidable but can be controlled in the design stage of a control system.

4 Case study

A case study of the simplified robot arm of Beagle 2 is addressed for fault diagnosis purpose in this section. Beagle 2's robotic arm in Mars robot mission was originally devised as a means to remove specific scientific instruments and tools from the Lander and deploy them in positions where they can study or obtain samples of the rocks and soil. The arm supports the panoramic cameras and deploys the crawling mole to gather subsurface soil samples, returning these to the on-board analytical laboratory. The position and speed of the end-effector is determined as key variables. Repeatability (or joint offset) is taken from the datasheet of Beagle 2 [1], it intends to generate faults for modelling errors.

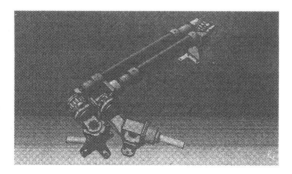

Figure 3: The robot arm of Beagle 2 Lander

4.1 Simulation results

Robot diagnosis, generally speaking, includes fault detection, fault isolation and fault identification [5]. The *FPDE* applies to first three links of the robot arm with 20 time intervals, simulation results are demonstrated in figures 4, 5 and 6, respectively. Solid-line trajectories describe the test position and speed; Dashed-line trajectories describe their corresponding upper bounds and lower bounds, the position with '*' symbol describes the characteristic value caused by a discrepancy in the x coordinate, position with 'o' symbol describes characteristic value caused by a discrepancy in the y coordinate. Fault analysis of the end-effector in Cartesian space is presented in figure 4, from which it clearly demonstrates discrepancy between the tested trajectories and their corresponding bounds. Due to the FPDE, this existing characteristic value in key priority parameter means the corresponding time interval existing robotic fault.

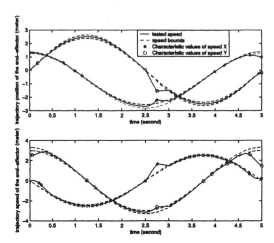

Figure 4: Fault analysis of trajectories of the end-effector

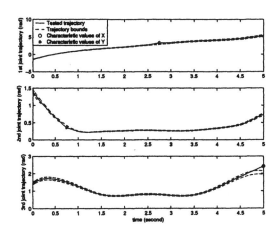

Figure 5: Fault analysis of the joint trajectories

The location of the robot fault is found in the fault isolation stage. In terms of the definition of robot components, the *FPDE* diagnoses motors and links of a robot in turn. The fault location is generated by the mapping of characteristic values of the end-effector based on robotics. The advantage of the *FPDE* for motor faults diagnosis is that it diagnoses joint fault decouplly. Figure 5 presents the characteristic values in the joint trajectories corresponding to the trajectories of the end-effector. Figure 6 presents the characteristic values in the joint speed corresponding to the speed of the end-effector. The figures

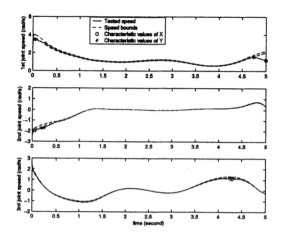

Figure 6: Fault analysis of the joint speeds

illustrate faulty time instants with symbols, respectively. For example, the characteristic values of the 1st joint in figure 5 allows FPDE to deduce that the fault in time interval 12 are caused by the 1st joint, this fault leads to faulty motion of the end-effector in both x and y coordinates. The fault of the 3rd joint in time interval 17 leads to the faulty motion of the end-effector at y coordinate. One of contributions of the $FPDE$ algorithm is to identify multiple faults in a time interval, for example, the speed fault of the end-effector in 1st time interval is caused by faults of joint 1 and joint 2.

4.2 Fault report

Fault report is used to conclude detected fault and to generate preparation for further fault reaction such as tolerant control or even system reconfiguration. The fault report of this case study is given in table 2. The motion process is divided into 20 time intervals, the symbol '$\sqrt{}$' means all data in corresponding time interval is not faulty by remaining within its corresponding bounds. The last column '$fault$' concludes reasons of the faults in the corresponding time interval. Where J_i denotes fault caused by the ith joint, M_j denotes fault caused by modelling error in the j parameter.

For example, fault in the 1st time interval, trajectory fault of the y coordinate is caused by modelling error, M_y, due to that J_y is with $\sqrt{}$. The fault of the speed in the x coordinate is caused by fault in the 2nd joint; the faults of the speed in the y coordinate are caused by fault in the 1st joint and 2nd joint.

5   Conclusion

The First Priority Diagnostic Engine has been proposed to deal with two common difficulties in robot diagnosis, computational efficiency and measurement noise. The first principle of the FPDE is that a robot is assumed to work well as long as its key variables are within acceptable bounds. Basically FPDE first calculates characteristic values for key variables of a robot in a predetermined interval time, then maps them into corresponding qualitative states to present their quantitative characteristics. Finally compare the characteristic values with their bounds to diagnose faults. The FPDE is composed of four modules: the bounds generator, interval filter, component-based fault reasoning (core of FPDE) and fault reaction. The paper ends with a presentation of simulation results and discussion of a case study.

Acknowledgements

The financial support from the Engineering and Physical Science Research Council, United Kingdom, under grant GR/S10773/01 and GR/S10766/01 is gratefully acknowledged. The authors also would like to thank their partners: Dave Barnes and Andy Shaw from University of Wales, Aberystwyth.

Notation

$\hat{\theta}_i, \hat{\dot{\theta}}_i$: ith estimated orientation angle and its velocity.

$\Theta_d, \dot{\Theta}_d$:   desired joint trajectory and its velocity of a robot.

$\Theta_b, \dot{\Theta}_b$:   bounds of a joint trajectory and its velocity.

Θ_{offset}:   joint repeatability.

$\Theta_s, \dot{\Theta}_s$:   joint trajectory from sensors and its velocity.

$\Theta^{\pm}$:   upper and lower trajectory bounds based on a kinematic model.

$\tilde{\Theta}^{\pm}$:   upper and lower trajectory bounds based on a dynamic model.

$\hat{\Theta}_b, \hat{\dot{\Theta}}_b$:   estimated bounds of a joint trajectory and its velocity.

$\hat{\Theta}_s, \hat{\dot{\Theta}}_s$:   estimated joint trajectory and its joint speed.

$\hat{\Theta}_i, \hat{\dot{\Theta}}_i$: ith estimated joint trajectory and velocity, respectively.

τ: computed torque of a robot.

CI_i: time instant of a characteristic value of a position interval in the i coord

CV_j: characteristic value of a position interval in the j coordinate.

CI_{iv}:   time instant of a characteristic value of a velocity interval in the i coord

CV_{jv}:   characteristic value of a velocity interval in the j coordinate.

J_i: Joint fault for the i coordinate.

$\hat{l}_i$:   estimated length of the ith link.

$\hat{X}, \hat{Y}$:   estimated position of an end-effector in x, y coordinates.

$\hat{\dot{X}}, \hat{\dot{Y}}$:   estimated speed of an end-effector in x, y coordinates.

	CI_x	CV_x	CI_y	CV_y	CI_{zv}	CV_{zv}	CI_{yv}	CV_{yv}	J_x	J_y	J_{zv}	J_{yv}	fault
1	√	√	178	.524	200	.591	53	.135	√	√	$J2$	$J1$	$J1,J2$
	√	√	178	.524	200	.591	53	.135	√	√	$J2$	$J2$	M_y
2	√	√	√	√	252	.749	√	√	√	√	$J2$	√	$J2,M_y$
3	750	.577	√	√	√	√	√	√	$J2$	√	√	√	$J2$
4	1000	−.05	√	√	√	√	√	√	√	√	√	√	M_x
5	1155	−.42	√	√	√	√	1250	2.500	√	√	√	√	M_x,M_{yv}
6	√	√	√	√	√	√	1431	2.442	√	√	√	√	M_{yv}
7	√	√	√	√	√	√	√	√	√	√	√	√	√
8	√	√	√	√	√	√	√	√	√	√	√	√	√
9	√	√	√	√	√	√	√	√	√	√	√	√	√
10	√	√	2500	.0312	2500	.032	√	√	√	√	√	√	M_y,M_{zv}
11	2750	−2.22	2750	−1.53	2750	−1.53	2750	−1.53	$J1$	$J1$	√	√	$J1,M_{zv},M_{yv}$
12	2752	−2.22	2752	−1.53	2752	−1.53	2752	−1.53	$J1$	$J1$	√	√	$J1,M_{zv},M_{yv}$
13	√	√	√	√	√	√	√	√	√	√	√	√	√
14	√	√	√	√	√	√	√	√	√	√	√	√	√
15	√	√	√	√	√	√	3750	−2.50	√	√	√	√	M_{yv}
16	4000	−.09	√	√	√	√	3930	−2.44	√	√	√	√	M_x,M_{yv}
17	4201	.365	√	√	√	√	4250	−2.04	√	√	√	$J3$	$J3,M_x$
18	√	√	√	√	√	√	4299	−1.95	√	√	√	$J3$	$J1,J3$
19	4750	1.125	√	√	4737	−.81	4750	.773	√	√	$J1$	$J1$	$J1,M_x$
20	5000	.984	5000	−.19	5000	−.19	5000	.193	$J3$	$J3$	$J1$	√	$J1,J3,M_{yv}$

Table 2: Robotic fault analysis at component level

References

[1] D. Barnes, E. Taylor, N. Phillips, A. Gossant, and G. Paar. Beagle2 simulation, kinematics calibration, and environment dem generation. *Proc. 7th ESA Workshop on Advanced Space Technologies for Robotics and Automation*, 2002.

[2] M. Blanke, M. Kinnaert, J. Lunze, and M. Staroswiecki. Diagnosis and fault-tolerant control. *Springer-Verlag Berlin Heidelberg*, 2003.

[3] B. Bouchon-Meunier and V. Kreinovich. From interval computations to modal mathematics: Applications and computational complexity. *ACM SIGSAM Bulletin*, 32(2):7–11, 1998.

[4] A. Castellet and F. Thomas. An algorithm for the solution of inverse kinematic problems based on an interval method. *in Advances in Robot Kinematics, M. Husty and J. Lenarcic (Eds.), Kluwer Academic Publishers*, pages 393–403, 1998.

[5] G. M. Coghill and Q. Shen. Towards the specification of models for diagnosis of dynamic systems. *Artificial Intelligence in Communications*, 14(2), 2001.

[6] J. De Kleer and B. Williams. Diagnosing multiple faults. *Artificial Intelligence*, 32:100–117, 1987.

[7] R. Dearden and D. Clancy. Particle filters for real-tim fault detection in planetary rovers. *13th international workshop on principles of diagnosis*, 2003.

[8] M. Grewal. Kalman filtering: Theory and practice. *Englewood Cliffs, NJ: Prentice-Hall*, 2001.

[9] U. Heller and P. Struss. g^+de:the generalize diagnosis engine. *12th international workshop on principles of diagnosis*, 2001.

[10] P. A. Naylor, O. Tanrkulu, and A. G. Constantinides. Subband adaptive filtering for acoustic echo control using allpass polyphase iir filterbanks. *IEEE Trans, on Signal and Processing*, 6(2), 1998.

[11] T. Parks and C. Burrus. Digital filter design. *New York: John Wiley and Sons, Inc.*, June 1987.

[12] R. Patton, P. Frank, and R. Clark. Fault diagnosis in dynamic systems (theory and applications). *prentice Hall International (UK) Ltd*, 1989.

[13] C. Perng, H. Wang, S. Zhang, and D. Parker. Landmark: a new technique for similarity-based pattern querying in time series databases. *Proceedings, ICDE*, 2000.

[14] J. Schroder. Modelling, state oberservation and diagnosis of quantised systems. *Springer-Verlag Berlin Heidelberg*, 2003.

[15] J. Schroder. Modelling, state observation and diagnosis of quantised systems. *Springer-Verlag Berlin Heidelberg*, Germany, 2003.

[16] P. Shiakolas, K. Conrad, and T. Yih. On the accuracy, repeatability, and degree of influence of kinematics parameters for industrial robots. *International journal of modelling and simulation*, 22(3):1 – 10, 2002.

[17] M. Visinsky, J. Cavallaro, and W. I.D. A dynamic fault tolerance framework for remote robots. *IEEE Transactions on Robotics and Automation*, 11(4):477 – 490, 1995.

[18] M. Visinsky, J. Cavallaro, and I. Walker. Robotic fault detection and fault tolerance: A survey. *Reliability Engineering and System Safety*, 46(2):139–158, 1994.

Automating the Analysis and Management of Power System Data using Multi-agent Systems Technology

Euan M. Davidson, Stephen D. J. McArthur, James R. McDonald
Tom Cumming, Ian Watt

University of Strathclyde
euan.davidson@strath.ac.uk
www.instee.eee.strath.ac.uk

Abstract

Earlier research [1] by the Institute of Energy and Environment and SP PowerSystems demonstrated that multi-agent systems technology could be used to integrate a number of software tools to automate the analysis and management of power systems monitoring data. This paper focuses on issues raised during the migration from an off-line prototype to an on-line multi-agent system for use at SP PowerSystems. The authors believe that the system described in this paper is one of the first of its type to be deployed in the electrical power industry for continual on-line use by operational engineers.

1. Introduction

System monitoring plays an increasingly important role in the management and operation of electrical power networks. Power system operators aim to keep customer interruptions to a minimum and increase commercial return from network assets such as power lines, cables, transformers, switchgear and associated protection, control and communication equipment; data from monitoring systems contains important information about the health of assets and the performance of the power system. As a result, monitoring data is of interest to those tasked with managing these assets as well as the engineers responsible for day-to-day operation of the power system. Staff wishing to utilise this data are faced with the following problems:

- Useful information contained within the data is often implicit. Due to the sheer volume of captured data, manual analysis and interpretation of the data is time-consuming if not impractical; and

- Data captured by different systems is often stored in different proprietary data formats in different databases in different physical locations. In many cases, data from different monitoring systems is related but there is no means of easily collating and managing the different types of data.

151

Previous research at the Institute for Energy and the Environment [1] demonstrated that multi-agent system technology could be employed to integrate a number of disparate data capture and analysis systems used by engineers to assess the performance of power system protection. A prototype system, named PEDA (Protection Engineering Diagnostic Agents), was built and tested in the laboratory using historical power systems data provided by SP PowerSystems. While the prototype was adequate to demonstrate the use of multi-agent systems for that particular application, it was not deemed suitable for industrial application for the following reasons:

- During the course of the PEDA project SP PowerSystems made enhancements to the monitoring system which impacted on the functionality required in the PEDA system;

- Engineers wished to manually append additional information, e.g. the results of fault investigations or any outstanding issues with the monitoring system, to the information produced by PEDA;

- It became apparent that selected information produced by the PEDA system was of interest to engineers in SP PowerSystems' business other than the protection engineers that PEDA was originally designed for. As a result, ways of tailoring the information for certain roles in the business became an additional requirement; and

- The prototype of the PEDA system was implemented using a toolkit for building multi-agent systems [2]. When the project began the toolkit was well supported by developers and implemented many of the FIPA (Foundation for Intelligent Physical Agents) [3] standards of the time. Since then maintenance of the toolkit has ceased and FIPA standards have been updated and expanded.

In this paper the authors present an overview of the problem that the PEDA system was designed to solve and how the issues above were resolved. The following section describes the monitoring data that SP PowerSystems' protection engineers use to assess the performance of the protection system for the transmission grid in central and southern Scotland.

2. Post-fault Analysis and Management of Power System Data related to Protection Operation

Due to the large investment that utilities make in power system plant, such as cables, power-lines, transformers and generators, it is vital that the plant is protected from the effects of disturbances to and faults on the power system. Weather is one of the root causes of disturbances to the power network. High winds, lightning, snow and ice can all be responsible for causing faults. Abnormal currents and voltages experienced during a disturbance can cause damage to plant or problems with power systems stability.

Power system protection is responsible for detecting disturbances and removing their effect on the network before plant is damaged. There are many different types of protection system for protecting specific items of plant (unit protection) or areas of the power system (non-unit protection).

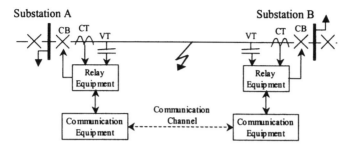

Figure 1. A unit protection scheme

Figure 1 shows a unit protection scheme that protects a line between two substations. At each substation, current transformers (CT) and voltage transformers (VT) are used to measure instantaneous voltage and current. If a fault occurs on the line, the relay equipment detects the fault and opens the circuit breakers (CB) in both substations, clearing the fault.

It is vital that the protection system operates correctly clearing faults before plant is permanently damaged or isolating permanently faulted items of plant. Protection engineers are tasked with maintaining the protection system and tracking its performance.

2.1 Monitoring Systems and Data sources

Protection engineers use data from a number of different monitoring systems to assess whether or not the protection system has operated correctly in response to a disturbance on the power system. The different monitoring systems are described below.

2.1.1 SCADA (Supervisory Control And Data Acquisition)

SCADA data (figure 2) is collated from substations around the transmission network. Protection engineers are primarily interested in the alarms related to the operation of the protection system. From the SCADA data the engineers identify 'incidents' and 'events'. An 'incident' is a group of alarms that relate to a disturbance on a particular circuit or item of plant. 'Events' are alarms or groups of alarms that make up a part of an incident, e.g. alarms indicating protection operation, circuit breakers opening and closing, or communication signals between substations. Once all the events for a given incident have been identified, engineers check for particular patterns of alarms which indicate either correct operation or that further investigation is required.

SCADA Alarms and Indications

13:54:14:720 SUBA SUBB	Unit Protection Optd	ON
13:54:14:730 SUBA SUBB	Trip Relays Optd	ON
13:54:14:730 SUBF	Battery Volts Low	ON
13:54:14:750 SUBF	Battery Volts Low	OFF
13:54:14:760 SUBA SUBB	Second Intertrip Optd	ON
13:54:14:760 SUBA cb1	OPEN	
13:54:14:790 SUBB SUBA	Distance Protection Optd	ON
13:54:14:800 SUBC T1	Trip Relays Optd	ON
13:54:14:800 SUBD	Pilot Faulty	ON
13:54:14:800 SUBB SUBA	Trip Relays Optd	ON
13:54:14:810 SUBD	Pilot Faulty	OFF
13:54:14:810 SUBB SUBA	Unit Protection Optd	ON
13:54:14:810 SUBE	Metering Alarms	ON
13:54:14:820 SUBB cb2	OPEN	
13:54:14:830 SUBA SUBB	Autoswitching in Progress	
13:54:14:850 SUBC cb3	OPEN	
13:54:14:860 SUBB SUBA	Second Intertrip Optd	ON
13:54:14:860 SUBB SUBA	First Intertrip Optd	ON
13:54:14:890 SUBB SUBA	Autoswitching in Progress	
13:54:14:900 SUBC T1	Autoswitching in Progress	
⋮	⋮	⋮
13:54:35:470 SUBC T3	Autoswitching Complete	
13:54:35:490 SUBC cb3	CLOSED	
13:54:37:710 SUBB cb2	CLOSED	
13:54:38:210 SUBA SUBB	Autoswitching Complete	
13:54:38:300 SUBA cb1	CLOSED	

Figure 2. Example of SCADA generated during a disturbance

Protection engineers access the SCADA data through a system called PSAlerts. The PSAlerts system stores the SCADA alarms in a database which engineers can query using PSAlerts-client software.

An advantage of the SCADA data is that engineers across the company can access it within seconds using the PSAlerts system. The disadvantage of the SCADA data is its volume; thousands of alarms are generated every day.

2.1.2 Digital Fault Recorder

Digital Fault Recorders (DFR) are located in various substations across the transmission network. They continuously monitor a number of power system parameters including instantaneous analogue values of voltage and current, breaker status, protection relay status, and communication signals sent or received between substations. DFRs can be set to trigger on changes in these parameters. When a DFR triggers, it captures time series data of all the measurands, with a pre-defined number of pre-trigger and post-trigger samples. This time series data forms a fault record (figure 3).

Typically there will be a number of fault recorders in substation monitoring circuits out of the substation (figure 4). If one of the fault recorder triggers, it also triggers the other fault recorders in the substation generating additional records.

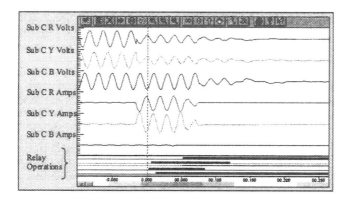

Figure 3. Fault Recorder Data

Figure 3 shows DFR data from a substation at one end of a circuit experiencing a disturbance. The fault record shows the three-phase voltages at the substation (Sub C Red Volts, Sub C Yellow Volts, Sub C Blue Volts) and also the currents on those 3 phases. The status of circuit beakers, relaying and communication equipment is displayed at the bottom of the record as digital signals.

When the fault occurs, the magnitude of the currents on the faulted phases increase. In the case above the fault is a red-yellow phase-to-phase fault. The voltage on the faulted phases is also depressed. When the local circuit breaker opens, the voltage on the line collapses.

Often when a disturbance occurs, high fault currents, such as those seen in figure 3, also cause the magnitude of the voltage in the surrounding parts of the network to dip. This can trigger other DFRs which are not directly experiencing the fault. This means that one disturbance can cause several of fault recorders to trigger.

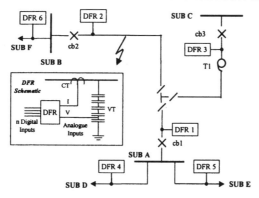

Figure 4. Fault recorders installed on a section of a transmission network

Engineers are primarily interested in the fault records from the substations at the ends of the circuits which have experienced disturbance. Using that data, engineers can classify the type of disturbance and assess the reaction of the protection to the particular disturbance. While SCADA data allows some analysis of protection operation, engineers need the detailed timing information and the nature of the disturbance found in fault records to truly validate the protection system's performance.

Fault records are retrieved from site using an 'auto-polling' system which connects to the recorder via a telephone line every 24 hours and retrieves any new data. In a month SP PowerSystems' fault recorder system can produce in excess of 2,000 records, although not all of these records due to faults. In a similar manner to SCADA data, the sheer volume of data makes analysis and management of the data problematic.

2.1.3 Travelling Wave Fault Locator

When a fault occurs on a line, a travelling electromagnetic wave is produced at the point of the fault which propagates up and down the conductor. Accurate timing information of when the wave and its reflection arrive at the substations allows an accurate fault location to be calculated. SP PowerSystems have a number of GPS-synchronised fault locators in substations across the transmission network. After a disturbance has occurred on a particular line, engineers retrieve records from the fault locators and determine where on the line the fault occurred.

2.2 Post-fault Analysis using Existing Software Tools

Engineers analyse the data above using the following steps:

1. Engineers identify an incident from the SCADA data. Some aspects of protection operation can be validated from the SCADA data, e.g. missing protection or inter-trip alarms suggest that part of the protection scheme may have failed to operate.

2. Once incidents have been identified from the SCADA, the engineers use the fault recorders' manufacturer's software to retrieve the fault records either from the record archive or from the fault recorders on site.

3. After the fault records pertaining to a particular incident have been retrieved engineers analyse the DFR data as follows:

   • The phases of the line involved in the disturbance are identified;

   • The fault inception time and the fault clearance time, i.e. the time between the start of the fault and it being cleared by the protection system, are determined;

   • An assessment of whether protection operated correctly or not is made; and

   • The location of the fault on the line is calculated based on the current and voltage measurements, and the impedance of the line.

4. Travelling wave fault locator records are also retrieved for the faulted circuit. These records tend to give a more accurate fault location than that derived from the DFR data.

Often it is not feasible to analyse all the data manually. Parts of steps 2 and 3 can be automated using the tools described in the following sections.

2.2.1 Telemetry Processor: an expert system for SCADA analysis

The disadvantage of the SCADA data is its volume. On the average day the SCADA system may produce 8000 alarms. During a storm conditions this can double or triple, overwhelming the engineers who have to analyse it. For example, a recent storm lasting less than a day generated 15000 alarms. It took protection engineers in excess of 10 man-days to analyse the data manually.

While expert systems had been built in the past for analysing SCADA for control room engineers [4][5], it became clear there was a requirement for a system for automating the interpretation of SCADA data for protection engineers. Knowledge of how the protection engineers manually analysed the data was elicited and embedded in a rule-based expert system named the 'Telemetry Processor'.

The telemetry processor analyses SCADA data by extracting the pertinent information about protection operations and presenting summary information to engineers (figure 5), effectively automating step 1 of the post fault analysis process.

Incident:	"13:54:14.720 SUB A / SUB B / SUB C Autoswitching Sequence Complete"
Events:	13:54:14.720 "Unit Protection Operated Successfully at SUBA -> SUBB
	13:54:14.810 "Unit & Distance Protection Operated Successfully ay SUBB -> SUBA
	13:54:14.860 "1ˢᵗ and 2ⁿᵈ Intertrips received at SUBB from SUBA
	13: 54:38.300 "Distance Protection at SUBA -> SUBB failed to operate

Figure 5. Summary information produced by the telemetry processor

The current version of the telemetry processor has been processing 'live' SCADA data from the PSAlerts system at SP PowerSystems since June 2003. Its results are stored in a database that can be accessed form anywhere on SP PowerSystems' corporate intranet, using a web front-end, within minutes of an incident occurring.

2.2.2 Model-based Reasoning Tool-set for Validation of Protection Operation

In step 3, engineers analyse the DFR data in detail. Previous research has resulted in rule-based expert systems which automate differing aspects of the analysis [6][7]. The Institute for Energy and Environment have developed a tool-set for analysing protection operation [8]. The toolset includes two core modules: a fault record interpretation module and a diagnostic engine.

The fault record interpretation module determines the fault inception and clearance times, and which phases have been faulted. The module also converts fault records into the format required by the diagnostic engine, producing files called interpreted fault records.

The diagnostic engine employs model-based reasoning to validate protection operation. By running fault records through a software model [9] of the protection scheme to be validated, it predicts how protection should have operated and compares that prediction with how it actually operated. The diagnostic engine identifies potential faulted components using a consistency-based approach [10]. The output of the diagnostic engine is a protection validation report containing details of the fault records analysed and the results of the analysis.

3. Protection Engineering Diagnostic Agents

The original aim of the PEDA project was to integrate the tools described in the preceding section to automate the post-fault analysis process. There were two reasons for this:

- Post-fault analysis using the tools described above still required engineers to manage the flow of data. Fault records still had to be matched with incidents identified by the telemetry processor. The fault records had to be run through the fault record interpretation software and the diagnostic engine. The results had then to be collated along with the fault location information and made available to various engineers across the business.

- At the start of the PEDA project, fault recorders had a limited storage capacity. Records were stored in a 'rolling buffer'. As new records were created, older records would be wiped from the buffer. Under storm conditions, when fault recorders can trigger many times, important data was being overwritten before engineers could dial into the recorder and retrieve the pertinent fault records. The original version of PEDA was designed to focus the retrieval of the fault records using the output of the telemetry processor, i.e. retrieve fault records from DFR on faulted circuits first, thus preventing important data from being lost.

Agent technology was attractive for a number of reasons. In a similar manner to the work described in [11], it provided a method of flexibly integrating the existing software systems while offering a degree of extensibility. This was important as it was envisaged that the integration of additional analysis tools and data sources, e.g. travelling wave fault locator data, might be required in the near future.

3.1 Agents and their Interactions

Details of the original design of PEDA and the design methodology employed can be found in [12]. The prototype comprised of 4 PEDA agents, an interface agent and 2 utility agents that were provided by the agent platform originally used for the project [2]. The PEDA agents effectively 'wrapped' the existing software systems as agents as follows:

- An Incident and Event Identification (IEI) Agent which 'wrapped' the telemetry processor;

- A Fault Record Retrieval Agent (FRR) Agent which prioritised the retrieval of fault records for different sites across the network;

- A Fault Record Interpretation (FRI) Agent which wrapped the fault record interpretation module of the MBR tool-set; and

- Protection Validation and Diagnosis (PVD) Agent which wrapped the MBR tool-set's diagnostic engine.

In addition to the four core PEDA agents, an interface agent was developed to collate the results and present them to the user. This agent simply subscribed to all PEDA agents for the results of their particular analysis.

The agent interaction diagram in figure 6 illustrates the communicative steps the core agents took in order to automate the post-fault analysis process. When agents joined the system they subscribed to other agents which offered the data they required. All agents subscribed to the IEI agent for incident information. The FRI agent subscribed to FRR for notification of new fault records. The PVD agent subscribed to the FRI agent for notification of newly interpreted fault records.

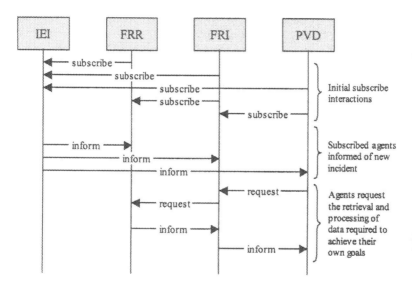

Figure 6. Interaction of the original PEDA agents

The process was driven by the identification of incidents by the telemetry processor (IEI agent). When a new incident was identified all subscribed agents were informed of the new incident. The PVD agent requested the interpretation of any captured fault records relating to that incident, i.e. fault records from specific substations during a specific time interval. If the FRI agent did not know of any fault records relating to the incident, it would send a request to the FRR agent to poll the required fault recorders. Retrieved and interpreted records would then be passed back to the PVD agent, via the FRI agent, so that protection operation could be validated.

4. Industrial Implementation of PEDA

4.1 Issues arising during industrial implementation

As stated in the introduction to this paper, a number of issues had to be addressed in order to make PEDA suitable proper industrial application.

4.1.1 Enhancements to the monitoring system

During the course of the PEDA project, engineers at SP PowerSystems enhanced the fault recorder system by installing data storage units in substations. Fault recorders now store captured records in these units. The storage capacity of these units is such that there is little chance of records being overwritten or lost due to a lack of local storage space. As a result, the PEDA system was no longer required to focus the retrieval of fault records. Instead engineers simply wait until the pertinent records are retrieved by the auto-polling process or they poll the fault recorder themselves if they want to see the records sooner. This means that there is approximately a 4 to 6 hour lag between identifying incidents and the retrieval of the fault records related to the incident. Under the original PEDA design every agent would have to store incident data locally for this period.

An alternative was to have the post-fault analysis process driven by the retrieval of new fault records rather than the identification of new incidents. As a result, the interactions between the agents had to be reconsidered.

4.1.2 Additional Requirements

Through discussion with the protection engineers, it was decided that a relational database containing the result of the PEDA system's analysis was required to allow engineers to search through recent and historical data and results. For each incident the database should store any associated fault records, the results of analysis of the PEDA agents and also allow engineers to append additional information such as the results of fault locations or any other investigations undertaken in response to the incident. The data was to be made available across the corporate intranet through a web front-end. From this front-end engineers should also be able to download the fault records associated with particular incidents.

It was also noted that the telemetry processor identified four basic types of incident: incidents related to circuit or line protection operation; incidents related to generator protection operation; incidents related to the operation of transformer protection; and incidents related to planned switching operations. Switching operations account for more than half of the incidents the telemetry processor identifies yet are of less interest to engineers than protection operations resulting from a system disturbance.

Different engineers are interested in different types of incident. Engineers responsible for managing and maintaining transformers, for example, are primarily interested in knowing when transformer protection operates. As a result, engineers requested that the PEDA system should be able to discriminate between these different types of incident. The meant that PEDA's ontology had to be extended to include new terms for these different types of incident.

4.1.3 Evolution of FIPA Standards

The authors wished to adopt the FIPA standards with the view that other multi-agent systems may be integrated with PEDA in the future. However, during the course of the project the FIPA standards for ACL, content languages and agent interactions were constantly evolving. For example, the FIPA-SL (Semantic Language) content language specification moved from a draft specification to a standard in 2002. The original ontology described in [1] was designed using a draft version of the FIPA-SL standard. The draft version of FIPA-SL contained greater-than (>) and less-than (<) operators which PEDA employed when sending request messages relating to the fault records captured between specific times. These operators are no longer part of FIPA-SL. As a result the ontology needed to be extended to include functional terms for comparing timing information.

4.2 Resolving issues related to industrial implementation

The decision was taken to port the PEDA system to a new multi-agent system platform [13] that was FIPA compliant and actively supported and updated as the FIPA standards evolved. Changes in the standards and user requirements meant that the ontology defined in [1] had to be revisited.

4.2.1 Extending the Disturbance Diagnosis Ontology

Figure 7 shows the class hierarchy of the ontology used by the PEDA agents. The terms marked with asterisks have been added to the ontology. These additional terms have been added to reflect the additional requirements identified in section 4.1.2. The removal of the greater-than and less-than operators from FIPA-SP has been dealt with by adding two new functional terms or predicates to the ontology which can be used to relate timing information: *startBefore* and *startAfter*.

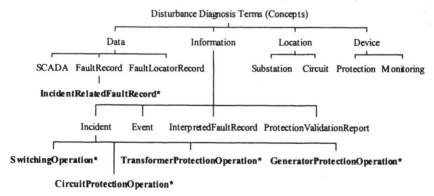

Figure 7. Disturbance diagnosis ontology terms

4.2.2 Accessing PEDA's Analysis

Currently there are two ways in which engineers can access the information generated by the PEDA system: through a database, which archives the results and using an engineering assistant agent (EAA).

Using the web front-end, engineers can immediately see the last two weeks worth of incidents separated into different categories. For each incident tabbed panes allow engineers to view fault record data relating to the incident, the results of the fault record interpretation agent and the protection validation and diagnosis agent, as well as additional information relating to fault location or the results of manual analysis entered into the database by engineers.

While the database and web-server allow staff to access the results of the PEDA system without running specific client software on desktop machine, use of the web front-end requires users to look at the PEDA intranet-site for new incidents and fault records. The authors have also developed prototype engineering assistant agents which inform engineers when new information becomes available. EAAs are similar in concept to Personal Assistant Agents [14]. The EAAs subscribe to the data the PEDA system produces that their owner engineer is interested in. For example, an EAA belonging to an engineer responsible for managing transformer assets can subscribe for transformer protection operation information from the IEI agent. As soon as the IEI agent identifies an incident involving protection it informs its owner.

The current EAA prototype appears as an icon in the user's systray. When an incident is identified, a pop-up box appears on the desktop containing summary information on the incident. It is anticipated that in the future EAAs will be able to gather information from other multi-agent systems for their user.

4.3   Agents and their interactions

In order to change the flow of data in the PEDA system, the interaction of the agents had to be modified so that the analysis process was driven by the retrieval of new fault records rather than the identification of incidents.

The communicative ability of the IEI agent had to be extended. The agent was modified to classify incidents as one of the four types in the extended ontology and its behaviour extended to allow other agents to subscribe for one of the four types of incident. While the original version of the agent could only perform FIPA-subscribe interactions, the new version of the IEI agent can also respond to query-ref type messages. This allows other agents to ask the IEI for any incidents that it has identified that fulfil certain criteria.

A collation (Col.) agent was added to the PEDA agent community. This agent subscribes to the data produced by all the other agents and stores it in the relational results database.

Figure 8 shows the agent interactions that automate the post-fault diagnosis process. When an incident is identified, the IEI agent informs only the collation agent and any EAA agents with an active subscription to that type of incident.

When a new fault record is retrieved, the FRR agent sends a *query-ref* message, which uses the *startBefore* and *startAfter* predicates, asking the IEI agent for any incident which occurred around the period the fault record was generated. The IEI agent responds by sending a set of incidents that it has identified as occurring around that time. If the fault record does not match any incident, the FRR agent takes no further action at that time If, however, the fault record does match an incident, the agent informs the FRI and Collation agents of its existence. Once the FRI agent has interpreted the record, it is sent to the PVD agent. The PVD performs its analysis and sends a protection validation report to the Collation agent. In this manner the post fault analysis process is automated.

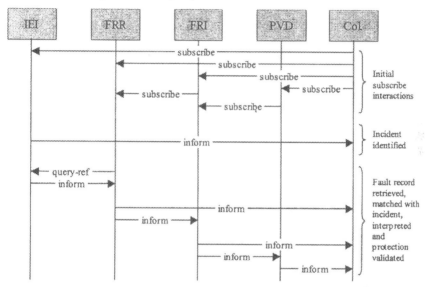

Figure 8. Interaction of industrial Implementation of PEDA

While the PEDA system analyses fault records related to disturbances first, fault records not related to disturbances may also contain information about emerging problems in voltage and current transformers, protection relays, circuit breakers and other items of plant. Analysis of this data is also required. It is planned that further agents will be added to allow all fault records to be interpreted, a task that is impossible to do manually given the volume of data. The addition of other data sources, such as the travelling wave fault locator systems, is also planned.

At the time of writing, the PEDA system was being installed at SP PowerSystems. The system had been tested off-line using a year's worth of SCADA and DFR data. 605 incidents were identified from 3 million alarms. The majority of incidents were related to planned switching operations (54.8%). 10.4% (66 incidents in total) of incidents were related to protection operations on circuits. Over the same period, 20,000 fault records were captured. 1800 records were related to incidents identified by the telemetry processor. Tests using historical data replayed at a real-time rate have shown that PEDA can inform engineers of incidents within a few seconds of them concluding. The analysis of fault records is completed within minutes of the fault record being retrieved. Storm data was also used to test the system's performance during a worst-case scenario where 15,000 alarms and 1695 records were generated in 24 hours. 166 incidents were identified, with nearly 88% associated with circuit protection operating (over double the number seen in the average year).

5. Concluding Remarks

While previous work has demonstrated the possibility of using multi-agent systems for automating the analysis of power systems data, in this paper the authors have presented some of their experience of implementing such a system for industrial application. On a daily basis, PEDA will assist engineers by allowing them to identify incipient faults quickly whilst reducing the burden of management and manual analysis of large quantities of data through the use of multi-agent system technology. In addition, PEDA will offer invaluable support during storm conditions, providing the result of its analysis to engineers across the company.

References

[1] J. Hossack, S.D.J McArthur, E.M. Davidson et al. "A multi-agent intelligent interpretation system for power system disturbance diagnosis" Applications and Innovations in Intelligent Systems X, 2002, 91-104.

[2] Zeus Agent Toolkit: Available: http://more.btexact.com/projects/agents/zeus/

[3] FIPA Specifications: Available: http://www.fipa.org/

[4] Z.A. Vale, et al "Better KBS for real-time applications in power system control centres: the experience of the SPARSE project" Comp. In Ind. 1998, 37 –111

[5] J.R. McDonald, G.M. Burt, D.J. Young. Alarm Processing and fault diagnosis using knowledge based systems for transmission and distribution network control. IEEE Trans. on Power Systems 1992; 7(3):1292-1298.

[6] M. Kezunovic, I. Rikalo, B. Vesovic, S.L. Goiffon, "The Next Generation System for Automated DFR File Classification", Fault & Disturbance Analysis Conference, May 1998.

[7] L. Cederblad, P.O. Gjerde "A Knowledge-based System for the Automatic Evaluation of Disturbance Recordings" *CIGRE*, Paris, Paper 34 – 204, August 1992

[8] E. Davidson, S.D.J. McArthur, J.R. McDonald, "A Tool-Set for Applying Model Based Reasoning Techniques to Diagnostics of Power Systems Protection", IEEE Trans on Power Systems, 2003:

[9] A Dysko, J.R. McDonald, G.M. Burt "Integrated Modelling Environment: a platform for dynamic protection modelling and advanced functionality", IEEE Transmission and Distribution Conf, April 1999.

[10] J. de Kleer, B.C. Williams "Diagnosing multiple faults" Artificial Intelligence, 1987, 32(1):97-130

[11] T. Wittig, N.R. Jennings, E.M. Mandani, "ARCHON – A Framework for Intelligent Co-operation" IEE-BSC Journal of Intelligent Systems Engineering, 3(3):168-179

[12] J.A. Hossack, J. Menal, S.D.J. McArthur, J.R. McDonald, "A Multi-Agent Architecture for Protection Engineering Diagnostic Assistance", IEEE Trans on Power Systems, 2003.

[13] Java Agent Development Framework (JADE): Available: http://jade.cselt.it/

[14] Maes, Patti. "Agents that reduce work and information overload" Communications of the ACM, 1994 37(7): 31-40

The Industrialisation of a Multi-Agent System for Power Transformer Condition Monitoring

V. M. Catterson

Institute for Energy and Environment, University of Strathclyde
Glasgow, United Kingdom

S. D. J. McArthur

Institute for Energy and Environment, University of Strathclyde
Glasgow, United Kingdom

Abstract

Electrical utilities have a pressing need for help with asset management, particularly for large plant items such as transformers. Transformer aging, problems and faults are intimated by partial discharge activity, which can be categorised into defect types. This can be achieved by a condition monitoring system using multiple intelligent classification techniques to provide accurate diagnoses. On-line operation of this system will remove the data processing burden from personnel, allowing for concentration on alleviating the fault's effects rather than interpreting raw data.

1 Introduction

Power transformers are a crucial part of the electrical grid infrastructure, transforming voltages between the levels used within the utility's transmission and distribution networks. Typically, bulk transmission of electricity occurs at 400kV and 275kV. Distribution of electricity occurs at 132kV, 33kV and 11kV voltage levels. These large items of electrical plant are very costly to purchase and install, creating incentive to prolong their working lives as much as possible. However, when catastrophic failure can result in the loss of millions of US dollars[1], or death to employees or the public, it is imperative that aging plant is managed carefully. This involves using condition monitoring to determine the health of transformers, and to diagnose faults as they arise. At that stage, engineers can intervene and alter the operating conditions of the transformer, thus keeping the plant in service, but reducing the possibility of failure.

Condition monitoring relies on sensors gathering data about the transformer, and highlights the occurance of unusual activity. However, the volume of raw data generated is simply too high for engineers to thoroughly process, and extracting meaningful information about the transformer from sensor readings is extremely difficult. A system incorporating intelligent diagnostic techniques as well as data capture provides significant benefits to engineers, as they can focus on validating the system's hypotheses and considering solutions, rather than sifting through potentially unrelated raw sensor data.

To this end, the Transformer COndition Monitoring Multi-Agent System (COMMAS) has been developed[2] [3] [4]. COMMAS encapsulates different classification techniques in separate agents, and makes fault diagnoses based on the defect probabilities calculated by agents. This method of corroborative diagnosis had previously been used to process sensor data off-line, but the next stage in producing a useful industrial tool was to consider aspects of the system's architecture pertinent to continual, on-line, utilisation throughout the electrical network. This included aspects which are likely to be improved and upgraded in the future. The system was modified to ensure further extensions could be applied with no changes to the core architecture, therefore offering flexible and easy implementation of the system in the field.

2 Transformer Condition Monitoring

A power transformer comprises low and high voltage windings suspended in a tank of oil, with bushings for connection to the outside world. There is no way of directly observing the internals of a transformer, other than draining the oil and sending in personnel. This is prohibitively expensive, as the transformer will be out of commission for at least two weeks, and it is a dangerous environment with serious health and safety requirements.

Various monitoring techniques have been proposed to provide a view of what is happening inside a transformer, such as ultra-high frequency (UHF) signal detection, acoustic emission detection, and dissolved gas analysis[5]. All are used to verify the integrity of the insulating material and identify oil contaminants, by looking for indications of partial discharge (PD) activity.

A PD is an electrical discharge which only partially bridges the insulation gap between conductors. This is caused by an electric field exceeding the local dielectric strength of the insulator. This situation may arise from a breakdown of the transformer's insulating material, or from conducting particles in the oil. As partial discharge activity generally precipitates complete failure, identifying the cause and location of PDs will inform what action should be taken to secure the transformer, and can help forcast its remaining lifespan.

Partial discharge-causing defects can be separated into six classes[6]:

Bad Contact: where electrical contact is intermittent, such as between a nut and bolt;

Floating Component: where a large, motionless object floats in the oil, usually having detached from the tank due to vibration;

Rolling Particle: where a metallic particle rolls across the insulation surface;

Suspended Particle: where a small object moves around in the oil;

Surface Discharge: where moisture has contaminated the oil; and,

Protrusion: where part of a winding has worn or was poorly manufactured, and is protruding into the oil.

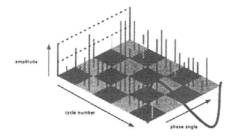

Figure 1: An Example Phase-Resolved Graph

UHF sensors can be used to detect PDs, as signals radiate from the electrical discharge in all directions. These signals can be recorded along with information about the transformer's input at that time, and a 3-dimensional graph can be constructed of signal strength against the cycle number and phase of the input voltage (see Figure 1). The different classes of defect each exibit different characteristics in these phase-resolved graphs, which can be exploited by intelligent classification techniques. This creates a very useful tool for engineers, as the relationships between graph features and defects are not always fully understood.

3 COMMAS

3.1 Functional Design

The aim of COMMAS is to record raw sensor data, perform analysis on it to diagnose faults, and provide information to engineers in a useful manner. This has been broken down into four separate tasks, represented by distinct layers of the COMMAS architecture. These are:

- The data monitoring layer;

- The interpretation layer;

- The corroboration layer; and

- The information layer.

The result is a flexible multi-agent system (MAS), where various data sources and interpretation techniques can be integrated easily as separate agents within the first two layers. The intrinsic MAS capability of service discovery allows multiple agents to be added and removed at the information layer, providing tailored information to different users.

COMMAS must bridge the gap between transformers operating in geographically distributed substations, and engineers located off-site. This presents the issue of how much of COMMAS should run on a computer at the substation, and which agents to run off-site. The communications link to a substation

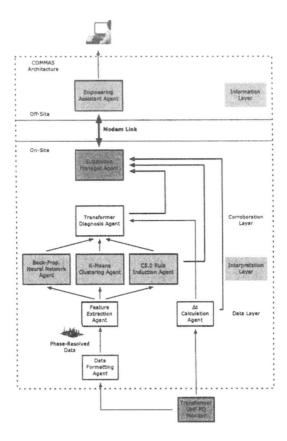

Figure 2: The COMMAS Architecture

is most often a telephone line, making dial-up modem access the only option. Further, computing resources on-site are not plentiful, compared with an engineer's off-site computer.

These two points create a tension, as they indicate that little computation should be done on-site, and little data transferred across the modem link. However, the more data processing performed at the substation, the more refined and compact the data becomes. The best balance is for the data monitoring, interpretation, and corroboration layers to run on-site, and for the information layer to be located off-site. This limits the telephone line traffic to corroborated fault diagnoses, and any raw data the engineer specifically requests. Additionally, the information layer can use increased computing resources to display 3-dimensional transformer models, or collect data from other sources, such as maintenance records.

The inclusion of an intermittent modem connection creates a need for a data management strategy. Engineers will use the information layer only when interested in recent activity. Conversely, the other layers will run continuously in order to record all partial discharges, potentially creating vast amounts of data. This should be collected and archived, ready for transfer to the information layer if needed. A Substation Manager agent fulfills this requirement, performing data collection and storage for the data monitoring, interpretation, and corroboration layers; and data provision for the information layer.

The COMMAS architecture is shown in Figure 2.

3.2 Detailed Design

3.2.1 Data Monitoring

The foundation of the data monitoring layer is the recording of phase-resolved UHF signals from partial discharges. This removes the need for engineers to check for sensor output, as it is automatically captured and processed into a standard format. The formatted data is then sent to a Feature Extraction agent, which creates a vector of standard basic, deduced, and statistical features from it[7]. This feature vector is made available to agents in the interpretation layer, which will use it as the basis of fault predictions.

In addition to agents for refining captured data, this layer also includes a Δt Calculation Agent. Multiple sensors can be used to capture UHF signals, and the difference in the time of arrival of the signals at those sensors will indicate where in the tank they originated[8]. This pin-points the location of the defect.

3.2.2 Interpretation

This layer contains multiple intelligent agents, each of which uses a different artificial intelligence technique to diagnose the cause of partial discharge. Each agent uses the feature vectors provided by the Feature Extraction agent to predict the probable transformer defect, and assigns a probability to each of the six classes. This information is then made available to the corroboration layer, which provides a single diagnosis based on all results from the interpretation layer.

COMMAS currently employs three classification techniques: K-Means clustering, Kohonen back-propagation, and C5.0 rule induction. The K-Means algorithm iteratively calculates cluster centres, where clusters correspond to the six defect classes. The Kohonen agent is a back-propagation neural network, with the weights trained to identify the fault class. C5.0 rule induction was used to derive rules to categorise defects based on observed PD activity. These rules are implemented within the C5.0 rule induction agent. A detailed discussion of the design and testing of all three interpretation agents can be found in references [2], [3], and [4].

Each of these techniques has particular strengths, classifying some fault types better than others[3]. For example, K-Means classification has difficulty distinguishing between Floating Components and Surface Discharges, but is very accurate with Bad Contact faults. Running feature vectors through all three interpretation agents in parallel ensures that the most appropriate technique will be used, and that agent will assign a higher probability to its diagnosis than other agents.

3.2.3 Corroboration

A single agent implements corroboration of all information from the data monitoring and interpretation layers. It collects the fault probabilities generated by interpretation agents, and compares those results. Supporting data, such as knowledge of the strengths of each classification technique and the Δt positioning data, can help improve the diagnosis.

The corroborated result is updated whenever new evidence is available. This enables different interpretation agents, such as knowledge based analysis, to be seamlessly added to the COMMAS architecture without the corroboration layer being informed. Additional supporting data, such as oil temperature readings, could also be integrated in the future, although the corroboration agent could not use this to improve diagnosis at run-time, without prior knowledge.

Whenever a corroborated diagnosis has been calculated, it is made available to the information layer, for presentation to the user.

3.2.4 Information

The information layer is an interface between the user and the diagnosis elements of COMMAS. It gathers corroborated fault predictions, and presents them to the user in an intuitive graphical format. While running, it automatically updates with new fault information, and can retrieve data about the intermediate diagnosis steps, if required. This functionality is provided by an Engineering Assistant Agent (EAA), which runs on a computer off-site.

The EAA is not constrained to run on a particular machine. As a result of this, multiple EAAs can run on different computers, allowing many engineers access to transformer data. Additionally, an EAA can monitor multiple substations, each containing varying numbers of transformers. Utilities will typically have over 100 substations, so creating a single point of contact for all transformers is a significantly beneficial feature.

This is achieved by running an agent platform on the computer at each substation. The Substation Manager agent is contactable by dial-up modem, so the telephone number of each substation must be known in advance. By querying the Substation Manager, the EAA constructs a list of monitored transformers, whose details can then be viewed.

All inter-agent messages in COMMAS are constructed according to FIPA standards for agent communication[9]. Specifically, COMMAS agents converse using messages corresponding to defined Communicative Acts[10], in exchanges governed by Interaction Protocols[11], where message content follows the syntax of the FIPA-SL Content Language[12]. When partial discharge activity occurs, corroborated fault predictions are sent to the EAA automatically, due to use

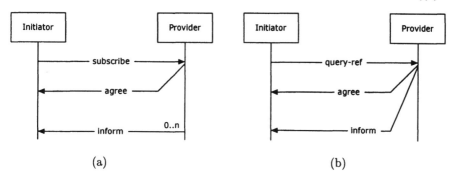

Figure 3: FIPA Interaction Protocols: (a) Subscribe, (b) Query Ref

of the FIPA Subscribe Interaction Protocol (shown in Figure 3a). If the user requires more detail about particular faults, such as the individual predictions made by the interpretation agents, the EAA can request more information from the appropriate Substation Manager, using the FIPA Query Ref Interaction Protocol (Figure 3b).

In this way, the EAA becomes a single point of contact for all transformer monitoring data, providing engineers with fault predictions, and allowing validation of the diagnostic steps.

4 Aspects of Extensible Design

As COMMAS makes the transition from its research and development environment to an industrial situation, certain elements of the system implementation require re-examination. In particular, COMMAS should be designed such that it facilitates future system enhancements, with no further changes to the core architecture. Additionally, system stability over long periods of time is a priority, as it may run in a substation for weeks or months before partial discharge activity commences.

Multi-agent systems are inherently upgradable, as functionality is separated into distinct agents. This reduces interdependancies, allowing changes in one agent to have minimal impact on others. Further, the MAS property of service discovery provides the potential for system reconfiguration: if one agent is replaced by another offering the same services, other agents can locate and use the new agent without difficulty.

However, there are still areas where small changes could impact every agent in the system, and these need to be addressed.

4.1 The Java Agent DEvelopment Framework (JADE)

When the COMMAS project originated, the Zeus multi-agent platform[13] was selected for use. At that time, it was well-featured and actively supported by its developers. Since then, maintenance has declined, and other platforms have gained popularity and abilities. Zeus does not support various FIPA standards which have been adopted in the intervening years, and is not robust enough for long-term field operation.

In order to combat these limitations, the JADE platform[14] was adopted. This actively maintained, open source platform does not suffer from Zeus's problems, and provides additional benefits. The behavioural model of agent operation allows for rapid prototyping, as tasks can be quickly decomposed into simple behaviours, which are built by extending one of the many behaviour classes provided. This greatly eased the conversion of COMMAS to the JADE platform, and will make future agent enhancements faster than Zeus would have allowed.

JADE facilitates the distribution of agents, as host computers need only be specified at run-time. This is realised by splitting the agent platform into containers: separate instances of the JADE runtime environment. Every platform has a Main Container for the utility agents, which provide services such as resource discovery. Any other containers need to be told at creation-time the address of the Main Container's host computer, to access these services.

COMMAS follows this model by running the Main Container on-site, providing agent services to the data monitoring, interpretation, and corroboration layer agents. The off-site EAA runs in its own container, which must know the address of the substation computer. This container can be created and destroyed many times while the Main Container is running, and may run on a different computer every time. This suits the model of engineers wanting access to the same substation data from different locations.

4.2 Ontology and Content Language

Agent communication is an area which is likely to be extended, as new agents are developed to provide more services and data sources. This has the potential to require changes to all agents, if not handled carefully from the beginning. The proper use of a content language and ontology should minimise this danger.

An ontology defines the lexicon used by agents, naming concepts, relationships, and actions which agents need to discuss. In the transformer condition monitoring domain, the ontology contains such things as Transformers, Substations, and FeatureVectors. Sentences are constructed from ontology elements using the grammar defined in a content language. As an example, the FIPA-SL content language renders "All FeatureVectors" as:

```
(all ?x (= ?x FeatureVector))
```

Creating a concept-based ontology is generally a much simpler task than identifying all the predicates that could be used in a domain. For this reason,

COMMAS was originally developed with only entity concepts defined. These concepts were included in basic FIPA-SL sentences, which were of fixed structure. This made the communication models very rigid, as agents performed pattern-matching on message content strings, rather than parsing them into content elements.

Updating the ontology to contain predicates and actions would dramatically alter the message structures, causing this previous method of content understanding to fail. A better solution is to break down content according to the grammar rules of FIPA-SL, for which JADE provides support. Essentially, agents can then understand the component parts of a message, rather than taking a particular content string as one symbol.

The usefulness of this feature can be demonstrated by an example. The FeatureVector concept contains slots for faultID, transformer, time, and fileType, in addition to the vector of features. Bursts of partial discharge activity are numbered sequentially with a faultID, and the time slot is a timestamp of the burst recording. The fileType indicates whether the data originated from a binary or text file format (see Section 4.3 for discussion of this), and transformer identifies in which transformer the PD occurred.

The user may be interested in all feature vectors of PD activity in one transformer, or a feature vector associated with a particular time. These separate expressions are written in FIPA SL as:

```
(all ?x (= ?x (FeatureVector
            :transformer (Transformer
                            :transformerName SGT1)))))
(any ?x (= ?x (FeatureVector
            :time 20040610T141224961Z)))
```

Providing COMMAS agents with the ability to break these expressions into constituent parts means that an agent can understand the content because it is grammatically correct, and not because it has prior knowledge of what expressions it will receive. In this example, an agent which can provide FeatureVectors will be prepared for messages about transformers, times, fileTypes, faultIDs, and features, but is not constrained to exact message templates.

Once the ability was in place for understanding more complex sentences, COMMAS could take advantage of a fuller ontology. However, design and management becomes more difficult with a large ontology, as JADE requires every concept to be a Java class, often with many methods for manipulating concept slots. The Protégé ontology editing tool[15] coupled with the JADE beangenerator[16] were found to help in this task (see Figure 4).

Protégé displays ontology elements as a graphical hierarchy, making relations instantly apparent. The JADE beangenerator is a plugin for Protégé, which creates a package of JavaBeans from the ontology specification. This package can then be imported into the agent classes, for creating and unpacking messages. Ontology creation in this way is very rapid and intuitive, as the lexicon is designed graphically, then converted to Java with a single button.

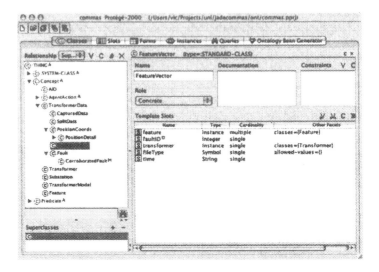

Figure 4: The COMMAS Ontology in Protégé

JADE and Protégé are both very actively maintained by their respective developers, and as a result, new versions are regularly released. This means issues are resolved quickly after discovery, but versions are not always backwards-compatible. The JADE beangenerator is developed separately again, and must be able to read Protégé files and generate JavaBeans for JADE to understand. This situation creates a version dependancy problem, where one of the tools cannot be upgraded unless compatible versions of the other two are also available.

Generally, minor version releases are compatible, and upgrading does not present a problem. However, both Protégé and JADE recently went through staggered major version changes (Protégé to 2.0 and JADE to 3.1), where compatibility was broken. This type of situation should be infrequent, but is difficult to manage none-the-less. The best solution is simply to wait until new versions of all three tools have been released before upgrading.

4.3 Raw Data Formats

Two types of equipment are currently available for recording the UHF signals caused by partial discharges. Each type has different advantages, and may be used in different situations, or even in conjunction. This impacts on the COMMAS structure, and particularly the interpretation agents. The COMMAS architecture needs to be flexible enough to handle data from the two types of recorders, and produce equally good results from both.

The first is the PortSUB Portable UHF Monitor, from Diagnostic Monitoring Systems Ltd. This is an expensive monitoring system which requires

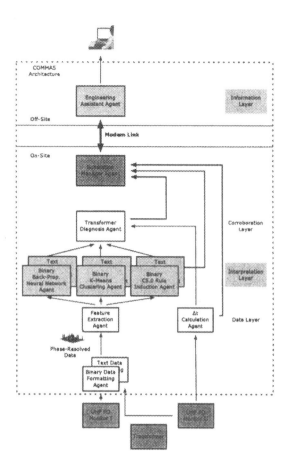

Figure 5: COMMAS with Multiple Data Capture Techniques

a supplementary computer, and stores the captured data in a binary format. Because of hardware limitations, there is no discernable difference in the arrival time of signals at different sensors, so the Δt positioning information cannot be calculated.

The second method of UHF monitoring is to use data capture cards in an ordinary computer. This stores data in text files, and Δt information is available. However, the throughput is not as good as on the PortSUB, and consequently some partial discharge activity is missed. This means that the phase-resolved graph of activity generated by this equipment is more sparse than that of the PortSUB, and the feature vectors calculated from data from the two systems for the same event will be completely different.

This presents difficulties for the classification agents at the interpretation layer. Each technique relies on training for one particular type of feature vector, and introducing a second will produce erratic and unreliable results. To combat this, separate sets of interpretation agents are needed to handle the different types. Additionally, separate data formatting agents take the binary and text files, turning them into the phase-resolved patterns required by the Feature Extractor agent.

The COMMAS architecture for a substation employing both monitoring techniques is shown in Figure 5. Ensuring that COMMAS can incorporate multiple techniques increases options for the future, as it is not yet known whether one type of equipment will become dominant.

5 Running COMMAS

As the COMMAS architecture has been designed to maximise extensibility, configurability at run-time is also desirable. Some factors are known only when the system is installed in a particular substation, such as which transformers to monitor, and which type of equipment is being used for data capture. This uncertainty is handled by having a substation configuration file: a simple text file containing such information as the number of transformers. It also provides the substation and transformer names, which directory to use for data storage, and the monitoring equipment type.

The system is started by launching a JADE platform on-site, containing the Substation Manager agent. This gathers substation information from the configuration file, and creates single instances of the Feature Extractor and Diagnosis agents. The number of interpretation agents is determined by how many data capturing techniques exist on-site. Every transformer has separate Δt agents, and the number of Data Formatting agents is the product of the number of transformers and data capture techniques. This process is shown in Figure 6.

Once all these agents have started, the system runs continuously.

6 Conclusion

The Transformer COndition Monitoring Multi-Agent System (COMMAS) has previously been shown to perform partial discharge defect classification in an off-line research environment. However, on-line use in an industrial setting demanded improvements in the areas of robustness and extensibility. These requirements were met by changing key aspects of the COMMAS architecture, which increased reliability and reduced the development cost of future alterations.

The result is a stable system supporting multiple users, which can be easily upgraded to incorporate new data sources and interpretation techniques. This allows COMMAS to be a new base for utility-wide asset management.

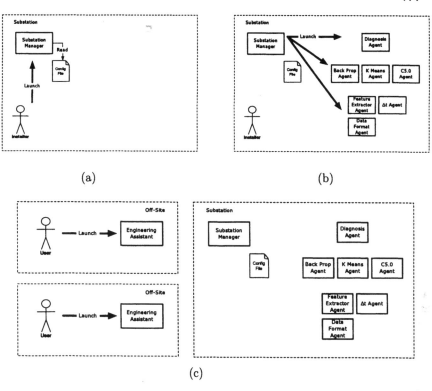

(a)

(b)

(c)

Figure 6: COMMAS Start-Up Sequence: (a) The Installer launches the Substation Manager Agent, which reads a configuration file describing the transformers and monitoring equipment; (b) Other agents are launched based on this information; (c) Users launch their own Engineering Assistant Agents, which communicate with the Substation Manager.

References

[1] A. Ottele and R Shoureshi, "Neural Network-Based Adaptive Monitoring System for Power Transformer", Journal of Dynamic Systems, Measurement, and Control, September 2001, Volume 123, Issue 3.

[2] S. D. J. McArthur, M. D. Judd and J. R. McDonald, "Advances in Intelligent Condition Monitoring and Asset Management of Power Transformers", Proc. Euro TechCon 2003, November 2003.

[3] S. D. J. McArthur, S. M. Strachan and G. Jahn, "The Design of a Multi-Agent Transformer Condition Monitoring System", To appear in IEEE Transactions on Power Systems.

[4] S. M. Strachan, G. Jahn, S. D. J. McArthur and J. R. McDonald, "Intelligent Diagnosis of Defects Responsible for Partial Discharge Activity Detected in Power Transformers", Intelligent System Applications in Power Systems Conf. (ISAP2003), 2003.

[5] Barry H. Ward, "A Survey of New Techniques in Insulation Monitoring of Power Transformers", IEEE Electrical Insulation Magazine, May/June 2001, Volume 17, Number 3, pp 16–23.

[6] G. P. Cleary and M. D. Judd, "An Investigation of Discharges in Oil Insulation using UHF PD Detection", Proc. 14th Int. Conf. on Dielectric Liquids (ICDL 2002), July 2002.

[7] E. Gulski, "Computer-Aided Recognition of Partial Discharges Using Statistical Tools", PhD Dissertation, Delft University Press, 1991.

[8] M. D. Judd, G. P. Cleary, and C. J. Bennoch, "Applying UHF Partial Discharge Detection to Power Transformers", IEEE Power Engineering Review, August 2002.

[9] Foundation for Intelligent Physical Agents (FIPA), http://fipa.org, 2003.

[10] Foundation for Intelligent Physical Agents, "Communicative Act Library Specification", http://fipa.org/specs/fipa00037/SC00037J.html, 2002.

[11] Foundation for Intelligent Physical Agents, "Interaction Protocol Specifications", http://fipa.org/repository/ips.php3, 2002.

[12] Foundation for Intelligent Physical Agents, "FIPA SL Content Language Specification", http://fipa.org/specs/fipa00008/SC00008I.html, 2002.

[13] British Telecommunications plc., The Zeus Website, http://more.btexact.com/projects/agents/zeus/, 2001.

[14] Telecom Italia Lab., http://sharon.cselt.it/projects/jade/, 2004.

[15] Stanford Medical Informatics, The Protégé Ontology Editor and Knowledge Acquisition System, http://protege.stanford.edu/, 2004.

[16] C. van Aart, The beangenerator Homepage, http://gaper.swi.psy.uva.nl/beangenerator/content/main.php, 2004.

SESSION 4:

CLASSIFICATION AND DESIGN

An Improved Genetic Programming Technique for the Classification of Raman Spectra

Kenneth Hennessy, Michael G. Madden, Jennifer Conroy and Alan G. Ryder

National University of Ireland, Galway, Ireland.
hennessy@vega.it.nuigalway.ie, michael.madden@nuigalway.ie
jennifer.conroy@nuigalway.ie, alan.ryder@nuigalway.ie

Abstract

The aim of this study is to evaluate the effectiveness of genetic programming relative to that of more commonly-used methods for the identification of components within mixtures of materials using Raman spectroscopy. A key contribution of the genetic programming technique proposed in this research is that it explicitly aims to optimise the certainty levels associated with discovered rules, so as to minimize the chance of misclassification of future samples.

1 Introduction

Raman spectroscopy may be described as the measurement of the intensity and wavelength of inelastically scattered light from molecules when they are excited by a monochromatic light source. The Raman scattered light occurs at wavelengths that are shifted from the incident light by the energies of molecular vibrations. The analytical applications of Raman spectroscopy continue to grow; typical applications are in structure determination [1], multi-component qualitative analysis and quantitative analysis [2].

Traditionally, multivariate data analysis techniques such as Partial Least Squares (PLS) and Principal Component Regression (PCR) have been used to identify the presence of specific compounds in mixtures from their Raman spectra [2]. However, Raman spectral elucidation suffers from several problems. The presence of fluorescent compounds, impurities, complex mixtures and other environmental and instrumental factors can greatly add to the difficulty in identifying compounds from their spectra [3]. Increasingly, machine learning techniques are being investigated as a possible solution to these problems, as they have been shown to be successful in conjunction with other spectroscopic techniques, such as the use of neural networks to identify bacteria from their infra-red spectra [4] and the application of neural networks to quantification of Fourier transform infra-red (FTIR) spectroscopy data [5]. Schultz et al. [6] used a neural network and PLS to identify individual components in biological mixtures from their Raman spectra, and

Benjathapanum *et al.* [7] used PCR and neural networks to classify ultraviolet-visible spectroscopic data.

In this paper, neural networks, PLS and PCR are compared with the evolutionary technique of genetic programming for predicting which of four solvents are present in a range of mixtures. Genetic programming offers an advantage over neural networks and chemometric methods in this area as the rules generated are interpretable and may be used in isolation or in conjunction with expert opinion to classify spectra.

In combination with the environmental and instrumental problems outlined above, a significant challenge that also arises in other machine learning problems, is in the high sample dimensionality and low sample number commonly found in this area. In many real laboratory applications, it is required to identify materials based on a small number of reference spectra. While commercial spectral databases typically contain spectra for some thousands of materials, they are organised into categories and for individual groups of materials such as the solvents considered here, spectra would be provided for only a small number of mixtures, if any. Machine learning models exhibiting poor generalisation and overfitting to the training data are a consequence of this problem.

In response to this, rather than aiming simply to evolve equations that classify the training data correctly, our approach aims to optimise selection of equations so as to minimize the chance of misclassification of future predicted samples and thereby minimize the problems associated with low sample numbers.

Not many research groups have published applications of genetic programming for the interpretation of spectra. Goodacre [8] discusses the application genetic programming to FTIR spectroscopy image analysis. Using the same genetic programming software, Ellis *et al.* [9] has quantified the spoilage of meat from its FTIR spectra and Taylor *et al.* [10] has classified *Eubacterium* species based on their pyrolysis mass spectra.

2   Description of Task

Raman spectra were recorded on a Labram Infinity (J-Y Horiba) equipped with a liquid nitrogen cooled CCD detector and a 488nm excitation source. All spectra were recorded at a set interval of ~400-3340 cm^{-1} with a resolution of ~11cm^{-1}. The liquid samples were held in 1 cm pathlength quartz cuvettes and mounted in a macro sample holder (J-Y Horiba). The macro lens has a focal length of 40mm, which focuses through the cuvette to the centre of the solution. The spectral data was not corrected for instrument response. Three spectra were taken for each sample, the raw data for each sample were then averaged and analysed using the Unscrambler chemometrics software package. The solvents (all spectroscopic grade), acetone, acetonitrile, cyclohexane, and toluene were obtained from Sigma-Aldrich and used as received. Solutions of different concentrations (Table 1) were made up by mixing known volumes of each solvent.

The objective is to be able to predict accurately whether or not a specific solvent is present in a mixture of other solvents. The 24 samples contain differing combinations of four solvents, Acetone (A), Cyclohexanol (C), Acetonitrile (Acn) and Toluene (T), with compositions as listed in Table 1. Identification of each solvent is treated as a separate classification task. For each solvent, the dataset was divided into a training/testing set of 14 samples and a validation set of 10. The validation set in each case contained 5 positive and 5 negative samples.

There are two challenging aspect to the dataset. Firstly, as mentioned earlier, the dimensionality of the data is very high, with 1024 points per sample and the number of samples is low. Secondly, for all four solvents, the most significant peaks occur in the same region of the spectra. This may be seen in Figures 2 to 4 (Section 4.1), which plot the Raman spectra of each pure solvent. The solvent mixtures detailed in Table 1 are a preliminary dataset produced for this study; the authors are currently collecting a more extensive and diverse dataset for future research.

Table 1 Chemical composition of samples used in this study

No.	A %	C %	Acn%	T %	No.	A %	C %	Acn%	T %
1	0	100	0	0	13	0	75	0	25
2	0	0	0	100	14	25	75	0	0
3	100	0	0	0	15	25	0	0	75
4	0	0	100	0	16	0	25	0	75
5	50	50	0	0	17	0	0	25	75
6	50	0	0	50	18	25	0	75	0
7	50	0	50	0	19	0	0	75	25
8	0	50	0	50	20	33	0	33	33
9	0	0	50	50	21	33	33	33	0
10	75	25	0	0	22	33	33	0	33
11	75	0	0	25	23	0	33	33	33
12	75	0	25	0	24	25	25	25	25

3 Analysis Techniques

3.1 Overview

This section outlines the use of standard chemometric techniques and neural networks to identify components in mixtures from their Raman spectra. It then goes on to describe an alternative technique based on genetic programming.

As mentioned in the Introduction, chemometric techniques are widely used for analysing spectra. While there are many such techniques, the two chosen in this study are PCR and PLS, as they are particularly well established for the classification of spectroscopic data [11,12,13]. Neural networks have been used successfully in conjunction with spectroscopic data in past research for classification purposes [4, 6]. Conventional feed-forward neural networks, however, can be hard to configure for a given problem and the means by which they form predictions are not particularly easy to interpret. Hence, they are often viewed as a 'black box' technique.

Genetic programming is a well-known and well documented technique in machine learning [14]. In the approach taken in this paper, we attempt to evolve a mathematical formula through which data may be classified. A particular benefit of this technique is that it develops classification rules that are quite easily interpretable, in so far as it can be seen which wavelengths in the spectrum are used as the basis for decisions and how they are combined.

3.2 Chemometric Methods

PLS and PCR were carried out on the data using the Unscrambler software (CAMO A/S). PLS and PCR are extensions of the multiple linear regression approach and they are both well suited for estimating linear regression models when the predictor variables are highly collinear [15]. Both PCR and PLS extract successive linear combinations of the predictors, called factors, so that there is no correlation between the factor score variables used in the predictive regression model. The techniques differ, however, in the methods used in extracting factor scores. PCR produces factors reflecting the covariance structure between the predictor variables, while PLS regression produces factors reflecting the covariance structure between the predictor and response variables [12].

One of the main advantages of PLS over PCR is that the factors created by PLS are directly related to the constituents of interest and may be informative. In PCR, the factors are created solely by the spectral data and represent the most common variation in the data, ignoring their relation to the constituents of interest until the final regression step [16]. In the chemometric analyses, positive values above or equal to 0.5 classified a solvent as present.

3.3 Neural Networks

For this analysis, conventional feed-forward neural network structures [17] are used, and are trained using the backpropagation with momentum algorithm. Such networks consist of layers of neurons, with outputs from neurons in one layer connected to inputs in the next. Each neuron sums a set of weighted inputs and then applies a non-linear activation function (*tanh*, in this work) to this sum to derive an output. A separate neural network was trained for identification of each solvent. The inputs corresponded to Raman spectra of mixtures and the single output corresponded to a prediction whether or not the solvent was present in the mixture. The neural network configurations for each solvent are detailed in Table 2. These settings were found through experimentation.

Table 2 Neural network configurations

Neural Network Setting	Cyclohexane	Acetonitrile	Acetone	Toluene
Number of Hidden Nodes	15	23	20	23
Input–Hidden Learning Rate	0.02	0.03	0.06	0.03
Hidden–Output Learning Rate	0.001	0.008	0.001	0.008
Momentum	0.002	0.001	0.001	0.001
Epochs	1000	1000	1000	1000

3.4 Genetic Programming

Genetic programming is a learning technique based on evolution. It views learning as a competition between individuals in an initially random population of potential solutions to a problem [14]. The approach attempts to find an optimal solution by breeding individuals in the population, chosen based on their fitness in partially or completely solving the problem, over a number of generations.

In this research, each individual in the population represents a mathematical formula, composed of functions and variables. The functions used are the simple mathematical operators + and −. (Others could have been used, but sufficiently good performance was achieved with just these.) The variables correspond to wavelengths in each spectrum. The population was initialised using random combinations of functions and variables to create trees with a maximum depth of 5 nodes. Together, the functions and wavelengths selected by an individual i form an equation E_i, which, when evaluated for a specific spectrum S_j, produces a value $E_i(S_j)$. We interpret this value as indicating the presence ($E_i(S_j) \geq 0$) or absence ($E_i(S_j) < 0$) of the corresponding solvent. Fitness is calculated based on performance in classifying the training data, and also on minimising future misclassifications, as discussed below in Section 3.5.

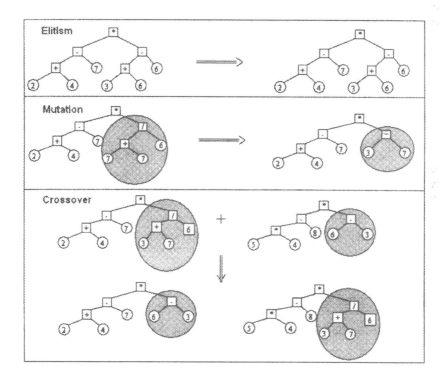

Figure 1 Schematic representation of genetic programming operations

For this analysis, we use a population of 2000 individuals. Once the fitness of each equation in the population is ascertained, the fittest ones are chosen to breed in order to create a new population. Our breeding strategy consists of elitism, crossover and mutation as illustrated schematically in Figure 1. *Elitism* involves selecting the top two fittest individuals from each population, and copying them without mutation into the next generation. *Crossover* is used to generate the rest of the next generation's population. This involves randomly selecting two individuals (according to a uniform distribution) from the top 1.5% of the preceding population and producing a new individual that combines features from both. The tree depth was set at a maximum of 5 nodes, and trees were prevented from becoming too large by addition of only the smaller of the two progeny to the population after crossover. *Mutation* involves random changes to an individual in the newly-generated population and is pre-configured to a fixed probability. The mutation rate in this experiment was set at 10%, i.e. one mutation in every 10 individuals. The algorithm was run until convergence, which took 50 generations.

3.5   Optimisation of Certainty of Equations

The primary goal of the individuals being evolved is, of course, to be able to classify all training data correctly. However, a secondary goal is to minimise the risk of future misclassifications. To achieve the primary goal, fitness is required to be defined in terms of classification performance on the training data. To achieve the secondary goal requires a mechanism whereby, if two individuals are equally good at classifying the data, the one with the greatest *certainty* is preferred. To this end, a two-level fitness function is proposed. To encourage achievement of the first goal, the first-level fitness of an individual i is calculated very simply as:

$$F_1(i) = Acc(i) \times N \tag{1}$$

where $Acc(i)$ is the classification accuracy of the individual and N is the number of training cases. Thus, a score of 1 is given for each correctly-classified individual, and a score of 0 is given for each incorrectly-classified one. To search for individuals with high levels of certainty, a measure of certainty is first required. We define the *certainty factor*, $C_i(S_j)$ of an individual i relative to a spectrum S_j as:

$$
\begin{aligned}
C_i(S_j) &= 0 \text{ if } S_j \text{ is misclassified by } i, \\
C_i(S_j) &= |E_i(S_j)| \text{ if } S_j \text{ is classified correctly by } i
\end{aligned}
\tag{2}
$$

To encourage achievement of the second goal, the second-level fitness of an individual i is calculated as:

$$F_2(i) = \min_j C_i(S_j) \tag{3}$$

In other words, it is equal to the lowest certainty factor for all spectra in the training set. Thus, if an individual does not classify all spectra correctly, its F_2 value will be 0. The overall fitness of an individual is the sum of these:

$$F(i) = F_1(i) + F_2(i) \tag{4}$$

The result of this is that F_2 does not affect fitness unless an equation correctly identifies all training set samples. Accordingly, F_2 does not affect the fitness rankings of equations that do not classify all spectra correctly, but acts as a tie-breaker for those that do, as their fitness is increased by the minimum certainty factor relative to all spectra. This encourages the evolution of equations with increasing levels of certainty, thereby reducing risk of misclassification on future spectra. Since the F_2 term arises from evaluating the equations, its order of magnitude may be completely different from that of the F_1 term. However, since individuals are selected for crossover according to a uniform distribution from the top 1.5% of the population (see Section 3.4), the fitness function is required simply to give a ranking of individuals rather than an estimate of their relative performance.

4 Experimental Results

4.1 Comparison of Techniques

The PLS, PCR, neural network and genetic programming techniques that were discussed in Section 3 have been applied to the task of predicting the presence/absence of each solvent (described in Section 2). For comparison purposes, the authors have also included results using three other popular general machine learning techniques, Naïve Bayes, Ripper and C4.5, as implemented in WEKA [18], using the default settings. For all algorithms, the same sub-divisions of the data were used for training, parameter tuning and final validation testing.

Table 3 provides details of the numbers of incorrect predictions made by each technique on the 10 validation samples for each solvent. As it indicates, PLS performed slightly better than PCR, with no incorrect classifications for cyclohexane. The neural network performed relatively badly on the cyclohexane test set but performed well on the others. In spite of large amounts of time spent exploring different configurations and parameter settings for the neural network to classify this solvent, the best result achieved was 3 incorrect. Naïve Bayes performed somewhat better than Ripper and C4.5 with an overall error rate of 17.5%; however, it did not perform as well as the other techniques. In contrast with this, our genetic programming technique classified all validation samples correctly with little configuration.

Table 3 Results of Analysis Techniques

Technique	Prediction (Number incorrect out of 10)				
	Cyclohexane	Acetonitrile	Acetone	Toluene	Overall Error Rate (%)
PCR	2	0	1	0	7.5
PLS	1	0	1	0	5.0
Neural Network	3	0	0	0	7.5
Naïve Bayes	0	2	1	4	17.5
Ripper	1	3	4	2	25
C4.5	0	2	4	4	25
Genetic Programming	0	0	0	0	0

Figures 2 to 5 show the equations chosen by the genetic programming algorithm for identification of each of the four solvents, the chemical structure of the solvents and also illustrate the position of the wavelengths chosen in each of the equations. The genetic programming equations for toluene and cyclohexane tend to focus principally on the most intense peaks of the spectra. This corresponds to the C-H region of the spectrum. Acetone has 6 C-H bonds in its structure and therefore its main peak (at 2925 cm^{-1}) coincides with significant peaks of toluene and acetonitrile. Presumably this is why the genetic programming equations do not identify this peak as useful for discriminating between the solvents, and instead focus on points around 1700 cm^{-1}. In fact, the peak around 1700cm^{-1} in acetone corresponds to the presence of a C=O functional group, which the other solvents do not have. Similarly, acetonitrile was classified using two points around a peak at 2255 cm^{-1}. This corresponds to the presence of a C$\equiv$N bond in acetonitrile, which is not present in any of the other solvents. This correlation between points chosen and chemical structure demonstrates the practicality of this method for use by chemists.

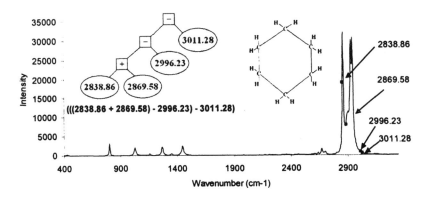

Figure 2 Raman spectrum of 100% cyclohexane sample showing data points used

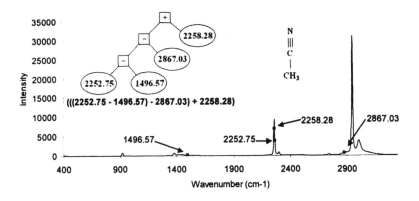

Figure 3 Raman spectrum of 100% acetonitrile sample showing data points used

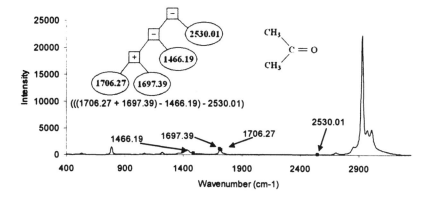

Figure 4 Raman spectrum of 100% acetone sample showing data points used

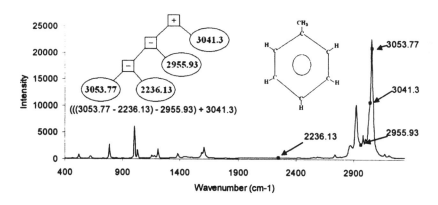

Figure 5 Raman spectrum of 100% toluene sample showing the data points used

4.2 Effect of Optimising Certainty of Equations

As was outlined in Section 3.5, a key aspect of our approach is that it seeks to promote the evolution of equations so as to maximise their certainty, with the intention that this should in turn minimise errors in subsequent prediction. Naturally, this assumes that increased certainty in the training set will correlate with increased certainty in the validation set. Such a correlation should be present if the two datasets are independently and identically distributed (IID). To verify this assumption empirically, Figure 6 presents plots for each solvent separately, comparing F_2 values (minimum certainty factor for all spectra) as calculated on training data with corresponding values calculated on testing data. Each point in a graph corresponds to a single equation evolved for a solvent, all unique equations generated for each solvent are shown. The figure shows that there is reasonably good correlation between the F_2 values for the training and testing data.

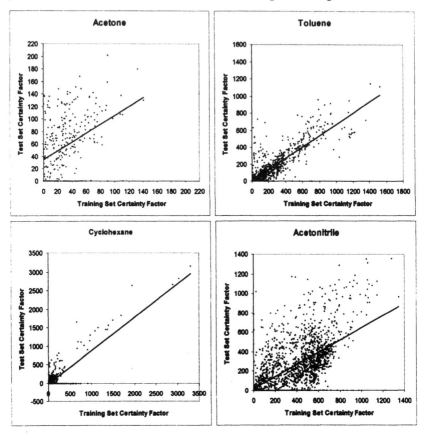

Figure 6 Comparisons of minimum certainty factors on training data relative to those of validation testing data

It is worthwhile to note that, in Figure 6, the equations plotted all have F_2 values for the training data that are greater than 0; in other words, they all classify all training samples correctly. On the other hand, several have F_2 values for the testing data that are equal to 0, indicating that they do not classify all test samples correctly. This highlights the need to select equations that not only classify the training data correctly, but that do so with as high certainty as possible. The graphs indicate that the strategy of maximising certainty on the training data generally results in improving performance on unseen data, though there are some exceptions.

It should be noted that the axes have different scales for the different solvents. The equations predicting acetone have significantly lower certainty levels than those of the other solvents, with the best acetone figure having a certainty level of just 208, compared to values of over 2000 for the other solvents. Accordingly, we expect the acetone predictions to be the most vulnerable to misclassification of future test samples.

5 Conclusions & Future Work

This paper has described the value of genetic programming for Raman spectral classification and has introduced an improved fitness function to reduce the risk of misclassification of future samples. Genetic programming identified all solvent samples correctly with little configuration and the equations generated provide an insight into how decisions are made which offers an advantage over other techniques such as PLS, PCR and neural networks. This is very important in 'real world' practical applications of machine learning techniques, as troubleshooting misclassifications by 'black box' techniques is difficult. The evolved rules allow for decisions to be made which take both human and machine opinion into account and are informative when viewed in conjunction with the chemical structure of the compound whose presence is being investigated.

The genetic programming technique developed in this research optimises the assurance levels associated with discovered rules, so as to reduce the likelihood of misclassification of future samples. This is useful in areas where the number of training samples is low. Future investigations in this area include the use of genetic programming in the prediction of chemical concentration from Raman spectra. We also propose in the future, to refine our fitness equations so that they can incorporate different misclassification costs for false positives and false negatives, as in some forensic applications one type of error is more serious than the other.

Acknowledgements

This work was supported by funding from Enterprise Ireland's Commercialisation Fund Technology Development Programme (TD/03/212) and by the National Centre for Biomedical Engineering Science as part of the Higher Education Authority Programme for Research in Third Level Institutions.

References

1. Ferraro J. R., Nakamoto K., Brown C. W., Introductory Raman Spectroscopy Second Ed., San Diego, Academic Press, 2003.
2. Shaver J.M. Chemometrics for Raman Spectroscopy. Handbook of Raman Spectroscopy: Practical Spectroscopy Series Vol. 28, Marcel Dekker Inc, New York, 2001.
3. Bulkin B.J. The Raman effect: an introduction. Analytical Raman Spectroscopy, Chemical Analysis, volume 114. John Wiley and Sons, Inc, 1991; 1-19.
4. Goodacre R., Timmins E. M., Rooney P.J. et al. Rapid identification of Streptococcus and Enterococcus species using diffuse reflectance-absorbance Fourier transform infrared spectroscopy and artificial neural networks. FEMS Microbiol Lett 1996; 140:233-239.

5. Yang H., Griffiths P. R., Tate J.D. Comparison of partial least squares regression and multi-layer neural networks for quantification of nonlinear systems and application to gas phase Fourier transform infrared spectra. Anal Chim Acta 2003; 489:125–136.

6. Schulze H.G., Greek L.S., Gorzalka B.B. et al. Artificial neural network and classical least squares method for neurotransmitter mixture analysis. J Neurosci Meth 1995; 56:155-167.

7. Benjathapanun N., Boyle W.J.O. and Grattan K.T.V. Classification of UV-Vis spectroscopic data using principal component analysis and neural network techniques. Measurement 1998; 24:1-7.

8. Goodacre R. Explanatory analysis of Spectroscopic data using machine learning of simple, interpretable rules. Vib Spectrosc 2003; 32:33-45.

9. Ellis D.I., Broadhurst D., Kell D.B. et al. Rapid and Quantitative Detection of the Microbial Spoilage of Meat by Fourier Transform Infrared Spectroscopy and Machine Learning. Appl Environ Microb 2002; 68:2822-2828.

10. Taylor J., Goodacre R., Wade W.G., Rowland J.J. and Kell D.B. The deconvolution of pyrolysis mass spectra using genetic programming: application to identification of some Eubacterium species. FEMS Microbiol Lett 1998; 160:237-246.

11. Ryder A.G., O'Connor G.M. and Glynn T.J. Quantitative analysis of cocaine in solid mixtures using Raman spectroscopy and chemometric methods. J Raman Spectrosc 2000; 31:221-227.

12. Estienne F., Massart D.L. Multivariate calibration with Raman data using fast Principal component regression and partial least squares methods. Anal Chim Acta 2001; 450:123-129.

13. Madden M.G., Ryder A. G. Machine learning methods for quantitative analysis of Raman Spectroscopy data. Proceedings of SPIE, the International Society for Optical Engineering 2002; 4876:1130-1139.

14. Koza J.R., Bennett III F.H, Andre D. et al. Genetic Programming III. Morgan Kaufmann, 1999.

15. StatSoft, Inc. Electronic Statistics Textbook, http://www.statsoft.com/textbook/stathome.html, 2004.

16. Berthold M., Hand D. J. Intelligent Data Analysis, Springer, 2003.

17. Brierley P. Visual Neural Data Mining, http://www.philbrierley.com, 2004.

18. Witten I.H., Eibe F. Data Mining: Practical machine learning tools with Java implementations, Morgan Kaufmann, San Francisco, 2000.

PROPOSE - Intelligent Advisory System for supporting Redesign

Marina Novak & Bojan Dolšak

Faculty of Mechanical Engineering, University of Maribor

Maribor, Slovenia

Abstract

Optimal design reached in the first attempt is rare in engineering. Design is an iterative process. How many iterations/cycles are needed directly depends on the initial design and appropriateness of the later redesign actions. The results of engineering analysis are often basic parameters for the redesign actions in design process. If the structure does not satisfy given criteria, certain optimisation steps, such as redesign, have to be taken. Yet, the existing CAD software still fails to provide any advice about these redesign steps. Thus, the selection of the appropriate redesign actions still depends mostly on the designer's knowledge and experience. The idea for our research work was to collect this kind of knowledge and experiences, organise them, and write them into a knowledge base of the intelligent system. The aim of this paper is to present PROPOSE, the intelligent consultative system for supporting modification of the design parameters during the embodiment design phase considering the results of the engineering analysis. The results of the evaluation of the system show that the prototype of the presented intelligent system can be applied either to design new products in practice or as an educational tool.

1. Introduction

Nowadays, designers work under the strong pressure of high technology. Modern world demands the products of high quality in short development time. Design process becomes very complex task [1, 2]. Designers are forced to use all modern methods and tools in order to be successful. In this respect, design and computing are inseparably linked in the modern development process of new products. Regarding this, design and computing are inseparably linked in the modern development process of new products. Computer Aided Design (CAD) applications cover different design activities, like modelling, kinematics simulations, structure analysis or just drawing technical documentation, but they fail to provide help in more creative parts of design process that involve complex reasoning, as for example when possible design solutions need to be evaluated.

In order to overcome this bottleneck we believe that the "intelligent behaviour" should be added to the present CAD systems [3, 4]. Knowledge-based Engineering (KBE) or Knowledge Aided Engineering (KAE) presents the link of Computer Aided Engineering (CAE) tools and methods of artificial intelligence.

KAE was born in aircraft and automotive industry [5, 6] and has been applied for some years, but mostly for specific products [7 - 10].

Designer with lack of experience needs advice to be able to make the right decisions within design process and consequently to design optimal structures. Traditional design optimisation systems that concentrate on numerical aspects of design process are not successful in integrating numerical parts with human expertise [11]. Our idea was to apply intelligent advisory system that will be able to provide "decision-making" support to design process.

In this paper, a prototype of the intelligent advisory system for supporting redesign (Fig. 1) is presented.

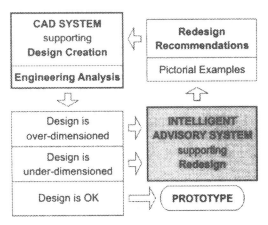

Figure 1 Intelligent redesign system

2. Analysis-Based Optimisation in Design Process

Every proposed design should be verified during embodiment phase of design process. The purpose of engineering analysis (using for example Finite Element Method - FEM) [12] in design process (Fig. 2) is to simulate and verify the conditions in the structure, as they will appear during its exploitation. If the structure does not satisfy given criteria, it needs to be improved by applying certain optimisation steps, such as redesign, use of other material, etc.

A substantial knowledge and experience is needed to be able to understand the results of the analysis and to choose the appropriate redesign actions. In spite of rapid progress in the field of computer graphics, the existing computer post-processing tools fail to provide advice about further optimisation/modification steps. The easiest design change is a selection of a different material. Yet, in many cases, it is not possible or financially justified. Fig. 3 presents a simple example of the initial design with some redesign possibilities. In case the structure is over-dimensioned, it could have unlimited life cycle, because it is too strong for its loading. Yet, it is usually too heavy and too expensive. Thus, redesign is justified. On the other hand, the redesign is urgent for under-dimensioned structure, which cannot bear the loadings and will fail during its exploitation.

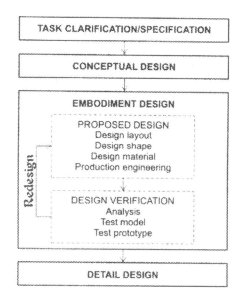

Figure 2 Four main phases of design process [1]

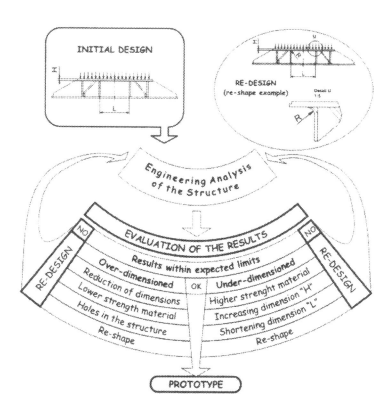

Figure 3 Example of redesign possibilities

As a rule, there are several redesign steps possible for design improvement. The selection of one or more redesign steps that should be performed in a certain case depends on the requirements, possibilities and on wishes. The level of knowledge about the principles of mechanics, structures and materials technology as well as the experiences are very important factors in determining the most appropriate redesign step.

Applying artificial intelligence to design optimisation based on engineering analysis is certainly one of the present important research activities. Most of the research work in this field supports the pre-processing phase of the engineering analysis and automatic optimisation [13-18]. A few recent research projects also address post-processing phase and further modification steps, but only for very specific products [19-23]. In this context, our idea was to encode the knowledge and experience about design and redesign (design modification) to create the rules for proposing the most appropriate redesign actions considering results of engineering analysis and to develop an intelligent advisory system for redesign recommendations.

3. Development of the Intelligent Redesign System

Development of the proposed system was performed in several steps. First and the most important step was development of the knowledge base, where knowledge acquisition was the most crucial task. The theoretical and practical knowledge about design and redesign actions were investigated and collected. A great amount of different knowledge is needed to perform redesign actions after the engineering analysis is performed. We acquired the redesign knowledge in three different ways, from literature survey and examinations of the old engineering analyses to the interviews of some human experts. It was not an easy task. The recommendations for redesign are scarce and dispersed in many different design publications [24-29]. Many reports about the analyses contain some confidential data and are not allowed to be used. On the other hand, interviews and examination of the existing redesign elaborates are conditioned by cooperation with several experts and can be time-consuming. Therefore, the scope of results is very much limited by the experts.

The production rules were selected as the appropriate formalism for encoding knowledge, because the actual rules used in design process are quite similar to them. Each rule proposes a list of recommended redesign actions that should be taken into consideration, while dealing with a certain problem, taking into account some specific design limits.

The rules are generalised and do not refer only to the examples that were used during the knowledge acquisition process. They can be used every time when the problem and limits match with those in the head of the rule. In such a case, the application of the appropriate rule would result in the list of recommended redesign actions for dealing with the given problem. Some pictorial examples were added to the system for additional help to the user to better understand the proposed redesign actions and to make an adequate chose.

The knowledge base development was time consumable task. Finally, we could developed the shell of the system named PROPOSE (Fig. 4) consisting of the user interface and the inference engine suited to the existent knowledge base. The knowledge base and the shell of the system are encoded in Prolog [30] syntax. Visual Prolog version 5.2 [31] was used for that purpose.

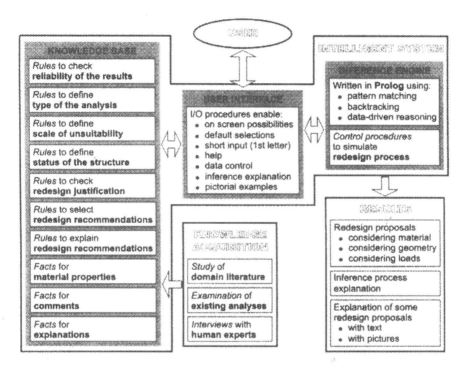

Figure 4 PROPOSE – an intelligent advisory system

4. The Knowledge Base

From the technical point of view, the most important rules in the knowledge base are those defining redesign recommendations. Let us present an example of the rule that define redesign recommendations for a certain design case. Figure 5 presents several redesign possibilities for reducing high stresses around the notch. These kinds of problems are quite frequent in design practice. Considering also some other redesign recommendations for this case, the following redesign rule was defined:

> **IF** stresses are too high
> **AND** area is around the notch
> **THEN**
>   Make a larger radius
>   Remove the material around the notch
>   Add smaller relief notch on both sides
>   Change the notch geometry to decrease stress concentration factor (K).

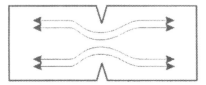

It is assumed that a notch of this sort
is to occur in this element.

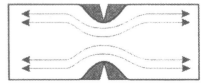

Removal of the material around the notch
would be a favorable way of reducing
the section, but the notch and the flat top
and bottom surfaces are eliminated.

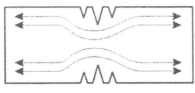

Stress concentration reduced but
notch retained.

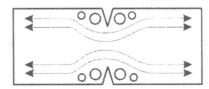

Stress concentration reduced but
notch and top and bottom
surfaces retained.

Figure 5 Design problem – reducing high stresses around the notch

In the knowledge base, the extended rule encoded in Prolog syntax has the following form:

```
actions([],
  ["make a larger radius",
  "remove the material around the notch",
  "add smaller relief notches on both sides",
  "change the notch geometry to decrease stress concentration factor
  (K)"],
  [], L) :-
  stresses(high),
  area_description(one,notch_area),
  L = ["Structure type is 3D","stresses are high",
      "problem area is one region with notch"].
```

However, there are many other rules that are also necessary for the system to be functional. For example, several rules are needed to define the status of the structure (not stiff enough, under-dimensioned, over-dimensioned or almost ideal). The status of the structure depends on the type of the engineering analysis, the parameters being analysed (stresses or deformations) and the deviations between computed and allowable values. Finally, the need for redesign is defined considering the status of the structure, the scale of the proposed changes (significant or minor) and justification for redesign.

In addition to the production rules, a part of the knowledge is written in the knowledge base in form of the facts, as for example:

```
significant_minor_ss(too_low,too_low,over_dimensioned,significant).
```

A set of such facts represent the Table 1, which shows the status of the structure and the scale of the proposed changes, considering deviations of the computed and allowable values for the stresses and deformations. Relative deviations within 10 percent are annotated as "low" or "high", while terms "too low" or "too high" are used for greater deviations.

Table 1 Relations for stress-strain analysis

Stresses	Deformations	Status	Changes	Comment
too low	too low	over-dimensioned	significant	changes only if justified
too low	low	over-dimensioned	minor	changes only if justified
too low	high	not stiff enough	minor	
too low	too high	not stiff enough	significant	
low	too low	over-dimensioned	minor	changes only if justified
low	low	almost ideal	no changes	optimal design!
low	high	not stiff enough	minor	
low	too high	not stiff enough	significant	
high	too low	under-dimensioned	minor	
high	low	under-dimensioned	minor	
high	high	under-dimensioned	minor	
high	too high	under-dimensioned	significant	
too high	too low	under-dimensioned	significant	
too high	low	under-dimensioned	significant	
too high	high	under-dimensioned	significant	
too high	too high	under-dimensioned	significant	

5. The Shell of the System

The shell of the system was encoded in Prolog. Prolog was chosen because of its built-in features: rule-based programming, pattern matching and backtracking, which are excellent tools for developing an intelligent system. Our work was concentrated on declarative presentation of the knowledge. Thus, we used the data-driven reasoning, which is again built in Prolog. However, some control procedures were also added to the inference engine of the system to adjust the performance of the program to the real-life redesign process. The actual data flow of the intelligent redesign system is presented in Figure 6.

More effort was put into development of the user interface to enable the appropriate communication between the user and the system. The user can be supported with help and reported with the information about the inference process. At any time the list of possible choices (between the square brackets, []), and a default selection (between the signs for smaller and greater, <>), are presented to the user.

In order to use the system, the user simply needs to run the executive version of the system with filename "PROPOSE.exe". The execution starts with the system introduction presented on the screen including some basic information how to use the system. From that point, the system leads the user from the specification of the problem to the final conclusions.

First, the user needs to present the qualitative manner of the information about the results of the engineering analysis: the results reliability, the type of the engineering analysis (strain-stress or thermal analysis), the results deviations from allowable limits, the type of the structure and the abstract description of the problem area (Fig. 7). In case the problem area can be described in different ways, it is advisable to do so, as the system will be able to propose more improvements that are possible.

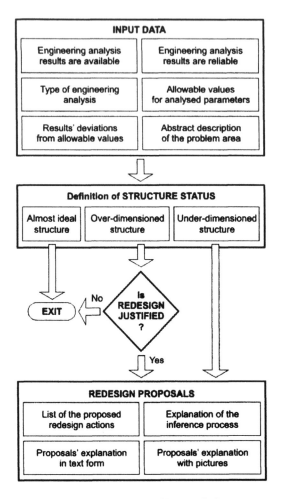

Figure 6 Data flow of the intelligent redesign system

Help is available through the whole data input process. For every problem area, the system searches for the redesign recommendations in the knowledge base. The results in form of the redesign recommendations are written on the screen. As it was mentioned before, the user can also get the insight into the inference process. If the user requires, the system presents all the steps that led to the final conclusion together with the list of redesign recommendations, as it can be seen in example presented in Fig. 14.

In addition to the explanation of the inference process, the user can also get more information about certain redesign proposals. This kind of information is provided not only for the geometry changes, but also to support the selection of more relevant material. Redesign proposals are explained with text or with pictorial examples. Some proposals are explained in either ways (Fig. 8 and Fig. 9).

```
PROPOSE
*****************************************************************************
This system currently deals with two types of structures: BEAM or 3D
*****************************************************************************

 Select the type of the structure
     - BEAM structure
     - 3D structure
 Your choice: < 3D structure > :


*****************************************************************************
THE ABSTRACT DESCRIPTION OF THE PROBLEM AREA IS THE FOLLOWING:
*****************************************************************************

Try to imagine your problem area as:
-- uniform area (examples: one region: 'around a hole' or
                                       'in corner')
-- combined area (examples: 'two regions: plate and rib' or
                            'three regions: two plates and screw')

 Select the problem area which is a combination of:
     - 1-one region
     - 2-two regions
     - 3-three regions
 Your choice: < 1-one region > :

 Select description of the problem area:
     - plate
     - tube
     - vessel
     - wide
     - short_narrow
     - notch_area
     - around_hole
     - in_corner
 Your choice: < plate > :n
```

Figure 7 Abstract description of the problem area

```
PROPOSE
---------------------------------------------------------------------------
More information about the proposal:
- change the notch geometry to decrease stress concentration factor (K)
[ yes, no, help ] <yes>  =>

To: change the notch geometry to decrease stress concentration factor (K)
- draw out the width of notch (wide V notch or bigger radius at U notch)
- change the notch shape (U shape is better than V shape)
- change the internal notch shape (rectangle change into quadrat or ellipse)

---------------------------------------------------------------------------
Show the picture to describe the proposed changes in detail?
[ yes, no, help ] <yes>  => _
```

Figure 8 Text explanation for the redesign proposal: Change the notch geometry to decrease stress concentration factor (K).

At the end of every application the user is asked to specify the name of the output file where the results are saved. The filename "Propose.rez" is proposed by the system, yet to build a record about the whole optimisation process, different filenames should be used for every consecutive application of the system. The output file contains the same information as the explanation of the inference process.

For the time being, the system is still in development phase and is written as the console application. As such, it is more convenient for testing and frequent immediate changes. In the future, the executive version of the system with graphical user interface is also planed to be made.

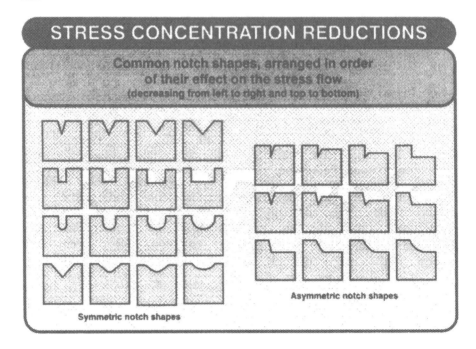

Figure 9 Pictorial explanation for the redesign proposal: Change the notch geometry to decrease stress concentration factor (K).

6.   Evaluation of the System

The evaluation of the system was performed in two ways:

- The experts, who were already involved in the knowledge acquisition process, evaluated the system.
- Some real-life examples were used to test the performance of the system.

The experts evaluated the system from two points of view. First they evaluated the user interface of the system by inspecting the way how the system helps and guides the user or even enables him or her to acquire some new knowledge. In addition, they also analysed the performance of the system while it was tested with some real-life examples, evaluating the suitability, clearness and sufficiency of the redesign proposals. All comments and suggestions, presented by the experts were taken into consideration and resulted into numerous corrections and adjustments of the system.

Most of the tests with real-life examples were performed by the last year mechanical engineering students. One of the testing examples was a connecting rod of a motorbike internal combustion engine that was originally modelled by the students.

The results of the FEM analyses (Fig. 10) predicted the gradients of the stresses in the ear of the connecting rod, and at the connection of the rod and the ear respectively.

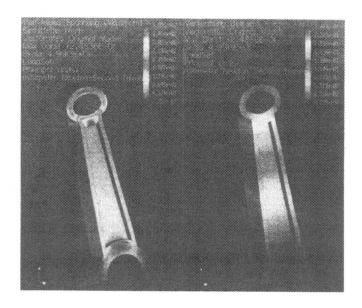

Figure 10 The results of the initial analysis

Similarly, the displacements in the ear of the connecting rod also exceeded the allowable value. In this respect, the redesign was certainly needed. The results of the analysis were presented to the system PROPOSE [32]. The redesign recommendations that were proposed by the system are presented in Fig. 11 and Fig. 12.

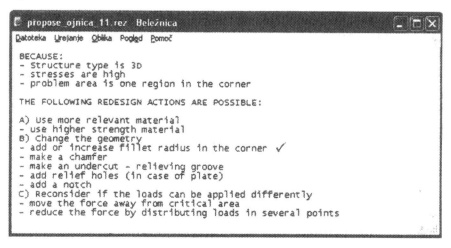

Figure 11 Redesign proposals ("in corner")

The proposals that were selected as the most appropriate to be applied in this particular case are ticked on the right hand side of the list in Fig. 11 and Fig. 12. The new design of the connection rod was developed by applying these proposals.

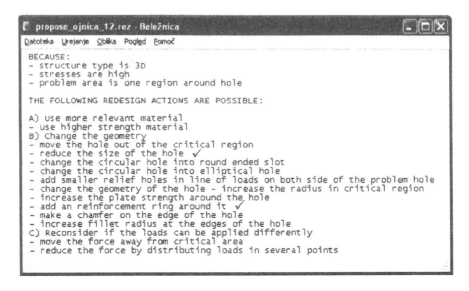

BECAUSE:
- structure type is 3D
- stresses are high
- problem area is one region around hole

THE FOLLOWING REDESIGN ACTIONS ARE POSSIBLE:

A) use more relevant material
- use higher strength material
B) Change the geometry
- move the hole out of the critical region
- reduce the size of the hole ✓
- change the circular hole into round ended slot
- change the circular hole into elliptical hole
- add smaller relief holes in line of loads on both side of the problem hole
- change the geometry of the hole - increase the radius in critical region
- increase the plate strength around the hole
- add an reinforcement ring around it ✓
- make a chamfer on the edge of the hole
- increase fillet radius at the edges of the hole
C) Reconsider if the loads can be applied differently
- move the force away from critical area
- reduce the force by distributing loads in several points

Figure 12 Redesign proposals ("around hole")

The new stress-strain FEM analysis was performed for the redesigned structure. It confirmed that the redesign actions were chosen correctly, as the stresses in the problem area were reduced significantly (Fig.13).

However, the deformations were still too high to be satisfied. Thus, the next task was to increase the stiffness of the connecting rod in the critical area. PROPOSE was applied once again. The connecting rod was changed according to the new proposals presented in Fig. 14.

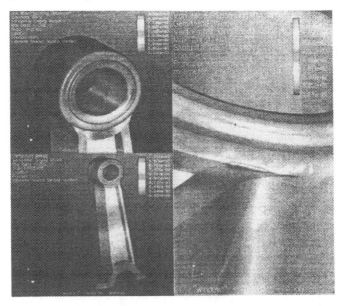

Figure 13 The results for the second version of the connecting rod

```
propose_ojnica_Z1.rez - Beležnica                              _ □ ×

Datoteka  Urejanje  Oblika  Pogled  Pomoč

Results of engineering analysis are available and reliable :: was told
Results represent strain-stress analysis :: was told
Allowable stresses/deformations for structure are known :: was told
The stresses do not exceed the allowable stresses :: was told
BECAUSE: The stresses do not exceed the allowable stresses
        The stresses are low :: was defined by rule
The stres. are lower than allow. stres. for less than 10%! :: was told
The deformations exceed the allowable deformations :: was told
BECAUSE: The deformations exceed the allowable deformations
        The deformations are high :: was defined by rule
The deform. are higher than allow. deform. for more than 10%! :: was told
BECAUSE: Stresses are low and deformations are high
        The structure is NOT STIFF ENOUGH :: was defined by rule
BECAUSE: Diff. of stresses < 10% and diff. of deformations> 10%
        SIGNIFICANT changes need to be done! :: was defined by rule
stiffness should be increased :: was defined by rule
BECAUSE: The structure is NOT STIFF ENOUGH
        Changes are JUSTIFIED :: was defined by rule
BECAUSE: Structure is NOT STIFF ENOUGH and changes are justified
        Redesign is needed :: was defined by rule


BECAUSE:
- stiffnes should be increased

THE FOLLOWING REDESIGN ACTIONS ARE POSSIBLE:

A) use more relevant material
- use higher strength material
B) Change the geometry
- increase the thickness        ✓
- add some reinforcement ribs    ✓
- shorten critical dimensions
C) Reconsider if the loads can be applied differently
- move the force away from critical area
- reduce the force by distributing loads in several points
```

Figure 14 Redesign proposals for the stiffness problem

By applying two of the proposed redesign changes (ticked), the next stress-strain analysis proved that the deformations were reduced bellow the allowable limit, while the stresses did not change significantly (Fig. 15).

Figure 15 The final result for the connecting rod

Conclusions

Development of the intelligent advisory system for redesign was mostly stimulated with our experiences acquired through design education process [33]. The aim of our research work was to develop an intelligent system, which would be able to support the user (designer or student) through design optimisation process based on the results of the engineering analysis. This paper presents a prototype of the system that was developed within this project.

When using the system PROPOSE, the user has to answer some questions stated by the system to describe quantitatively the results of the engineering analysis. In addition the critical areas within the structure need to be quantitatively described to the system. These input data are then compared with the rules in the knowledge base and the most appropriate redesign changes that should be taken into account in certain case are determined and recommended to the user. The system provides constant support to the user's decisions in terms of explanations and advises. At the end, the user can get the explanation how the proposed redesign changes were selected and also some more precise information how to implement a certain redesign proposal including some pictorial examples.

At the moment, the system is an independent console application that could be used just after the results of stress-strain or thermal engineering analysis are acquired with any CAD or other engineering program. A proper integration of the system with a selected CAD program is planned for the future.

It is anticipated; the presented intelligent system will be used not only for designing new products in practice, but also in design education. The students are typical representatives of inexperienced designers. Thus, the use of the presented system could be very useful in design education process. In this case, the important feature of the knowledge-based systems, the ability to explain the inference process, will be specially welcome and could enable the students to acquire some new knowledge. It may help them to learn more about basic principles of design process and to avoid many wrong conclusions and mistakes, which are now quite frequent due to lack of experience. We believe the application of our system in the education process can help to prepare the students for their future engineering profession, when their work will be exposed to the competitive "battle" on the market, where optimal design solutions are more and more indispensable.

Acknowledgements

Development of the intelligent system presented in the paper was financially supported by the Ministry for Education, Science and Sport, Republic of Slovenia. We would specially like to thank to the experts from companies AVL-AST and RTI in Maribor, Slovenia, who were willing to act as a medium for transfer of their knowledge and experience. Thanks also to Dr. T.K. Hellen from UK for sharing with us his numerous ideas that were essential to build the first prototype of the system. A great part of the research work presented in this paper was done during our visits to Department of engineering design and CAD, Faculty of engineering sciences, University of Bayreuth in Germany, headed by Professor Frank Rieg.

References

1. Pahl G., Beitz W. Engineering Design – A systematic Approach. Second Edition, Springer-Verlag, 1996.

2. Pugh S. Creating Innovative Products Using Total Design. Addison-Wesley, 1996.

3. Giddings J. CAD/CAM Project. Automotive Engineering Design, 1999.

4. Barlow R, Amirudin R. Structural Steelwork Planning and Design Evaluation – A Knowledge-Based Approach. Proc. of the Information Technology in Construction, W78 Workshop Construction on the Information Highway, University of Ljubljana, Slovenia, June 1996.

5. Liening A, Blount GN. Influences of KBE on the Aircraft Brake Industry, Aircraft Engineering and Aerospace Technology, Volume 70, Number 6, pp. 439-444, 1998.

6. Kochan A. Jaguar uses Knowledge-based Tools to Reduce Model Development Times. Assembly Automation, Vol. 19, No. 2, pp. 114-117, 1999.

7. Vajna S, Zirkel M, Rhinow S, Klette G. Wissensbasierende Konstruktion in der Praxis. CAD-CAM Report Nr.7, 2003.

8. Schneider T. Industrieller Einsatz von wissensbasierenden Systemen. CAD-CAM Report Nr. 8, 2003.

9. Susca L, Mandorli F, Rizzi C. Cugini U. Racing Car Design using Knowledge aided Engineering. Artificial Intelligence for Engineering Design, Analysis and Manufacturing, 14, pp. 235-249, 2000.

10. Harper AP. Knowledge-based Engineering. Engineering Designer, January/ February 1999.

11. Lee D, Kim S-Y. A Knowledge-based Expert System as a Pre-Post Processor in Engineering Optimisation. Expert Systems with Applications, Vol. 11, No. 1, pp. 79-87, 1996.

12. Zienkiewicz OC, Taylor RL. The Finite Element Method – Basic Formulation and Linear Problems. McGRAW-HILL, London, 1988.

13. Rodriguez-Velazquez J, Seireg A. Optimizing the Shapes of Structures via a Rule-based Computer Program. Computers in Mech. Eng., Vol. 4, pp. 20-28, 1985.

14. Jozwiak S. Artificial Intelligence: The Means for Developing more Effective Structural Optimisation Programs. Proc. Int. Conf. on Comp. Mechanics (ICCM 86), Tokyo, pp. 103-108, 1986.

15. Arora J, Baenziger G. Uses of Artificial Intelligence in Design Optimisation. Computer Methods in Applied Mechanics and Engineering, Vol. 54, pp. 303-323, 1986.

16. Rajeev S, Krishnamoorthy C. Expert Systems for Optimal Design of Structural Steel Members. Knowledge Based Expert Systems in Engineering: Planning and Design, Ed. D. Sriram and R. Adey, Computational Mech. Pub., pp. 405-419, 1987.

17. Balachandran M, Gero J. A Knowledge-based Approach to Mathematical Modelling and Optimisation. Engineering Optimisation, Vol. 12, pp. 71-115, 1987.

18. Rinderle J, Balasubramaniam L. Automated Modelling to Support Design. Proc. 2nd ASME Design theory and Methodology Conf., Chicago. Engineering Design research Centre EDRC 24-31-90, 1990.

19. Sahu K, Grosse I. Concurrent Iterative Design and the Integration of Finite Element Analysis Results. Engineering with Computers, Vol. 10, pp. 245-257, 1994.

20. Calkins D, Su W, Chan W. A Design Rule-based Tool for Automobile Systems Design. SAE Special Publications, Vol. 1318, Paper 980397, pp. 237-248, 1998.

21. Smith L, Midha P. A Knowledge-based System for Optimum and Concurrent Design and Manufacture by Powder Metallurgy Technology. Int. Journal of Prod. Res., Vol. 37, No. 1, pp. 125-137, 1999.

22. Pilani R, Narasimhan K, Maiti S, Singh U, Date P. A Hybrid Intelligent Systems Approach for Die Design in Sheet Metal Forming. Int. Journal of Advanced Manufacturing Technology, Vol. 16, pp. 370-375, 2000.

23. Lambert J. Strategic Selling: Integrating ANSYS and Knowledge Based Engineering for Real Time Custom Product Engineering during the Sales Cycle. ANSYS User Group Conference, Pittsburgh, USA, 2000.

24. Young WC, Budynas RG. Roark's Formulas for Stress and Strain. Seventh Edition, McGraw-Hill, 2002.

25. Gross D, Hauger W, Schnell W, Wriggers P. Technische Mechanik, Band 4: Hydromechanik, Elemente der Höheren Mechanik, Numerische Methoden, 4. Auflage. Springer-Verlag, 2002.

26. Roth K. Konstruieren mit Konstruktionskatalogen, Band II. Konstruktions-kataloge, Springer-Verlag, 2001.

27. Mattheck C. Design in Nature, Learning from Trees. Springer-Verlag Berlin, 1998.

28. Koller R, Kastrup N. Prinziplösungen zur Konstruktion technischer Produkte. 2. Auflage, Springer-Verlag, 1998.

29. Pilkey WD. Formulas for Stress, Strain, and Structural Matrices. John Wiley & Sons, 1994.

30. Bratko I. Prolog: Programming for Artificial Intelligence. Second Edition, Addison-Wesley, 1990.

31. Prolog Development Center A/S. Visual Prolog 5.x – Language Tutorial. Copenhagen, Denmark, 2001.

32. Novak M. Intelligent Computer System for supporting Design Optimisation, PhD Thesis, University of Maribor, Faculty of Mechanical Engineering, 2004.

33. Novak M, Dolsak B, Jezernik A. Expert Supporting System for Teaching Design. Proceedings of the 6th International Design Conference - DESIGN'00, pp. 477–482, 2000.

The Designers' Workbench: Using Ontologies and Constraints for Configuration

David W. Fowler, Derek Sleeman
University of Aberdeen,
Aberdeen, UK
dfowler@csd.abdn.ac.uk

Gary Wills
University of Southampton,
Southampton, UK

Terry Lyon, David Knott
Rolls-Royce plc,
Derby, UK

Abstract

Typically, complex engineering artifacts are designed by teams who may not all be located in the same building or even city. Additionally, besides having to design a part of an artifact to be consistent with the specification, it must also be consistent with the company's design standards.

The Designers' Workbench supports designers by checking that their configurations satisfy both physical and organisational constraints. The system uses an ontology to describe the available elements in a configuration task. Configurations are composed of features, which can be geometric or nongeometric, physical or abstract. Designers can select a class of feature (e.g. Bolt) from the ontology, and add an instance of that class (e.g. a particular bolt) to their configuration. Properties of the instance can express the parameters of the feature (e.g. the size of the bolt), and also describe connections to other features (e.g. what parts the bolt is used to hold together).

1. Background

Engineering designers typically have to find configurations of parts that implement a particular function. The engineering design process is constraint orientated, and requires the recognition, formulation and satisfaction of constraints [15]. To assist designers, most organisations have built up a large number of design rules and standards, usually held as large volumes of text. Designers must try to ensure that their configurations satisfy these constraints, but it is often easy to overlook some. Novice designers often have a hard task in learning the constraints. On occasion, constraints may be modified or become obsolete. Also, new constraints may be added. In practice, it is often hard to find which constraints apply in a given situation. Additionally, in a collaborative environment, where many designers are working on subsections of a common component, it is common for changes made by one designer to affect the options available to another, but for this to go unnoticed until much later, causing expensive and time consuming redesigns.

It would clearly be useful to have some way of automating the design checking process, so that all applicable constraints are checked, without the designer having to manually initiate a search for the constraints. In our approach, we use an ontology to describe the available features and check the constraints automatically. A constraint is specified by the conditions of applicability (which types of features it applies to), and the logical or mathematical expression that allows a constraint check to be performed.

2. Aims of Designers' Workbench

The Designers' Workbench deals mainly with problems that lie in the domain of configuration. Mittal and Frayman [17] define a configuration problem as selecting parts from an existing set of types, and connecting them using specified ports in such a way that certain constraints are satisfied and that particular functions can be performed by the resulting configuration. Brown [2] discusses the adequacy of this definition. For our purposes, we will assume that ports can be described by properties of a feature, so that ``normal" properties may have values that are simple data values to further describe the feature, whereas ``port" properties have values that are other features. For an example, consider a class corresponding to bolts. An instance of this class will have properties that describe the size and shape of the bolt (real numbers or integers). There will also be properties that have values that are instances of other classes—for example, the has_material property might have a value steel, an instance of the Material class.

The current version of Designers' Workbench allows designers to build a configuration and to check that all the appropriate constraints hold. We have used the term features, rather than parts or components, as we wish to emphasise the fact that features can be abstract entities (such as temperatures, holes in other features, etc). Brown [3] discusses a large number of different uses of the word ``feature", including functional features that we are also interested in. The designer can select a feature class from an ontology, and add an instance of it to the configuration. Each instance can have properties that are defined for the class that it belongs to. The properties that are defined for a particular type of feature can be of two kinds: *datatype* (integers, strings, reals etc), which are parameters of the feature; and *objecttype* (other feature instances), which correspond to ports (connections to other features).

In a real engineering situation there may be many thousands of constraints, which means that it is easy to overlook some of them. We define constraints as generic, in that they apply to particular *types* of subconfigurations of features, rather than to specific features. It is not necessary to have any actual features defined before defining a constraint. For example, there may be a constraint that applies to neighbouring features such that if feature X is made of metal A, and feature Y is made of metal B, then the features are incompatible. This constraint could be added without any knowledge that such a pair of features exists in a design. Constraint checking becomes a process of finding such subconfigurations and checking that they satisfy the constraints. We have concentrated on checking that constraints are satisfied by a configuration produced by a human designer, rather than finding a solution. This has implications for tractability, in that solving a CSP is an NP-complete problem, whereas checking a solution can be done in polynomial time. The system has been implemented so that the human designer is free to use his or her engineering expertise to override constraints that are not deemed applicable to the current situation.

3. Related work

In this section we examine some approaches to the configuration problem, dividing them according to whether they use constraints, or ontologies, or both. A general introduction to constraints can be found in [13], and [6] is an introduction to ontologies.

3.1 Constraint-based approaches

Bowen et al. [1] describe a constraint based language, LEO, which enables parts of a design to be represented as a collection of variables, with domains that are not necessarily finite (for example, rational numbers or reals). The system allows constraints to be specified over these variables. Constraint checking, rather than solving, is preferred, because:

> "A constraint monitoring system ... allows the designer to exercise his creativity, while relieving him of the drudgery of making many routine inferences and checks, thereby ensuring that the design choices he makes are consistent with good performance in all significant aspects of the product's life cycle. Furthermore, constraint monitoring is less expensive, computationally, than constraint satisfaction." [1]

A disadvantage of this approach, from the perspective of configuration, is that all variables must be declared at the outset. Also, the variables are not structured using classes. Variables corresponding to properties of features must be declared individually, whereas a structured system would associate properties with each feature class, and declare them automatically.

Mittal and Falkenhainer [18] introduce *Dynamic Constraint Satisfaction Problems* (DCSPs), for representing and solving configuration problems. A DCSP is similar to a CSP in that it consists of variables with prespecified finite domains, together with constraints that specify which values particular subsets of variables may take simultaneously. In addition, a DCSP variable may be *active* or *inactive*, and may switch during search. As well as standard constraints on variables, *activity constraints* may require that variables become active or inactive, dependent on the values (or activity) of other variables. For example, in a car configuration problem, variables Package and Sunroof might have domains {luxury, deluxe, standard} and {sr1, sr2} respectively. An activity constraint might require that if Package=luxury then Sunroof must be active (and can take a value from its domain). In this way, non-luxury cars will not have sunroofs, whereas luxury cars will have a choice of two sunroof types. ``Normal'' constraints (corresponding to CSP constraints) are only enforced on currently active variables.

Algorithms are given to solve DCSPs. One disadvantage is that all variables must be specified in advance, making it awkward to represent problems whose solution may require several of the same type of component. For example, a configuration might require many bolts, but the exact number is not known before searching for a solution. Using a DCSP would require the declaration of a variable for every bolt that might possibly be needed.

Sabin and Freuder [20] define *composite CSPs* which allow configuration problems to be represented in a hierarchical fashion. In a composite CSP, some variables can be assigned a subproblem, rather than a simple value. In this way, components can be selected at a higher level, before being specified in terms of subassemblies. The example used in [20] is also car configuration. The car is divided hierarchically: for example, the power plant system is divided into an engine, exhaust system, electrical system, and so on. Each of these can be represented by a variable that has a domain that is a subproblem. For instance, the engine variable could have a domain that has two values, gasoline engine and diesel engine. During search, if one of these values is selected, a subproblem will need to be solved, containing variables such as pistons, rods, valves, etc. An advantage of the approach is that existing CSP search algorithms can be easily adapted to solve composite CSPs, by dynamically adding and retracting variables and constraints as required.

3.2 Ontology-based approaches

Lin et al. [16] give an ontology for describing products. The main decomposition is into *parts, features, and parameters*. Parts are defined as ``a component of the artifact being designed''. Features are associated with parts, and can be either geometrical or functional (among others). Examples of geometrical features include holes, slots, channels, grooves, bosses, pads, etc. A functional feature describes the purpose of another feature or part. Parameters are properties of features or parts, for example: weight, colour, material. Classes of parts and features are organised into an inheritance hierarchy. Instances of parts and features are connected with properties *component_of, feature_of,* and *subfeature_of.*

McGuinness and Wright [19] describe the application of a description logic to configuration. *Concepts* can be defined, corresponding to the classes of an ontology, and *individuals* correspond to instances. The use of a description logic enables consistency checks to be made quickly. Forward chaining rules can be defined, which are ``associated with concepts, but are applied only to individuals''. These rules are used to enforce constraints that are generic, i.e. defined over classes of objects, rather than over specific objects.

3.3 Combining constraints and ontologies

Stumptner et al. [21] introduce an extension of CSP, *Generative CSP,* which uses complex variables, each of which has an associated type. The type of a variable determines its *attributes* (datatype properties), and its *ports* (objecttype properties).

The types are formed into a simple hierarchy. The constraints here include activation constraints and compatibility constraints, introduced by Mittal and Falkenhainer [18]. In addition, resource constraints are used, being global constraints over all variables of a particular type.

Junker and Mailharro [11] describe a system, ILOG Configurator, that combines the power of description logic (to describe the parts used in a configuration), with constraint programming (to solve the configuration problem). The description logic uses classes that are either abstract or concrete. Concrete classes are the leaf classes of the ontology, corresponding to actual parts. Abstract classes are the nonleaf classes. Properties are used to describe the instances of a class. Alternative methods can be used to specify the instances that can be part of a solution, ranging from an explicit list of instances, to an implicit list, where instances can be freely chosen from an infinite universe of instances. Generic constraints can be defined in a constraint language that allows numeric and symbolic constraints. To solve a configuration problem, a description logic representation of the class hierarchy and the constraints are converted into a constraint satisfaction problem.

Laburthe [14] extends CSPs to cases where variables have domains that are taken from a hierarchy. This differs from the approach of the Designers' Workbench (as well as that of [11] and [19] described above) in that we are concerned with constraints over values of properties of instances (ultimately datatype values). Laburthe's approach aims to find the entities in a hierarchy that will satisfy the constraints. It is possible that this approach could be used to find suitable types for elements of a configuration.

4.   An illustrative example

To illustrate the use of an ontology to describe a configuration, we will use the simple ontology whose class hierarchy is shown in Figure 1. We have used the concept of *feature* as the root of the ontology. Features have then been divided into *concrete features* (those that have a material), and *abstract features* (holes, temperatures, etc).

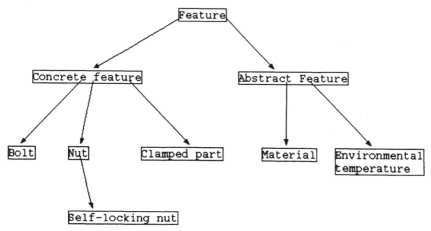

Figure 1 The class hierarchy of a simple configuration ontology

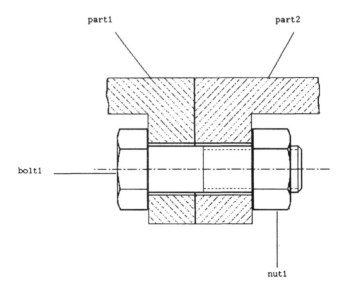

Figure 2 A bolted joint [image adapted from French, Vierck and Foster, ``Engineering Drawing and Graphics Technology'', McGraw-Hill Inc.]

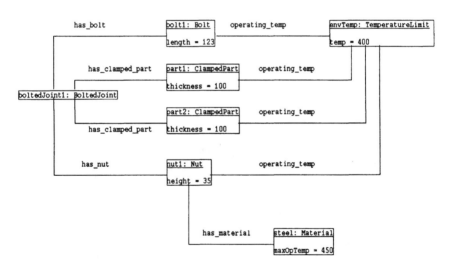

Figure 3 A configuration using the ontology

Using this ontology, we can describe the simple arrangement of a bolted joint shown in Figure 2, subject to a particular environmental temperature. This is shown in Figure 3. Example constraints might include:

- Any concrete feature must have a material with a higher operating temperature than the prevailing environmental temperature;

- The length of the bolt in a bolted joint must exceed the sum of the thicknesses of the clamped parts, plus the height of the nut. Note that for simplicity, we have ignored issues such as tolerances of dimensions, although this can be dealt with, for example by defining a Measurement class of feature, with a real valued properties dimension and tolerance.

The first constraint will apply to all features that have a has_material property and an environmental_temperature property defined. The second constraint is more complicated, and applies to all bolts, nuts, and clamped parts that are part of a bolted joint.

5. Functionality

An ontology written in DAML+OIL [7] describes available feature types. In the Designers' Workbench, the designer can select a feature class from the ontology and create an instance of that class. The property values of the instance can then be filled in: datatype values by literals of the appropriate type, and object type values by selecting an instance from a list of all instances of the appropriate type.

Constraints are handled in a two stage process:

- Identify feature values that should be constrained;

- Formulate a tuple(s) of values for each set of feature values, and check that the constraint is satisfied by these values.

The constraint processing uses RDQL (RDF Query Language) [10] to find the constrained features. A disadvantage of using RDQL is that it cannot return arbitrary numbers of values from a query, making constraints on arbitrary numbers of features impossible to express. For example, the constraint on the sum of thicknesses of clamped parts cannot be expressed. To get around this, it is possible to have separate constraints for 1, 2, 3, ..., n parts, where n is some arbitrary number, but this is clearly not ideal. Part of the future work will be to investigate other query languages or mechanisms to overcome this difficulty.

After using RDQL to extract the values that are constrained, SICStus Prolog [22] is used for the process of checking that the constraints hold.

The RDQL query that locates features affected by the material temperature constraint is:

```
SELECT ?arg1,?arg2 WHERE
  (?feature,<dwOnto:has_material>,?mat),
  (?mat,<dwOnto:max_operating_temp>,?arg1),
  (?feature,<dwOnto:operating_temp>,?optemp),
  (?optemp,<dwOnto:temperature>,?arg2)
  USING dwOnto FOR <namespace>
```

The values of the returned variables ?arg1 and ?arg2 are the maximum operating temperature of the material of the feature, and the current operating

216

temperature, respectively. The check that the values must satisfy is represented by the SICStus predicate

```
op_temp_limit(MaterialMaxTemp, EnvironTemp) :-
    EnvironTemp =< MaterialMaxTemp.
```

Using the values of ?arg1 and ?arg2, the query

```
op_temp_limit(MaterialMaxTemp, EnvironTemp).
```

is formed, and checked. This process is repeated for each set of values returned by the RDQL query, and for each constraint that has been specified.

6. Additional features of the Designers' Workbench

A screenshot of the Designers' Workbench is shown in Figure 4, with closeups of the main panels in Figure 5. In this section, we describe the system's additional features.

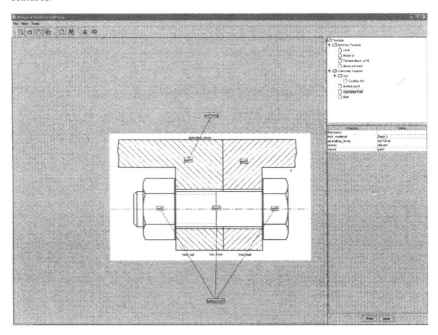

Figure 4 The Designers' Workbench

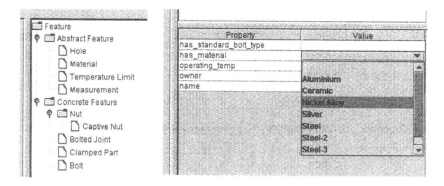

Figure 5 Closeups of the Designers' Workbench panels: the feature ontology (left), and properties of the selected feature (right)

6.1 Graph-based display of configuration

In the current implementation of Designers' Workbench, the designer can import a drawing and annotate it with features. The drawing is really a visual aid—the designer can ``mark up" an existing drawing or construct a configuration without a drawing. Features can be selected from an ontology. Features that are added by the designer are shown as labels overlaying the background drawing. Properties that connect features are represented by arcs. Features can be selected, and their properties viewed and modified using the table displayed beneath the ontology. Datatype properties are set by typing values into the field, whereas object properties are set using a drop down list of values representing the valid possibilities for the property. For example, if the property has_bolt is specified to have range of class Bolt, the list will consist only of instances of Bolt.

6.2 Checking incomplete configurations

Before checking constraints, it is not necessary to specify values for every defined property of every feature. Instead, the designer can fill in values for whichever properties he or she desires, and request a constraint check. The RDQL query will only return results for the features that have sufficient values specified, so that only certain constraints will be checked. This allows designers to operate in an exploratory way, defining small parts of a configuration, checking them, and then gradually extending the configuration until it is complete.

6.3 Constraint rationales

Each constraint has an associated rationale (currently a short text string, but which in future may have more structure), and an (optional) URI for a source document explaining the rationale in more depth. When a constraint violation is reported, the designer is presented with a list of the features involved in the violation, the rationale, and link that can be clicked on to read the source document. In this way, the designer can learn more about the constraint, and decide if it is in fact appropriate. As the constraint checking proceeds, an experienced designer may decide to override the constraint.

7. Preliminary evaluation

In order to get feedback on the Designers' Workbench an informal interview was carried out with an engineer with six years experience at Rolls-Royce. The format of the interview was: an overview of the system was given by the developer, followed by the engineer attempting a series of tasks, and finally a discussion of the pros and cons of the system took place. The main findings were:

1. the interface was intuitive to use, although some details needed to be refined (for example, the exercise revealed some mismatches between the original ontology and the domain);

2. it was reasonably straightforward to add features to a design, although the engineer would have preferred textual items rather than icons. This could be implemented as an option that the user can set as required;

3. the engineer prefers that constraint checks are performed automatically, and an error message pops up, rather than the current arrangement of the user requesting that constraint checks be performed. Again, this could be an option that the user could enable or disable as required;

4. the engineer requested an additional feature, namely that links to previous designs or documents referring to similar features or issues be provided, enabling the user to find relevant past material quickly. Currently, previous designs or documents can be searched, but only by a text-based search;

5. the engineer did not currently use software that provides the same functionality as the Designers' Workbench.

Clearly, point 4 provides the most challenge. To find previous documents relating to particular features will require that the documents are annotated with reference to the same ontology as used by the Designers' Workbench. This means that authors of these documents must be provided with editors that will enable them to make these annotations as painlessly and as automatically as possible.

8. Future work

The Designers' Workbench is still at an early stage of development. In this section we describe some possible future avenues of research.

8.1 Propagation of values

A useful feature would be to reflect the designers' choices by maintaining domains for property values, and reducing them by removing values that are incompatible with the constraints. A problem arises here: a designer may have only tentatively selected a value for a particular property, and may deliberately wish to select an incompatible value for another property. A possible solution would be to display all the values in the domains for the designer to choose from, but highlight in some way the values that are incompatible with the currently selected values for other properties. The implementation of this feature will require the use of the constraint solving libraries of SICStus to maintain variable domains and perform propagation, rather than the simple predicate checking that is used currently.

8.2 Functional descriptions

The current version of Designers' Workbench does not deal explicitly with the functions of features. (Functions have been described using ontologies by Iwasaki et al. [9] and Kitamura et al. [12].) Nor does it deal with the various possible different states of features; for example, a shaft will have to operate successfully at different temperatures, pressures and rotational speeds. Adding functions to the Designers' Workbench will allow users to specify the intended functions of each feature, or group of features. Using an ontology of functions should allow for a fairly straightforward integration with the current system.

8.3 Design rationale storage (argumentation)

It would be very useful to capture and store the reasoning that the designer performs during the configuration process (design rationale capture). More details on processing design rationales can be found in [4] and [5]. Designers can examine current and past solutions to find out the reasons for particular decisions, why alternatives were discarded, and avoid repeating past mistakes.

8.4 Constraint input

To add a new constraint currently requires coding a query in RDQL, and a predicate in SICStus Prolog. This is quite a laborious task, and can only be done by a programmer. It would be useful if a new constraint could be formulated in an intuitive way, by selecting classes and properties from the ontology, and somehow combining them using a predefined set of operators. This would enable designers to have control over the definition and refinement of constraints, and presumably to be able to have greater trust in the results of constraint checks. We also intend to investigate alternative approaches to the underlying representation and querying of constraints. It is likely that the mixed RDQL/Prolog method may be replaced by a single framework, possibly Colan/CIF [8].

8.5 Ontology change

Occasionally the available features described in the ontology may have to be increased (new parts or techniques become available), or decreased (obsolete parts removed). It is also possible that extensive changes may be made to naming conventions, or the arrangement of the feature class hierarchy. It is important to ensure that:

- previous designs can still be accessed using Designers' Workbench (possibly by recording the original ontology as part of each design);

- that existing constraints can be kept up to date.

A constraint that is defined on a class of features will automatically apply to a new subclass of that class. The problem of removals can be overcome by retaining the class, but flagging it in some way as obsolete. The most difficult situation will be the restructuring of a class hierarchy, which may require complex processing to ensure that existing constraints will still apply where necessary.

9. Summary

The Designers' Workbench allows designers to specify a configuration by selecting features from an ontology. Parameters of a feature can be specified by setting datatype property values, and the connections to other features are specified with objecttype properties. Constraints are defined on classes of features, but are applied to instances of features. A configuration can be checked for constraint violations at any time, even if some features are only partially specified. We have concentrated on assisting a human designer by checking constraints, rather than attempting to find solutions automatically. Constraint checking is performed by searching the configuration for applicable features, and passing the values of appropriate properties to a SICStus Prolog checker. A graphical display enables the designer to easily add new features, set property values, and perform constraint checks.

10. Acknowledgements

The authors would like to acknowledge the assistance of engineers and designers in the Transmissions and Structures division of Rolls-Royce plc, Derby, UK. The work was carried out as part of the EPSRC Sponsored Advanced Knowledge Technologies project, GR/NI5764, which is an Interdisciplinary Research Collaboration involving the University of Aberdeen, the University of Edinburgh, the Open University, the University of Sheffield and the University of Southampton.

References

1. J. Bowen, P. O'Grady, and L. Smith. A constraint programming language for life-cycle engineering. Artificial Intelligence in Engineering, 5(4):206 – 220, 1990.
2. D. C. Brown. Defining configuring. AI EDAM, 12:301 – 305, September 1998.
3. D. C. Brown. Functional, behavioral and structural features. In J. C. Borg and P. Farrugia, editors, Proc. KIC5: 5th IFIP WG5.2 Workshop on Knowledge Intensive CAD, Malta, July 2002. Available at: http://www.cs.wpi.edu/~dcb/Papers/KIC5/KIC5-Features.html. Accessed on 1st September 2004.
4. S. Buckingham Shum. Design argumentation as design rationale. In A. Kent and J. G. Williams, editors, The Encylopedia of Computer Science and Technology, pages 95 – 128. Marcel Dekker, Inc., 1996.
5. R. Bracewell and K. Wallace. A tool for capturing design rationale. In ICED03, 14th International Conference on Engineering Design, pages 185 – 186, Stockholm, Sweden, 2003.
6. B. Chandrasekaran, J. R. Josephson, and V. R. Benjamins. What are ontologies and why do we need them? IEEE Intelligent Systems, 14(1):20 – 26, Jan/Feb 1999.
7. The darpa agent markup language homepage. http://www.daml.org/. Accessed on 1st September 2004.
8. P. Gray, K. Hui, and A. Preece. An expressive constraint language for semantic web applications. In IJCAI-01 Workshop on E-Business and the Intelligent Web, pages 46 – 53, Seattle, USA, August 2001.
9. Y. Iwasaki, R. Fikes, M. Vescovi, and B. Chandrasekaran. How things are intended to work: Capturing functional knowledge in device design. In IJCAI-93, pages 1516 – 1522, 1993.
10. Jena—a semantic web framework for java. http://jena.sourceforge.net/index.html. Accessed on 1st September 2004.
11. U. Junker and D. Mailharro. The logic of ilog (j)configurator: Combining constraint programming with a description logic. In Proceedings of IJCAI'03 Workshop on Configuration, 2003. Available at: http://www2.ilog.com/ijcai-03/Papers/IJCAI03-03.pdf. Accessed on 1st September 2004.
12. Y. Kitamura, T. Sano, K. Namba, and R. Mizoguchi. A functional concept ontology and its application to automatic identification of functional structures. Advanced Engineering Informatics, 16(2):145 – 163, April 2002.
13. V. Kumar. Algorithms for constraint-satisfaction problems: A survey. AI Magazine, pages 32 – 44, Spring 1992.
14. F. Laburthe. Constraints over ontologies. In Proceedings of CP2003, pages 878 – 882, 2003.
15. L. Lin and L.-C. Chen. Constraints modelling in product design. Journal of Engineering Design, 13(3):205 – 214, September 2002.
16. Jinxin Lin, M. Fox, and T. Bilgic. A requirement ontology for engineering design. Concurrent Engineering: Research and Applications, 4(4):279 – 291, September 1996.

A Visualisation Tool to Explain Case-Base Reasoning Solutions for Tablet Formulation

Stewart Massie   Susan Craw   Nirmalie Wiratunga

School of Computing
The Robert Gordon University, Aberdeen

sm@comp.rgu.ac.uk   smc@comp.rgu.ac.uk   nw@comp.rgu.ac.uk

Abstract

Case Based Reasoning (CBR) systems solve new problems by reusing solutions of similar past problems. For knowledge intensive tasks such as design it is not sufficient to merely retrieve and present similar past experiences. This is because the user requires an explanation of the solution in order to judge its validity and identify any deficiencies. Case retrieval with k-nearest neighbour relies heavily on the availability of cases, knowledge about important problem features and the similarity metric. However, much of this information, utilised by the system, is not transparent to the user. Consequently there is a need for tools that can help instil confidence in the system by providing useful explanations to the user. This paper proposes an approach that explains the CBR retrieval process by visualising implicit system design knowledge. This is achieved by visualising the immediate neighbour hood and by highlighting features that contribute to similarity and to differences. The approach is demonstrated on a pharmaceutical tablet formulation problem with a tool called FormuCaseViz. An expert evaluation provides evidence to support our approach.

1 Introduction

The problem being considered here is the formulation of a pharmaceutical tablet for a given dose of a new drug. Inert excipients (e.g. Lactose, Maize Starch, etc.) are chosen to mix with the new drug so that the tablet can be manufactured in a robust form. In addition to the drug, a tablet consists of five components each with a distinct role; i.e. Filler, Disintegrant, Lubricant, Surfactant, and Binder (see Figure 1). The formulation task entails identifying a suitable excipient and amount for each chosen component. Each chosen excipient must be suitable for its desired role and be compatible with each other and the drug. A more detailed description of the problem domain is available in [3].

A case-based reasoning (CBR) system solves new problems by reusing solutions from previously correctly solved similar problems [9]. Case retrieval is the first stage of the CBR cycle in Figure 2. For a tablet formulation, given a description of the new drug's chemical and physical properties together with specific requirements for the tablet, a similar case or a subset of similar cases useful for solving the new problem are retrieved from the case-base. Depending on the differences between the current problem and the retrieved cases some adaptation of the retrieved cases might be necessary before the retrieved solution can be reused. Here the proposed system solution will be the excipients names and quantities that would enable the manufacture of a

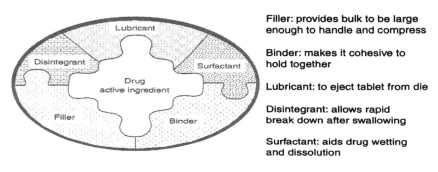

Filler: provides bulk to be large enough to handle and compress

Binder: makes it cohesive to hold together

Lubricant: to eject tablet from die

Disintegrant: allows rapid break down after swallowing

Surfactant: aids drug wetting and dissolution

Figure 1: Tablet formulation problem

viable tablet. Subsequent stages include verification of the proposed solution and, if necessary retention of the new problem and the modified solution with the aim of reusing it in the future.

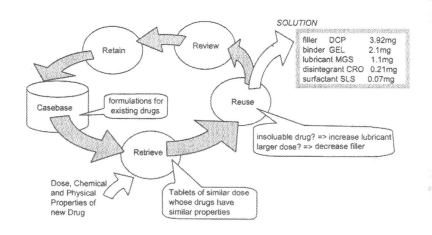

Figure 2: CBR cycle applied to the tablet formulation domain

An obvious advantage of CBR is its ability to present similar past experiences to an end-user instead of, for example a set of rules from a rule-base system. Clearly humans find it easier to relate to similar past experiences, however with domains such as tablet formulation where a case is described using 35 features simply presenting the cases will not aid the end-user's understanding of the reasoning behind the retrieval or even the proposed system solution. Mechanisms that aid human understanding of the system's problem solving process is vital because it helps instil confidence in the system and may eventually determine the success of the system's deployment in the real world.

In this paper we look at the retrieval stage of the CBR cycle and tackle the problem of improving comprehension of this important stage by incorporating a visualisation tool. Our approach is applied to the tablet formulation domain but should be generally applicable across a wide range of domains. The usefulness of this approach is measured by conducting an expert user evaluation.

In Section 2 we explore in more detail the importance of explaining the solution in CBR. Section 3 discusses the information that different users expect from an explanation in order to increase their acceptance of the CBR system. The initial tablet formulation tool which provided the user with a textual solution is discussed in Section 4. A knowledge-light approach to providing an explanation of the solution is presented in Section 5. In Section 6 the design of the user evaluation is described along with the results. In Section 7 we review recent CBR research in this area. Finally we provide conclusions and recommendation for future work.

2 Solutions Require Explanations

Case Based Reasoning (CBR) is experience based problem-solving that mimics the approach often used by humans. One of the many advantages associated with CBR is its understandability as it can present previous cases to support or explain its conclusions [10]. Recent research provides evidence to support this view that a solution based on a previous experience is more convincing than one based on rules [4].

In contrast to the idea that the CBR methodology is understandable, King et al. [8] grade classification algorithms based on the *comprehensibility of the results*. The k-nearest neighbour (k-NN) algorithm, generally used in CBR systems, was graded at only 2 out of 5 by users, with only neural network algorithms being graded lower. One reason is that the similarity measure, usually compacted into a single value, hides the knowledge gained during system development and encoded into the design [2]. Revealing this knowledge aids interpretation of results, exposes deficiencies and increases confidence in the system.

Explanation of CBR solutions is typically based on presenting the single most *similar* case to the new problem, and possibly a similarity value. While this level of explanation might suffice in relatively simple, easily understood domains, it is not sufficient for tasks that are knowledge intensive. Individually the nearest case can provide an explanation. However, as with CBR solutions that can be improved by using several cases to provide a combined solution, likewise there is added value in providing an explanation based on several *similar* cases. This is particularly true if the similarities and differences within these cases can be made explicit; e.g. with the aid of visualisation.

In this paper we address this apparent contradiction that the CBR paradigm is transparent and understandable, yet the results of k-NN retrieval are not easy to comprehend. The CBR process draws heavily on knowledge held in the knowledge containers. Vocabulary, case and retrieval knowledge are three of the CBR *knowledge containers* proposed by Richter [13]. In order to encourage user acceptance of the system the contents of these containers should be visible to the user. We present an approach that explicates this underlying knowledge to generate an explanation of the system solution formed on the basis of one or more nearest neighbours.

3 What Needs to be Explained

Knowledge intensive tasks require a better explanation than simply a proposed solution and a set of retrieved cases. This is particularly true of design problems, such as tablet formulation, where the case-base does not contain all possible designs. The proposed solution is only an initial draft, which may need to be adapted to compensate for differences between retrieved similar problems and the current problem at hand. The domain expert requires additional information and explanations to make the decision making process more transparent and to allow him to judge the validity of the solution. A visualisation tool for explanation must therefore highlight knowledge that not only drives the retrieval stage (e.g. retrieval knowledge containers), but also that suggests the need for adaptation (e.g. problem and solution differences).

3.1 Knowledge Containers

Knowledge elicitation for a CBR system, particularly applied to design tasks, can be substantial. A retrieve only CBR system will utilise the following knowledge containers:

- the case representation, generally containing two parts (the problem and solution), normally consists a set of attributes and values but can be a more complex structure. It is important for the user to be able to verify that this representation is suitable for the problem-solving task at hand.

- the case-base is the main knowledge source of a CBR system and usually determines its competence. It is not sufficient to expect the user to accept that the case-base provides representative problems. The user must be able to judge its quality and coverage in order to decide if it is suitable to address current problems. This will allow gaps in the case-base knowledge to be addressed and rectified.

- the retrieval process usually involves a similarity function that compares the cases held in the case-base with the new problem. This can be a Euclidean distance function or some domain specific function. The importance of individual features is often identified by feature weighting. The user needs to be able to decide if the similarity function is appropriate and if the importance of features is correctly represented.

This knowledge is often hidden from the user and can result in two effects: the user may accept the hidden knowledge as fact and not question it, or alternatively, confidence in the system may be harmed due to a lack of understanding of the hidden process. Either of these effects can be harmful to the usage of a CBR system.

3.2 The Proposed Solution

In addition to general information about the underlying CBR model being used, local information specific to the current problem must be visible to the user. This will allow a judgement to be made on the quality of the proposed solution and provide the relevant information to make manual adaptations. Visible, local information helps identify deficiencies in the current problem solving experience (e.g. quality of case-base, similarity function). It can be provided by comparing the new problem with either the case-base as a whole or with the most similar cases identified by the similarity function (its nearest neighbours). Local information is required in the following areas:

- **Similarities & Differences within Best Matching Cases and the Problem.** Easily interpretable information is required that allows the user to identify the attribute values that are common to both the problem and the best matching cases. More importantly it allows specific attribute value differences to be identified. This is the information needed to allow adaptation of the proposed solution. A one dimensional similarity value can hide these differences and is often not sufficient.

- **Relationship Between Neighbourhood & Case-base.** This allows the user to identify whether the case-base coverage is sufficient in the local region for this particular problem and allows an area of the problem space to be highlighted. Any deficiencies in coverage can be addressed by adding new relevant cases to the case-base.

4 Textual FORMUCASE

Our initial version of this application, called FORMUCASE, was developed along traditional CBR lines. Each case has a problem and solution represented by a list of attribute values. The problem attributes consist of five physical properties describing the drug itself and twenty chemical properties which describe how the drug reacts with possible excipients. All these attributes have numerical values. The solution has ten attributes; five with nominal values identifying the excipients used and five numeric values identifying the quantity of each excipient. When formulating a tablet for a new drug the attribute values representing the drug are entered and its nearest neighbours identified using the k-NN algorithm. The multi-component proposed solution to the problem is a weighted majority vote of its nearest neighbours to determine excipients and a weighted average for excipient quantities.

The output from FORMUCASE (see Fig. 3) is presented in report format displaying the nearest neighbours, their problem and solution attribute values and their similarity to the new problem. The feature values of the proposed solution are then displayed. This retrieve-only system forms the first step in a tablet formulation. Differences between the new test problem and the retrieved cases may indicate the need to refine the predicted solution by manual adaptation.

An initial evaluation of FORMUCASE identified two problems. Firstly, confidence in the retrieval stage of the system's low as there was a reluctance to accept that the

```
1 Nearest Neighbour: DrugT-200          Percentage match : 85.54%
PROBLEM: Drug Solubility        : 0.8   SOLUTION: Filler; Amount      : Lactose 154.59mg
         Drug Contact Angle   : 56.0             Disint; Amount      : Croscarmelose 9.8mg
         Drug Yield Press     : 75.24            Binder; Amount      : PreGelStarch 6.9mg
         Drug Yield PressFast : 81.36            Lubricant; Amount   : MgStearate 3.43mg
         Drug Dose            : 200              Surfactant; Amount  : null 0.0mg
         Stabilities: 99.6; 100; 100; 99.5; 0.0


2 Nearest Neighbour: DrugQ-100          Percentage match : 70.27%
PROBLEM: Drug Solubility        : 1.0   SOLUTION: Filler; Amount      : Lactose 182.2mg
         Drug Contact Angle   : 42.0             Disint; Amount      : NaStarchGlyc 12.6mg
         Drug Yield Press     : 24.84            Binder; Amount      : PreGelStarch 6.3mg
         Drug Yield PressFast : 45.6             Lubricant; Amount   : MgStearate 3.1mg
         Drug Dose            : 100.0            Surfactant; Amount  : null 0.0mg
         Stabilities: 100; 100; 100; 92.8; 0.0


Suggested Tablet Formulation :
  Filler; Amount           : Lactose 167.04mg
  Disintegrant; Amount     : Croscarmelose 11.06mg
  Binder; Amount           : PreGelStarch 6.63mg
  Lubricant; Amount        : MgStearate 3.28mg
  Surfactant; Amount       : null 0.0mg
```

Figure 3: FormuCase report format output

similarity metric used provided similar cases to the current problem. Secondly, it was difficult to perform adaptation because differences between the new problem and the retrieved cases were not obvious. A revised version of this application, called FORMUCASEVIZ, was developed to alleviate these problems.

5   FORMUCASEVIZ

We demonstrate our approach to explanation using visualisation with this tablet formulation problem. Our hypothesis is that the visual version (FORMUCASEVIZ) will help explain the CBR process and increase user confidence in the solution. The problem and solution are displayed in parallel coordinate plots in order to address the issues discussed in Section 3.

A parallel co-ordinate graph's primary advantage over other types of statistical graphics is its ability to display a multi-dimensional vector or case in two dimensions. Fig. 4 shows a plot with five dimensions. Each attribute is represented by a labelled vertical axis. The value of the attribute for each case is plotted along each axis. The points are then connected using horizontal line segments such that each case is represented as an unbroken series of line segments which intersect the vertical axes. Each axis is scaled to a different attribute. The result is a *signature* across n dimensions for each case. Cases with similar data values across all features will share similar signatures. Clusters of like cases can thus be discerned, and associations among features can also be visualised.

The basic layout of the graphical display for the tablet formulation task takes the form of three panels each containing a two dimensional parallel coordinate graphs (see Fig. 5). The top graph contains twenty axes and provides attribute value information for the drugs chemical properties. The lower left graph contains five axes with the

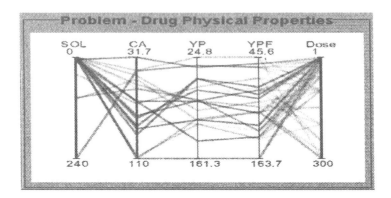

Figure 4: Parallel co-ordinate plot showing the drug physical properties of a case-Base

drugs physical properties and the lower right graph displays the solution attribute values. Thus the top and lower left panel contain attributes from the problem domain and the lower right graph contains attributes from the solution space.

Loading a case-base results in the vertical axes being drawn and labelled with an attribute's name and minimum and maximum value. The case lines, intersecting the axes, are also shown (see Fig. 4). A visual picture of case-base coverage can now be seen with darker regions representing well covered areas of the problem space and gaps being visible as portions of the axis without case lines. The encoded retrieval knowledge in the form of feature weights is represent by the width of each axis. Fig. 4 shows a case-base displayed on the drug physical properties graph. It can be seen that the attributes *SOL* and *Dose* have the highest weights.

We see in Fig. 5 that on entering a new problem a black line representing it is drawn on the two problem domain graphs. This provides information on the local coverage provided by the case-base in relation to this particular problem. As no solution is yet available there is no black line representing the problem in the solution panel.

Fig. 6 shows a solution to a problem. The nearest neighbours are identified in the case-base and displayed as coloured dashed lines. The nearest neighbour solutions are also displayed in the solution panel along with the proposed solution for the new problem. A new axis is added to the drug physical properties problem panel showing the similarity value between the problem and its NN along with labels for each case. This visualisation allows the similarities and differences to be viewed in terms of the real data aiding interpretation of the proposed solution and making the adaptation stage easier. For example, in Fig. 6, it can be seen that the best matching cases disagree on which filler to use. *LAC* is the proposed solution but reference to the chemical stabilities show *DCP* would be a better choice as it has a higher chemical stability.

5.1 Ordering the Attributes

The order or arrangement of the attributes is important when using parallel co-ordinate graphs. The arrangement can improve the visualisation by helping to identify trends

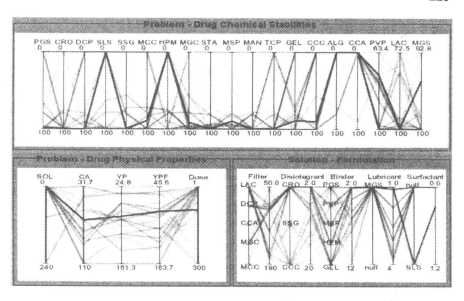

Figure 5: Output screen of FORMUCASEVIZ with an unsolved problem entered

or correlations within the case-base. Many approaches to multi-dimensional data visualisation arrange the attributes arbitrarily, possibly in the order that they appear in the case representation. We have taken the approach of arranging the attribute axis based on their similarity to each other in order to reduce line crossing on the graph. To achieve this axis arrangement we first use an axes similarity function to identify the pairwise similarities between the axes and then determine an arrangement so that similar axis are placed adjacent to each other.

An obvious way to measure axis similarity is to compare values across the cases. The similarity between axes A_i and A_j is measured using the attribute value similarity across the *cases*, rather than across the attributes as for case similarity. Thus, when case c_k is described by the n-tuple of attribute values $(a_{1k}, \ldots a_{nk})$, the axis similarity from cases $c_1 \ldots c_m$ is defined as follows:

$$Similarity(A_i, A_j) = \sum_{k=1}^{m} similarity(a_{ik}, a_{jk})$$

where similarity is the inverse Euclidean distance defined for individual (normalised) attribute values.

Determining a linear arrangement for the axes such that similar axes are placed close to each other is still not straightforward. We adopt the approach of first looking at the pairwise similarity values between the axes and picking the most similar pair. These are placed to the left of the graph. The most similar unallocated axis is placed next to it. This process continues until all the axes have been allocated a position in the graph.

230

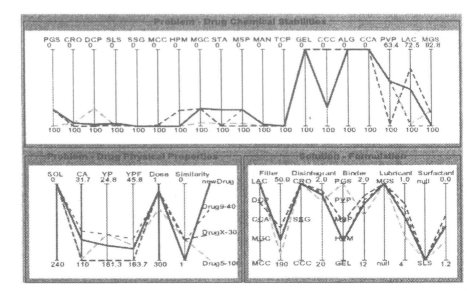

Figure 6: Output screen of FORMUCASEVIZ with a problem and proposed solution

An alternative approach, which may give an optimal arrangement, is to find the order with the minimum total similarity when adjacent axis similarities are summed. However Ankerst et al [1] show that this problem is NP-complete. The use of a heuristic approach such as genetic algorithms or optimisation may suit.

The arrangement of the axes can be carried out from a global or local context. The global arrangement looks at the whole case-base and takes no account of the current problem. This approach is best for looking at case-base coverage or when trying to identify trends within the case-base. It also has the benefit that it can be used prior to a problem being entered and is more stable as it remains unchanged as each new problem is entered. The local arrangement only looks at a portion of the case-base, typically around the new problem by only using its nearest neighbours in the calculation of the axes similarities.

FORMUCASEVIZ was implemented with the global arrangement on the two problem domain panels as it was found that the continual rearranging of axes gave problems in interpreting the results. However in other domains the advantages of a local approach may outweigh this disadvantage. No ordering of axes was applied to the solution panel as a fixed order was found to be more easily understood.

6 User Evaluation of FormuCaseViz

The purpose of the domain expert evaluation was to investigate how well FORMU-CASE and FORMUCASEVIZ explain their solution and the process undertaken to arrive at the solution. This was done by looking at how easily the solutions could be interpreted and the confidence the domain expert has in the system's solution.

Three new tablet formulation problems were created to act as test queries for these evaluations. Test case 1 and 2 were created by making minor changes to an existing case held in the case-base. As a result, these test cases had similar nearest neighbours and a competent proposed solution was generated by the system. The third test case was created by removing an existing formulation from the case-base and making minor variations to it. This had the effect of creating a test case that had no similar cases in the case-base. There was considerable variation within the solutions of the retrieved nearest neighbour cases and confidence in the proposed solution was expected to be lower.

The questionnaire, containing thirty questions in total, was designed to ascertain the evaluators confidence in the system given the tool's ability to explain its reasoning. It contained three parts. Part A and B involved answering questions, as the three test cases were solved, using FORMUCASE and FORMUCASEVIZ respectively. The questions varied from specific questions e.g. *What is the similarity value of the best matching case?* to more abstract questions e.g. *Are you more confident in excipient prediction for the Filler or the Binder?.* Part C contained general questions comparing the advantages and disadvantages of two versions of the application.

Two domain experts were given both versions of FORMUCASE, a case-base and the three sample problems to solve. The evaluation required the expert to fill out the questionnaire while solving the three different test problems, on the same case-base, first with FORMUCASE and then with FORMUCASEVIZ. While the results of the evaluation are not published in detail here, we summarise our findings by highlighting some of the interesting observations.

- The experts agreed that FORMUCASEVIZ explains the CBR process of generating a solution better than the textual output version.

- There was a reluctance to accept a similarity value alone as a measure of the case-base's competence to answer a specific problem. In answer to the question *does the case-base contain similar cases to the problem?* with FORMUCASE an *unsure* answer was usually given. In contrast, when presented with the same problem on FORMUCASEVIZ a definite and expected answer was always given.

- There was generally more confidence in the solutions provide by FORMUCASEVIZ and it was possible for alternative solutions to be suggested by the expert as would be required during the manual adaptation stage of the CBR cycle.

- The evaluators were better able to answer questions requiring them to identify differences within the nearest neighbours and between the problem and the neighbours. One evaluator commented *The graphical display is excellent and shows up similarities and differences in a very clear way.*

- Exact numerical values cannot be read from FORMUCASEVIZ as the values have to be interpolated from the axes. This is not ideal with one expert commenting *the absence of easily readable numerical data is a big problem.* This deficiency needs to be addressed.

The positive results from our evaluation suggest that FORMUCASEVIZ provides a useful and more informative explanation of the proposed solution than FORMUCASE.

7 Related Work

CBR systems using decision tree guided retrieval typically provide their explanations by highlighting feature values of decision nodes traversed in order to reach the leaf node [4]. This is similar to the methods adopted in rule-based expert systems which often show rule activations [14]. Such rule-based explanation is not possible in systems using only k-NN retrieval because a set of discriminatory features is not identified as part of the algorithm. In these systems a typical approach is to present an explanation in terms of feature value differences between the query and the retrieved case. Cunningham et al. [4] suggest that explanations, expressed in terms of similarity only, can be useful in some domains (e.g. medical decision support) but is inadequate in others. McSherry's [12] approach to explaining solutions is based on identifying features in the target problem that support and oppose the predicted outcome. Discovery of the supporters and opposers of a predicted outcome is based on the conditional probabilities, computed from the cases available at run time, of the observed features in each outcome class.

Hotho et al. [6] provide explanations that are not solely similarity based. In their approach text documents are formed into clusters using a similarity metric and k-means clustering. The importance of the features or words in each cluster are ranked and the most *important* are used to represent the cluster. The relationship between clusters can then be identified using WordNet concept hierarchies. An explanation can now be given not only by the similarity of a document to other members in its cluster, but also on the relationship to other clusters.

Another approach to providing an explanation is through visualisation. McArdle & Wilson [11] present a dynamic visualisation of case-base usage by using a spring based algorithm. The algorithm uses the attraction and repulsion of the *springs* to spread the cases around a two dimensional graph in an attempt to preserve the n-dimensional distances between cases. This provides more insight into the similarity assessment than the usual single dimensional value. However, the knowledge held within the similarity metric is still hidden. Although this approach is used for supporting the maintenance of large case-bases it could also be adopted to visualise retrieved cases. An alternative approach is the parallel coordinate plot, originally proposed and implemented by Inselberg [7]. Falkman [5] uses this approach to develop an information visualisation tool, The Cube, which displays a case-base using three dimensional parallel co-ordinate plots. This approach allows the underlying data to be visualised as well as the similarity metric. We exploit this approach by also using a parallel coordinate plot to display the case-base but in addition we display underlying knowledge from the CBR knowledge containers and the retrieval process itself .

8 Conclusions and Future Work

A user gains confidence in a system that provides correct results. However confidence is also improved in systems where the decision making process is transparent and deficiencies can be identified and resolved. The explanation of results should be a key design criterion in CBR systems.

In this paper we have identified some of the reasons why CBR systems, particularly those using k-NN retrieval, are not as successful as they might be. We have presented an approach that can address some of these problems using a parallel co-ordinate visualisation of the problem and solution. This approach has been demonstrated on FORMUCASEVIZ in a tablet formulation problem domain in which thirty-five dimensional data is viewed in one representation. A user evaluation confirmed that this explanation based approach made interpretation of the results easier than on the textual version, and better explained the CBR process. The need for exact numerical values to be available on the visualisation was also identified. While we have used tablet formulation in this paper our approach would be applicable across a wide range of CBR problem domains.

Future work will look at providing more local information related directly to the problem rather than to the case-base as a whole. This may involve a rearranging of the attribute axes. Alternative, we may look at identifying or highlighting attributes in the problem domain that have the biggest impact in determining specific parts of the solution. This could be done by looking for correlations between axes in the problem and solution space. In addition we will look at providing a more dynamic visualisation that allows the user to interact directly with the data, for example to change the problem or highlight certain areas of the case-base.

Acknowledgments

We acknowledge the assistance of PROFITS, Bradford University for funding the FORMUCASE demonstrator, providing the tablet formulation data and supplying willing domain experts for user evaluations.

References

[1] M. Ankerst, S. Berchtold, and D. A. Keim. Similarity clustering of dimensions for an enhanced visualization of multidimensional data. In *Proceedings of IEEE Symposium on Information Visualization*, pages 52–60. IEEE Computer Society Press, 1998.

[2] R. Bergmann. *Experience Management: Foundations, Development Methodology, and Internet-Based Applications*. Springer, 2002.

[3] S. M. Craw, N. Wiratunga, and R. Rowe. Case-based design for tablet formulation. In *Proceedings of the 4th European Workshop on Case-Based Reasoning*, pages 358–369. 1998.

[4] P. Cunningham, D. Doyle, and J. Loughrey. An evaluation of the usefulness of case-based explanation. In *Proceedings of the 5th International Conference on Case-Based Reasoning*, pages 122–130. Springer, 2003.

[5] G. Falkman. The use of a uniform declarative model in 3D visualisation for case-based reasoning. In *Proceedings of the 6th European Conference on Case-Based Reasoning*, pages 103–117. Springer, 2002.

[6] A. Hotho, S. Staab, and G. Stumme. Explaining text clustering results using semantic structures. In *Principles of Data Mining and Knowledge Discovery, 7th European Conference*, pages 217–228. Springer, 2003.

[7] A. Inselberg. The plane with parallel coordinates. *The Visual Computer*, 1:69–91, 1985.

[8] R. King, C. Feng, and A. Sutherland. Statlog: comparison of classification algorithms on large real-world problems. *Applied Artificial Intelligence*, 9(3):259–287, 1995.

[9] J. Kolodner. *Case-Based Reasoning*. Morgan Kaufmann, San Mateo, CA, 1993.

[10] D. B. Leake. CBR in context: The present and future. In D. B. Leake, editor, *Case-Based Reasoning: Experiences, Lessons and Future Directions*, pages 3–30. MIT Press, 1996.

[11] G. P. McArdle and D. C. Wilson. Visualising case-base usage. In *Workshop Proceedings of the 5th International Conference on Case-Based Reasoning*, pages 105–124. NTNU, 2003.

[12] D. McSherry. Explanation in case-based reasoning: an evidential approach. In *Proceedings of the 8th UK Workshop on Case-Based Reasoning*, pages 47–55. 2003.

[13] M. Richter. Introduction. In M. Lenz, B. Bartsch-Sporl, and S. Wess, editors, *Case-Based Reasoning Technology: From Foundations to Applications*, pages 1–15. Springer, 1998.

[14] R. Southwick. Explaining reasoning: an overview of explanation in knowledge-based systems. *Knowledge Engineering Review*, 6:1–19, 1991.

SESSION 5:

ANALYSIS AND EVALUATION

Formal Analysis of Empirical Traces
in Incident Management

Mark Hoogendoorn, Catholijn M. Jonker, Savas Konur,
Peter-Paul van Maanen, Viara Popova, Alexei Sharpanskykh,
Jan Treur, Lai Xu, Pınar Yolum

Department of Artificial Intelligence, Vrije Universiteit Amsterdam
De Boelelaan 1081a, 1081 HV Amsterdam, The Netherlands.
Email: {mhoogen, jonker, skonur, pp, popova,
sharp, treur, xu, pyolum}@few.vu.nl
URL: http://www.few.vu.nl

Abstract

Within incident management an important aspect is the analysis of
log files describing traces of incident management processes and the
errors made in them. Automated support of such an analysis can be
helpful. In this paper some results are shown on automated support
for analysis of errors in traces of incident management. For such
traces it can be checked automatically which dynamic properties
describing good functioning hold and which fail. The potential of the
approach is shown in the formal analysis of a given empirical trace.
The approach can also be applied in conjunction with simulation
experiments.

1. Introduction

Disasters are unforeseen events that cause great damage, destruction and human
suffering. The question that keeps rising is: "Could we have done anything to
prevent this?" The key element is the distinction between incidents and disasters.
Incidents are disturbances in a system that can lead to an uncontrollable chain of
events, a disaster, when not acted on properly.

Incidents will keep occurring. People can make mistakes and nature can be
unpredictable. Typically this causes chaotic situations and the resulting problems
are very complex and have to be solved within limited time. Examples of incidents
that took on disastrous proportions because of inadequate human intervention are
the crash of a Boeing 747 in an urban area in Amsterdam and the Hercules disaster
in Eindhoven in the Netherlands.

Research in incident management has been fruitful for the past few years. To
manage an incident usually many parties have to cooperate. Because of this
multidisciplinary and distributive character of incident management, research is
mainly focused on the design and development of information systems to support
both multi-party communication and decision making. Systems like IMI [13] and

237

the GIS-based information exchange system for nuclear emergencies in the Netherlands [14] belong to this category.

But incident management has a very dynamic and adaptive character too. Organising multi-party cooperation in a dynamic and adaptive manner, while minimising the number of errors, is one of the main challenges. There have been some attempts. For example COMBINED systems [5] tries to tackle the problem in such an adaptive multi-agent manner.

Finally, of course simulations are very important for the analysis of crisis response and the development of training systems. Such as simulations of strategic management [3].

This paper shows how formal modelling techniques from the area of AI enable automated support for the analysis of empirical or simulated traces (temporal description of chains of events) of incident management. More in particular, it is shown on the one hand how an empirical trace can be formalised to enable automated analysis, and on the other hand how dynamic properties that are essential for an incident management process can be formalised. Moreover, it is discussed how such dynamic properties can be (and actually have been) checked automatically for a given formalised trace. By pinpointing the failing dynamic properties, this automated analysis shows where things have gone wrong in the incident management process. Currently several incident domains are subject of study, such as plane crashes and environmental disasters, with a focus on local and regional as well as national and international processes. Empirical traces are constructed by hand, by means of the analysis of reports and the interviewing of experts. The formalisation of the traces is done by hand as well. However, for the future there are plans to develop a methodology that supports non-expert users in making formalised traces.

In Section 2 and 3 of this paper an informal analysis of traces of real life case studies is presented. In Section 4 a first categorisation of the types of errors is made. In Section 5 an outline is given of the adopted modelling approach. Section 6 shows a formalisation of the trace of one of the case studies. Section 7 discusses a number of essential dynamic properties that have been formalised and automatically checked for the formalised trace from Section 6. Section 8 is a final discussion.

2.   The Hercules Disaster

The informal analysis of the Hercules disaster presented here is based on [8] and a formalisation can be found in Section 6.

On October 16th, 1996 at 6:03 p.m. a Hercules military airplane crashed at the airport of Eindhoven, in the Netherlands. This disaster involves many examples of miscommunications and lack of communication and is therefore a well known example of a non optimal working disaster prevention organisation. An informal description of the events that took place during the rescue phase is presented below.

The Air-Traffic Control Leader on duty anticipated an accident and activated the so-called crash bell at 6:03 p.m. and hereby initiated the alarm phase. Trough the intercom installation he announced that a Hercules plane had landed with an accident and pointed out the location of the plane. The Assistant Air-Traffic Control Leader at the same time contacted the Emergency Centre of the Fire department at the Airbase and reported the situation. The Fire department immediately took action.

The Airbase Fire department must, when reporting to external authority, report which scenario is applicable. There are three different types of scenarios: Scenario 1: A maximum of 2 people involved, Scenario 2: More than 3 and less than or equal to 10 people. Scenario 3: More than 10 people. This all can be found on a checklist and also has consequences for the activities that should take place and the amount of authorities that need to be informed.

The Air-Traffic Control Leader on duty knew that at least 25 people were on board of the plane, this was due to a private source. He called the Emergency Centre of the Fire department at the Airbase around 6:04 p.m. with the order to call 06-11 (the national emergency number at that time).

The Chief of the Airbase Fire department ('On Scene Commander', OSC) asked Air-Traffic Control for the number of people on board of the plane at 6:04 p.m. According to this person, the answer was 'nothing known about that'. Following from this the OSC reported Scenario 2 through the walkie-talkie. The Emergency Centre operator says not to have heard this but does not want to state that this has not been said.

At 6:06 p.m. the Emergency Centre operator calls 06-11 and is connected to the Central Post for Ambulances (CPA). From that point on, the Emergency Centre operator got help from a fire fighter. Together they tried to inform several governmental officials.

At 6:12 p.m. the Regional Emergency Centre of the Fire department (RAC) Eindhoven phoned air-traffic control with the question whether backup was needed, the response was 'negative'. At 6:12 p.m. the Emergency Centre employee and the aforementioned fire fighter decided to follow Scenario 2 of the disaster plan (there were at least 4 people on board of the Hercules because that is the usual crew for this type of plane). At 6:15 p.m. the first civil fire trucks pulled out.

Besides alarming and informing all parties, actions on the scene were taken during that same period. Immediately after the announcement of the Air-Traffic Control Leader the Airbase Fire department went to the scene with a Land Rover Command vehicle (LARO) with the OSC and two Major Airport Crash Tenders (MAC's) each manned with a crew of 3 people. The OSC thought that only the crew was on board of the plane and till the moment passengers had been found he handled accordingly.

At 6:05 p.m. the LARO arrived at the scene and directed the MAC's to the plane. At 6:07 p.m. the MAC's took their position of attack, the plane was on fire across the full length of the body. According to the procedures, the extinguishing was aimed at making the body fire-free. At 6:09 p.m. this was the case and the rest of the fire did not spread anymore. In this situation, the survivors could escape from the plane by themselves.

Around 6:10 p.m. one of the MAC's was empty and the other one only had a quarter of the water-supply left. The OSC decided to have a fire fighter switch the empty one for another one that was still full. After 6 minutes the fire fighter was back with a full MAC.

At 6:19 p.m. there was complete control over the fire at the right wing and engine. Thereafter, at 6:25 p.m. the first civil fire trucks arrived on the scene. After their arrival the OSC contacted the chief of the first fire truck who was told that probably four people were on board of the plane. After pumping water to the MAC's at 6:38 p.m. they started extinguishing the left engine.

6:33 p.m. was the exact time point when the decision was made to go inside the plane and use a high-pressure hose to extinguish some small fires inside the plane. After that, at 6:37 p.m. the fire fighters were in the plane for the first time and shortly thereafter the first casualty was discovered. Almost at the same time 20 to 30 other casualties were discovered.

3.   The Dakota Disaster

The informal analysis of the Dakota disaster presented here is based on [9].

The plane crash of a Dakota PH DDA in 1996 in The Netherlands is another examined disaster. The plane had 6 crew members and 26 passengers on board and crashed into the Wadden Sea.

In the Dakota disaster, other factors are involved in the emergency rescue process. For instance, some officers are not familiar with emergency procedures/protocols for the disaster. The wrong procedures/protocols are picked up. An inefficient rescue procedures/protocols consequently is followed. Another example is that an overload of some of the partners can potentially cause some mistakes during the rescue process. However, miscommunications and inappropriate decisions are also involved in the rescue process.

On September 25, 1996 a Dakota PH DDA of the Dutch Dakota Association (DDA) left Texel International Airport Holland. The plane had 6 crewmembers and 26 passengers on board. Shortly after take off the crew reported engine trouble to Texel International Airport Holland (TIA). Around 4:36 p.m. the crew contacted the Navy airbase The Kooy (MVKK) and stated that it wanted to make an emergency landing on The Kooy. After a short while, The MVKK observed the Dakota disappear from the radar screen.

The MVKK immediately sent a helicopter, initiated a team of rescue helicopters and alarmed the coast guard centre (KWC). At 4:46 p.m. the KWC passed the correct information of the disaster to Regional Alarm Centre northern part of Noord-Holland (RAC) and asked the RAC to alarm the relevant partners. Unfortunately, the RAC only organised the rescue boats and vessels and did not alarm other parties, that should be warned in the disaster.

At 4:55 p.m., the KWC reported the disaster to Noord Hollands Dagblad (a Dutch newspaper) and RTL TV station. Consequently, the KWC got many requests for information from the ANP (Dutch press office). The KWC is thus under a lot of pressure.

Through the ANP, the National Centre for Coordination (LCC) got the message that the Dakota had crashed. At 5:03 p.m. the LCC contacted the KWC, the KWC asked the LCC to help by providing a trauma team.

Coincidentally, a big drill for ambulances was ready to start. The Drill leader asked the president of the Dutch health service (GGD) whether the drill should still go on. At 5:05 p.m. the president of the GGD called RAC to inquire if the accident is for real. The RAC responded that neither the KWC nor the harbour office (HK) knew what was going on. The GGD even agreed to start the drill.

At almost the same time, the KWC asked the MVKK to take care of the wounded and told the LCC that the trauma team should be sent to MVKK. At 5:07 p.m. the LCC made an appointment with the Ministry of Public Health, Wellbeing, and Sports (VWS), VWS finally arranged the trauma team.

At 5:17 p.m. the first helicopter with casualties landed at Gemini Hospital (Gemini), the Gemini called the RAC to ask what the purpose of this is. The RAC replied that they only knew a plane had crashed and did not know anything more.

At 5:20 p.m. the RAC asked the KWC to get a trauma team from Gemini to MVKK. Meanwhile the centre for ambulances (CPA) of Amsterdam, the mayors of Den Helder and Wieringen, and the commander of the regional fire department are notified. After a while the arrangements of a crisis centre finally set up at the Navy. At 6:44 p.m. all bodies are found and transported. There is only one survivor of the disaster.

4.   Categorisation of Error Types

Based on the above informal traces of the Hercules and Dakota disasters, in this section a first attempt is made to categorize the probable causes of the mistakes made during the incident management phase after the crashes.

Incomplete Information
First of all a property of urgent situations would be that a lot of decisions are made based on incomplete information. There may not be enough time or resources to gather all relevant information to support a decision, and therefore a wrong decision might be made.

For example, in the Hercules case the operator of the Airbase Fire department has no knowledge of the amount of people on board of the plane, while he has to decide on who to call and what kind of backup to request, without this information. An approach that can be used for planning (which is a typical task in incident management) using incomplete information is for example presented in [6].

Contradictory Information
A second property is that a lot of decisions are made based on contradictory information. One might think of urgent situations in which a decision is made, in spite of a lacking sound support for it, which causes mistakes. For example, in the Dakota disaster two numbers are mentioned to be the main information telephone number for relatives of the casualties.

Incorrect Information

Similar to the above properties, information can also be incorrect. Incorrect information obviously misleads incident management, and may cause errors. This incorrectness might be caused by, among others, ill communication, accident, or misinterpretation.

For example, in the Hercules disaster the air-traffic control leader knew how many people were on board of the plane, however he replied a request of the on scene commander for the amount of passengers with a denial of the fact that he knew the amount of people on board.

Decision making with incorrect information can be incorporated in reflective agents, an example of the modelling of reflective agents can be found in [2]. In [7] a constraint satisfaction framework for decisions under uncertainty is presented.

Use of Different Protocols

Another property is that in larger scale incidents a lot of parties are involved, and therefore it becomes more probable that different rules or protocols are used in situations where the same should have been used. In these situations parties might expect others to have different behaviours than they have in reality.

For example, in the Hercules case the operator of the Airbase Fire department had in mind that the protocol involved calling 06-11. This was however another protocol in case of a less severe accident. This caused unnecessary delays. In the Dakota disaster for example, the coast guard did not act according to the prescribed policy for disasters in the Wadden Sea, but instead used that of the North Sea, and hence the national level organizations got involved in the regional ones, which caused a lot of delay and misunderstandings.

Exception Handling

If disaster plans do not deal with different scenarios, or parties are not familiar enough with such plans, it is possible that exceptions are not handled well. For instance, in the Dakota disaster the commander of the regional fire department is surprised when he hears from the Regional Alarm Centre about the disaster and that the region is not involved in its management. Because it was not asked, the commander did not take any further action. If he had, it probably would have been very helpful. In these cases a back-up plan should be available.

Work Overload

Finally, if tasks are not delegated properly to parties, or a party is not aware of the possibility of delegation, work overload most probably occurs, and might be another cause for errors. For example, in the case of the Dakota disaster, during the first period after the crash, the coast guard had a lot to do, and therefore did not pay enough attention to initiating or delegating activities ashore. In these kinds of situations the coast guard should be relieved of the tasks that can be performed by others.

Software agents can be a very useful help in supporting people to cope with all the incoming information and making the right decision, see for example [4].

5. Modelling Approach

To formally specify dynamic properties that are essential in incident management processes, an expressive language is needed. To this end the *Temporal Trace Language* is used as a tool; cf. [11]. In this paper for the properties occurring in Section 6 both informal or semi-formal and formal representations are given. The formal representations are based on the Temporal Trace Language (TTL), which is briefly defined as follows.

A *state ontology* is a specification (in order-sorted logic) of a vocabulary. A state for ontology Ont is an assignment of truth-values {true, false} to the set At(Ont) of ground atoms expressed in terms of Ont. The *set of all possible states* for state ontology Ont is denoted by STATES(Ont). The set of *state properties* STATPROP(Ont) for state ontology Ont is the set of all propositions over ground atoms from At(Ont). A fixed *time frame* T is assumed which is linearly ordered. A *trace* or *trajectory* γ over a state ontology Ont and time frame T is a mapping $\gamma : T \rightarrow$ STATES(Ont), i.e., a sequence of states γ_t (t $\in$ T) in STATES(Ont). The set of all traces over state ontology Ont is denoted by TRACES(Ont). Depending on the application, the time frame T may be dense (e.g., the real numbers), or discrete (e.g., the set of integers or natural numbers or a finite initial segment of the natural numbers), or any other form, as long as it has a linear ordering. The set of *dynamic properties* DYNPROP(Σ) is the set of temporal statements that can be formulated with respect to traces based on the state ontology Ont in the following manner.

Given a trace γ over state ontology Ont, the input state of a role r within an incident management process (e.g., mayor, or fire fighter) at time point t is denoted by

state(γ, t, input(r))

analogously

state(γ, t, output(r))
state (γ, t, internal(r))

denote the output state, internal state and external world state.

These states can be related to state properties via the formally defined satisfaction relation $\models$, comparable to the Holds-predicate in the Situation Calculus: state(γ, t, output(r)) $\models$ p denotes that state property p holds in trace γ at time t in the output state of role r. Based on these statements, dynamic properties can be formulated in a formal manner in a sorted first-order predicate logic with sorts T for time points, Traces for traces and F for state formulae, using quantifiers over time and the usual first-order logical connectives such as $\neg$, $\wedge$, $\vee$, $\Rightarrow$, $\forall$, $\exists$. In trace descriptions, notations such as

state(γ, t, output(r)) $\models$ p

are shortened to

output(r) | p

To model direct temporal dependencies between two state properties, the simpler *leads to* format is used. This is an executable format defined as follows. Let α and β be state properties of the form 'conjunction of literals' (where a literal is an atom or the negation of an atom), and e, f, g, h non-negative real numbers. In the *leads to* language $\alpha \rightarrow\!\!\!\rightarrow_{e, f, g, h} \beta$, means:

> *If state property α holds for a certain time interval with duration g,*
>
> *then after some delay (between e and f) state property β will hold for a certain time interval of length h.*

For a precise definition of the *leads to* format in terms of the language TTL, see [12]. A specification of dynamic properties in *leads to* format has as advantages that it is executable and that it can often easily be depicted graphically.

6. Formalisation of an Empirical Trace

Informal traces of events, such as the trace presented in Section 2 of the Hercules disaster, can be formalised using the formal language TTL as briefly described in Section 5; see also [11]. The translation from an informal trace of events to a formal trace is currently done by hand. However, for the future there are plans to develop a methodology that supports non-expert users in making this translation.

Formalising a trace has several benefits. First of all, specific properties which should hold for a trace can be verified. An example of such a property in the case of an airplane crash is that a fire truck should be at the disaster area within 3 minutes according to the International Civil Aviation Organisation (ICAO). Some properties (like the example just mentioned) can often easily be checked by hand, but in more complex cases, a mistake may have been caused by a wrong chain of events. These types of causes are usually difficult to determine, and the formalisation can help for this purpose.

Another benefit of the formalisation is in the case where the protocol for the disaster prevention organisation was incorrect. After the protocol has been rewritten it can be formalised by means of executable properties and the scenario in which the previous protocol failed can be used as an input. Resulting from this, a simulation can be performed which in turn will result in a trace of the functioning of the disaster prevention organisation when using the new protocol. By means of this trace the properties that failed with the previous protocol can again be verified to see whether the new protocol has indeed improved the functioning. In case the properties are again not satisfied the cause of this failure can be determined and the protocol can be revised until the desired properties are all satisfied.

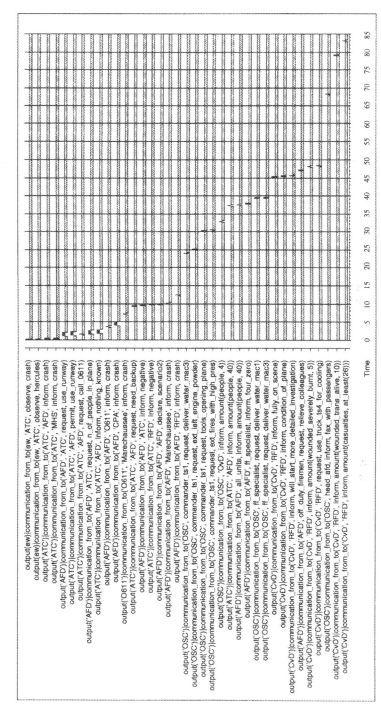

Figure 1: Formalised empirical trace of the Hercules disaster

An example of a formalisation of a trace is shown in Figure 1. It models the events that occurred during the Hercules incident. Only a part of the trace is shown for the sake of brevity. On the left side of the picture the atoms are shown that are present in the trace. All atoms have the format

output('role')|communicated_from_to('src', dst', 'type', 'information')

The 'role' indicates the role that outputs this information, whereas the 'src' and 'dst' model the source and destination role (notice that 'role' = 'src' always holds). A list of all the abbreviations used for the roles is shown in Table 1.

The types of communication are based on speech acts [1]. In the full trace also atoms containing input are present. Behind the atom there is a time line, indicating when the atom is true in the trace.

Abbreviation	Abbreviates
AFD	Airbase Fire Department
ATC	Air Traffic Control
CPA	Central Post Ambulances
MAC	Major Airport Crash tender
OSC	On Scene Commander
OSO	On Scene Operations
MHS	Medical Health Servies
OvD	Officer On Duty
CvD	Commander on Duty
0611	The national emergency number

Table 1: A list of all abbreviations

For example, the first atom

output(ew)|communication_from_to(ew, 'ATC', observe, crash)

which states that the external world outputs a crash of a Hercules to air-traffic control, is true during the first minute after the crash, as he observes the crashed plane during that period.

A verification of properties that should hold for the disaster prevention organisation is presented in the next section.

7. Validation of a Trace

After having obtained a formalised trace, either by formalisation of an empirical trace or by a simulated trace, it is useful to verify essential dynamic properties of an incident management process for the trace. By means of this verification one can determine what precisely went wrong in the example incident management process described by the trace.

Such dynamic properties can be verified using a special software environment *TTL Checker* that has been developed for the purpose of verifying dynamic properties specified in the Temporal Trace Language TTL (see Section 4 or [11]) against simulation traces.

The software environment takes a dynamic property and one or more (empirical or simulated) traces as input, and checks whether the dynamic property holds for the trace(s). Using this environment, the formal representation relations presented below have been automatically checked against the trace depicted in Figure 1. Traces are represented by sets of Prolog facts of the form

holds(state(m1, t(2)), a, true).

where m1 is the trace name, t(2) time point 2, and a is a state formula in the ontology of the component's input.

It is indicated that state formula a is true in the component's input state at time point 2. The programme for temporal formula checking basically uses Prolog rules that reduce the satisfaction of the temporal formula finally to the satisfaction of atomic state formulae at certain time points, which can be read from the trace representation. Examples of such reduction rules are:

sat(and(F,G)) :- sat(F), sat(G).

sat(not(and(F,G))) :- sat(or(not(F), not(G))).

sat(or(F,G)) :- sat(F).

sat(or(F,G)) :- sat(G).

sat(not(or(F,G))) :- sat(and(not(F), not(G))).

Below a number of properties are expressed that in particular are relevant for the Hercules case (Section 3.1), are represented in structured semi-formal format, and finally have been formalised using TTL.

P1: Information Correctness

At any point in time t1,
if AFD generates a request for ATC about the number of people on the plane,
then at a later point in time t2 ATC will communicate the correct answer to AFD

Formalization of the property P1:

∀t1 [state(γ, t1, input('ATC')) |= communication_from_to ('AFD','ATC', request, n_of_people_in_plane)
⇒ ∃t2>t1 state(γ, t2, output('ATC'))|= communication_from_to('ATC','AFD', inform, amount(people, 40))]

Automated verification showed that this property is not satisfied in the given trace.

P2: Choice of Protocols

At any points in time t1 and t2, t2≥t1,
if ATC generates information to AFD about the plane crash at t1,
and that the number of passengers is more than 10 at t2,
then at a later point in time t3 AFD declares Scenario 3.

Formalization of the property P2:

∀t1, t2, x [t2≥t1 ⇒ [state(γ, t1, input('AFD')) |= communication_from_to ('ATC','AFD', inform, crash)
& x>10 & state(γ, t2, input('AFD'))|= communication_from_to('ATC, 'AFD', inform, amount(people, x))]
⇒ ∃t3>t2 state(γ, t3, output('AFD'))|= communication_from_to('AFD','AFD', declare, scenario3)]

This property is not satisfied for the given trace.

P3: Timely Information Delivery

At any point in time t1,
if ATC generates information for AFD about the plane crash,
then at a later point in time t2, t2 ≤ t1+2 AFD will communicate this information to RFD.

Formalization of the property P3:

∀t1 [state(γ, t1, input('AFD')) |= communication_from_to ('ATC','AFD', inform, crash)
⇒ ∃t2≤ t1+2 state(γ, t2, output('AFD'))|= communication_from_to('AFD','RFD', inform, crash)]

This property is not satisfied for the given trace.

P4: MAC Timely Arrival at the Disaster Area

At any point in time t1,
if AFD receives information from ATC about the plane crash,
then at a later point in time t2 MAC will join AFD, and at a still later point in time t3 will come to the
disaster area in less than 3 minutes upon the plane crash information reception.

Formalization of the property P4:

∀t1 [state(γ, t1, input('AFD')) |= communication_from_to ('ATC','AFD', inform, crash)
⇒ ∃t2>t1 state(γ, t2) |= member_of('MAC', 'AFD') &
∃t3≤ t1+3 & t3>t2 & state(γ, t3)|=member_of('MAC', 'OSO')]

This property is satisfied for the given trace.

P5: Sufficient Number of Ambulances, Called Immediately

At some time point t1,
if CPA generates information about the number of ambulances, sent to the disaster area to RFD,
then at no later point in time t2 CPA will ask for additional ambulances.

Formalization of the property P5:

∀t1, x,y
[state(γ, t1, input('RFD')) |= communication_from_to ('CPA', 'RFD', inform, amount(ambulance_sent, x))
⇒ ¬∃t2>t1
state(γ, t2, output('CPA'))|= communication_from_to('CPA', 'CPA', request, amount(ambulance_needed), y)]

This property is not satisfied for the given trace.

The property P5 is meant to verify if CPA sent a sufficient number of ambulances
to the scene immediately.

As can be seen from the results of properties verification, given above, 4 from 5
properties are not satisfied over the trace. By analyzing the obtained results one can
get insight in which types of errors occurred in the scenario and which points of the
disaster plan were not fulfilled.

8. Discussion

In this paper it was shown how automated support of the analysis of errors in traces of incident management can be obtained. The potential of the approach was shown in the formal analysis of a given empirical trace. However, the approach can also be applied in conjunction with simulation experiments. If a large number of simulated traces are generated, for example by varying parameters or initial information, for these simulated traces it can be checked automatically which dynamic properties hold or fail for which of the traces.

Usually one can specify dynamic properties at different aggregation levels, from global properties, to more local properties, and establish hierarchical inter-level relations between the properties. If one of the global properties does not hold, then verification of properties at intermediate levels can follow to identify were the cause of the problem can be found. The verification process can be continued up to the lowest level, consisting of the simplest local properties. See [10] for more details of this diagnostic approach. The approach put forward in this paper can be extended to include such a hierarchical diagnostic approach as well.

Further potential uses of the checking of dynamic properties is by investigating whether or not certain mistakes would still exist after a modification of the relating protocols. The possibility to check such properties formally, can provide a clue to get to solutions or recommendations in terms of improved protocols.

References

1. Austin, J.L. How to do things with words. Oxford University Press, 2nd edition, 1976.
2. Brazier, F.M.T., Treur, J. Compositional modelling of reflective agents. International Journal of Human-Computer Studies, vol. 50, 1999, pp. 407-431.
3. Breuer, K., Satish, U. Emergency Management Simulations-An approach to the assessment of decisionmaking processes in complex dynamic environments. In Jose J. Gonzalez (eds), From modeling to managing security: A system dynamics approach, HoyskoleForlaget, 2003, pp. 145-156.
4. Brown, S. M., Santos Jr., E., Banks, S. B., Stytz, M. R. Intelligent interface agents for intelligent environments. In: Proceedings of the 1998 AAAI Spring Symposium on Intelligent Environments, 1998, pp. 145-147.
5. Burghardt, P. Combined Systems: The combined systems point of view. In: Carlé, B., Walle, B. van der (eds.), Proceedings of the International Workshop on Information Systems for Crisis Response and Management '04, Brussels, Belgium. 2004.
6. Etzioni, O., Hanks, S., Weld, D., Draper, D., Lesh, N., Williamson, M., An approach to planning with incomplete information. In: Proc. 3rd Int. Conf. on Principles of Knowledge Representation and Reasoning, 1992, pp. 115-125.
7. Fargier H., Lang J., Martin-Clouraire R., Schiex T. A constraint satisfaction framework for decision under uncertainty. In: Proc. of the 11th Int. Conf. on Uncertainty in Artificial Intelligence, 1995, pp. 167-174.

8. Inspectie Brandweerzorg en Rampenbestrijding, Vliegtuigongeval Vliegbasis Eindhoven 15 juli 1996, SDU Grafische Bedrijf, The Hague, 1996.
9. Inspectie Brandweerzorg en Rampenbestrijding, Dakota-incident Waddenzee 1996, SDU Grafische Bedrijf, The Hague, 1997.
10. Jonker, C.M., Letia, I.A., Treur, J. Diagnosis of the dynamics within an organisation by trace checking of behavioural requirements. In: Wooldridge, M., Weiss, G., and Ciancarini, P. (eds.), Agent-Oriented Software Engineering, Proc. of Second Int Workshop AOSE'01. Lecture Notes in Computer Science, vol. 2222. Springer Verlag, 2002, pp. 17-32.
11. Jonker, C.M., Treur, J. Compositional verification of multi-agent systems: a formal analysis of pro-activeness and reactiveness. International. Journal of Cooperative Information Systems, vol. 11, 2002, pp. 51-92.
12. Jonker, C.M., Treur, J., and Wijngaards, W.C.A., A Temporal Modelling Environment for Internally Grounded Beliefs, Desires and Intentions. Cognitive Systems Research Journal, vol. 4, 2003, pp. 191-210.
13. Lee, M.D.E. van der, Vugt, M. van. IMI – an information system for effective multidisciplinary incident management. In: Carlé, B., Walle, B. van der (eds.), Proceedings of the International Workshop on Information Systems for Crisis Response and Management '04, Brussels, Belgium. 2004.
14. Ridder, M. de, Twenhöfel, C. The design and implementation of a decision support and information exchange system for nuclear emergency management in the Netherlands. In: Carlé, B., Walle, B. van der (eds.), Proceedings of the International Workshop on Information Systems for Crisis Response and Management '04, Brussels, Belgium. 2004.

Modelling Expertise for Structure Elucidation in Organic Chemistry Using Bayesian Networks

Michaela Hohenner, Sven Wachsmuth, and Gerhard Sagerer

Applied Computer Science Group, Faculty of Technology

Bielefeld University, Germany

Abstract

The development of automated methods for chemical synthesis as well as for chemical analysis has inundated chemistry with huge amounts of experimental data. To refine them into information, the field of chemoinformatics applies techniques from artificial intelligence, pattern recognition and machine learning. A key task concerning organic chemistry is structure elucidation. NMR spectra have become accessible at low expenses of time and sample size, they also are predictable with good precision, and they are directly related to structural properties of the molecule. So the classical approach of ranking structure candidates by comparison of NMR spectra works well, but since the structural space is huge, more sophisticated approaches are in demand. Bayesian networks are promising in this concern, as they allow for contemplation in a dual way: provided an appropriate model, conclusions can be drawn from a given spectrum regarding the corresponding structure or vice versa, since the same interrelations hold in both directions. The development of such a model is documented, and first results are shown supporting the applicability of Bayesian networks to structure elucidation.

1   Introduction

Structure elucidation is a routine task in organic chemistry whenever a new compound has been isolated or synthesised. Due to modern methods such as combinatorial chemistry and automated laboratory pathways, the number of new compounds is ever growing, leading to a need for automating the structure elucidation process as well [1].

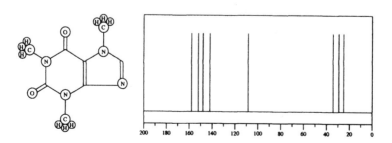

Figure 1: Molecular structure and ^{13}C NMR spectrum of Caffeine ($C_8H_{10}N_4O_2$)

NMR (*nuclear magnetic resonance*) spectroscopy is the most important category of methods in this context. It allows the conclusion of structural features based on the electromagnetic interference of atom nuclei in a strong homogeneous magnetic field [2]. The field of NMR spectroscopy has evolved rapidly, both concerning the development of new sophisticated techniques and the improvement of established methods. Thus it technically meets the requirements of modern science as to time exposure and sample size, but a new bottleneck arises with respect to evaluating the great amounts of complex data now easily being accumulated. Tools for automated NMR spectra evaluation in support for the structure elucidation process are therefore highly desirable.

Carbon NMR spectra focus on the carbon atoms forming the backbone of organic molecules. Each carbon evokes a peak (see figure 1: there are eight peaks corresponding to eight carbons), which appears in a characteristic interval depending on the "type" of the carbon. The spectrum thus provides evidence concerning the presence of certain carbon types, but the crucial point is their definition: On the one hand, the interval where the peak appears is primarily determined by the carbon's bond types (e.g. double bonds) and the chemical elements of its neighbours, but on the other hand, focusing on such a small neighbourhood leads to an overlap of intervals associated with different types. In fact, the influences of chemical element and bond types are propagated throughout the whole molecule. They are, however, therefore far too complex to be taken into account with any desired degree of precision. This problem is addressed in more detail when outlining the modelling in section 4.

2 Related Work

A well-practised approach of modern structure elucidation follows a two-step classical paradigm: First, a set of candidate structures is determined, and then every member of the candidate set is validated by comparing a well-chosen property of the candidate with the experimental findings of the unknown. The investigated property should be of a type such that it can be predicted well for a given structure and is also easily accessible in experiment with respect to the unknown. NMR spectra meet these requirements.

To generate the candidate set, nowadays structure generators such as CO-CON [5] or MOLGEN [3] are usually employed, calculating all possible structures given a certain molecular formula. The resulting set of candidates might well turn out to be very large even for small molecules with few heavy atoms[1]: For example, histidine ($C_6H_9N_3O_2$) has 89.5 million isomers[2], though it can be considered a relatively small molecule.

As to the validation step, one has to keep in mind that neither the prediction nor the experimental acquisition of NMR spectra can be performed without any uncertainties. Therefore, one cannot expect to always find a single candidate whose spectrum exactly matches the experimental spectrum, and even if one

---

[1]atoms other than hydrogen

[2]structures meeting the same molecular formula

is found, it need not necessarily be the correct structure. Usually the outcome of automated structure elucidation is a ranked list of candidate structures. The ANALYZE system [4], for example, ranks MOLGEN structure proposals by predicting the corresponding NMR spectra using neural networks and then comparing them with the experimental spectrum of the unknown compound.

The generating of the candidate set is not always based on molecular formula information only, and is often tightly linked to the subsequent ranking process. The idea behind this is the aim to restrict the structural space to be generated, since the time-consuming process of generating a huge number of candidate structures and predicting a huge number of corresponding spectra for means of validation is the major disadvantage of strictly keeping the two steps separate.

The concept of *good lists* or *bad lists* can be applied for this purpose in order to generate only those candidates containing certain required fragments or not containing certain forbidden fragments. In the StrucEluc system [8], for example, good or bad lists can either be given by the user or may be generated automatically. In other systems, additional information beyond the mere molecular formula is used for the same purpose. There may be connectivity information derived from COSY[3] experiments, as in the CHEMICS system [5], or a database of substructure-subspectrum-correlations can be searched, as in SpecSolv [6]. Still these approaches have their drawbacks: COSY experiments unfortunately are quite time-consuming and often result in under-determined ambiguous findings, and the database search is a hard problem with respect to all possible decompositions of the experimental spectrum.

The restriction of the structural space seems to be accomplishable best in another way, that is, not combining structure generation and validation as self-contained steps executed successively. The GENIUS system [1] rather interlaces the two steps iteratively, thereby reaching an even stronger integration than described above: A genetic algorithm is used for structure generation, its fitness function based on the deviation of the predicted spectrum of a candidate from the experimental spectrum of the unknown. In principle this reflects the assumption that similar structures evoke similar spectra. Nevertheless other approaches than genetic algorithms are imaginable to implement a stronger integration of the principles of structure candidate generation and candidate validation by spectra interpretation.

3 Bayesian Networks

In the field of probabilistic methods, *Graphical models* [9, 10] nowadays receive much attention in several domains, e.g. speech recognition and understanding [12] as well as bioinformatics [13], but also for the approach itself [7, 14] in order to utilise its advantages and to enhance its potentialities. Their main advantages, of course, also hold for the structure elucidation application: For one thing, uncertainties and vague information can be handled easily. The interrelation of NMR spectral and molecular structural properties involves such

---

[3]correlation spectroscopy, a two-dimensional NMR technique

254

kind of soft information, as will be explained in more detail in section 4. Also, the possibility of explicitly incorporating expert knowledge leads to a great perspicuity of results. Furthermore, experimental data is not required in principle, and thereby applicability to any class of organic molecules is granted independent of their presence in a given training set.

Thus, graphical models in general and Bayesian networks in particular provide some favourable qualities for the field of automated or computer assisted structure elucidation, but most notably they allow for a dual point of view, integrating aspects of spectra interpretation and spectrum prediction: Provided an appropriate model, conclusions can be drawn on the one hand as to the expected ^{13}C NMR absorption given a carbon in a certain molecular neighbourhood, but on the other hand, the same inherent chemical and physical laws hold for the inference of structural information from spectral properties. Given a model properly reflecting this causal interrelation, the propagation of evidences within the network simultaneously draws conclusions from both structural information (causal evidences) and spectral properties (diagnostic evidences) in a single run. Therefore, it can be regarded as dynamically integrating the structural point of view (which is usually dealt with in structure generation) and the spectral point of view (which is brought to bear when validating structure candidates).

A *Bayesian network* is a graphical model focused on causal relationships among events of interest in a given domain; it is a directed acyclic graph where the nodes are probability variables representing certain events. All variables $A, B, \ldots$ have an individual finite set of discrete states[4] representing different qualities of the event modelled by the respective variable. The directed edges of the graph are to be interpreted as causal links pointing from a cause A to the effected event B. An example network is shown in figure 2.

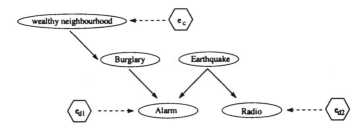

Figure 2: Example of a Bayesian network adapted from [10]: *Let all variables be binary with states "yes" and "no". The* ALARM *is caused to go off by a* BURGLARY. *But it can also be triggered by an* EARTHQUAKE. *However, only the earthquake will cause a* RADIO *report. Entering the diagnostic evidences e_{d1} and e_{d2} concerning the alarm and the radio allows for computation of the likelihood of a burglary taking place. Causal evidence e_c can easily be integrated, e.g. by adding a variable to represent that a* WEALTHY NEIGHBOURHOOD *is likely to increase the risk of a burglary.*

---

[4]The topic of continuous nodes is left out here.

Each variable B also has a conditional probability table $P(B|A_1 \ldots A_n)$ associated with it, which quantifies the influence of the causes $A_1 \ldots A_n$ on the modelled event. (Let B =ALARM, A_1 =BURGLARY, A_2 =EARTHQUAKE in figure 2.) For variables without parents (e.g. EARTHQUAKE and WEALTHY NEIGHBOURHOOD) there are unconditional prior probabilities $P(B)$ given. The joint probability over all variables of a Bayesian network is the product of all those (conditional and prior) probabilities (see [9] pp. 19–20). It allows calculation of the probability of any event within the model given evidence, i.e. the probability of a hypothesis given an observation. The actual probability distributions can either be derived from well-founded theories for the respective application, they can be estimated empirically, or they may even just be set to any value a human expert might consider convenient.

When developing a Bayesian network, the crucial point is building an appropriate causal model, i.e. to define the events of interest and to develop a structure properly reflecting their interdependencies. Firstly, the *hypothesis variables* have to be designed, that is, the events about which information is desired have to be identified and have to be represented as variables and variable states. As these typically are not directly observable, *information variables* have to be introduced, which model the findings of an experiment. Now investigating the causal relationship between information and hypothesis variables may lead to immediate causal links from one to the other, but often *mediating variables* will be necessary, because mediating events between the observables and the hypotheses have to be taken into consideration in order to compactly represent the interrelation of events in the actual domain. At this stage of the modelling task, a good understanding of the application domain is required.

4 Modelling

The development of a causal model for structure elucidation purposes is quite a demanding task, since the model has to meet the requirements of *both* views, spectrum interpretation as well as spectrum prediction. Therefore the task can be regarded as in fact building two models at the same time.

To develop a model, one has to understand about the domain and its applicable laws, as well as common approximations, which might prove helpful when strictly following the well-founded theory is infeasible for any reason. In the following, some basic ideas concerning NMR spectra will be given along with the resulting modelling decisions for the Bayesian network being developed.

4.1 Spectral and Structural Subunits

In terms of pattern recognition, the actual task is to be associated with pattern analysis, rather than pattern classification: A spectrum is not to be regarded as an atomic pattern to be classified, but subunits of the complex spectral pattern are contemplated in the context of each other, accommodating the fact that each carbon (structural subunit) evokes an NMR peak (spectral subunit).

This perspective can as well be found in other structure elucidation systems: Meiler and Meringer [4], for example, use nine neural networks corresponding to different types of carbon atoms to compute each peak individually before assembling the spectrum, which is then used for ranking structure hypotheses.

The *chemical shift* of a carbon (position of the corresponding peak) depends on the shielding effect of its surrounding electrons when the sample is put into the magnetic field of the spectrometer[5]. The density of the electron cloud, and thereby the shielding effect, is determined by the associated atom's type and the types of its neighbours, where an atom's type is given by its chemical element, the types of bonds it has formed (*hybridisation*) and the types of its neighbours. This 'recursive definition' accommodates the fact that influences are in fact propagated throughout the molecule.

The HOSE code (hierarchically ordered system of spherical environments [11]) is a good means of organising structural subunits. Focusing an atom, its neighbourhood is described as *spheres*, as can be seen in figure 3: the first sphere contains all direct neighbours (distance 1), the second sphere contains the neighbours' neighbours (distance 2), and so on.

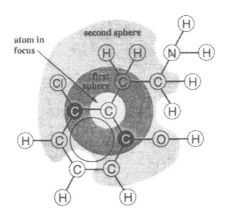

Figure 3: Exemplary compound depicting how the molecular environment is organised into spheres. The first sphere consists of all atoms one bond away from the atom in focus (direct neighbours), the second sphere consists of all atoms two bonds away.

Following just the two ideas of hybridisation and spherical environments, the great variety of organic compounds can be put down to basic building blocks. Four types of carbons can be distinguished, which are essentially different in hybridisation and therefore also differ in their typical chemical shift. It makes sense to develop an individual model for each type. In modelling, though, the same concept is applicable for each of the four types: Influences of the molecular neighbourhood on the chemical shift, as opposed to the hybridisation-dependent influence, are to be incorporated according to spheres.

---

[5]The influence of the spectrometer frequency is eliminated by normalisation.

Thus it appears to be a good starting point to focus on one carbon type at first, developing a showcase model which provides the opportunity to investigate the influence of individual modelling decisions. With respect to the challenge of the dual point of view on spectrum prediction and interpretation, this will without much doubt prove invaluable: The development of models for the other three types of carbons will be straight forward, following the very same ideas and schemes as in the development of the showcase model.

4.2   Aromatic Carbons

Aromatic carbons were chosen for the first exemplary network. *Benzene derivatives*, which contain a six-jointed ring of aromatic carbons as their common structural element (see fig. 4), are a large group of compounds of considerable importance in organic chemistry, so the first tentative scenario was framed to distinguishing substitution patterns on benzene derivatives.

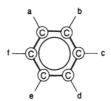

Figure 4: Schematic representation of benzene derivatives. In benzene itself, positions a–f are occupied by hydrogen atoms. There are n^6 combinations of n different admissible substituents (some of which are identical due to symmetry).

A *substitution pattern* is the combination of types and relative positions of *substituents* in positions a–f. With respect to focusing the single aromatic carbon, the corresponding event to be modelled is the occurrence of a substituent, and hypotheses are the different admissible residues (e.g. –OH, –NH$_2$). The corresponding *aromatic carbon* variable is the hypothesis variable of the network. Yet it has to be remarked that its states do not exactly represent the whole substituent, but the first sphere only (e.g. –O– for the –OH residue or –N< for NH$_2$, respectively). As has been stated previously, second sphere influences are to be incorporated separately (see section 4.3).

Figure 5 shows the hypothesis variable and the information variables, which are the initial building blocks of the network. The observables to draw conclusions from are the peaks in the spectrum and the molecular formula. Since each carbon atom causes only one peak, the respective peak is also the only one taken into account. A discretisation of the chemical shift is implemented in the *peak position* variable. As to the molecular formula, it is valuable information to know whether there are atoms of a certain chemical element in the compound. If not, influence of their characteristic type can be ruled out to affect the peak in focus. Molecular formula information is represented in a binary variable per chemical element, stating its presence or absence. Carbon, however, does not need to be represented, because it is always present in organic molecules.

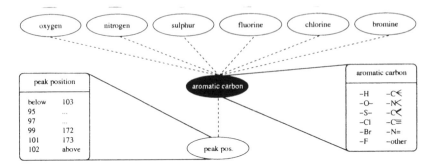

Figure 5: Initial building blocks of the causal model. *Aromatic carbon* is the hypothesis variable (its states are shown in the box on the right) while the other variables represent the information available to draw conclusions from. The variables on the top are all binary with states YES and NO, the peak position variable's states (shown in the left box) represent a discretisation of the spectrum's x-axis.

4.3 Laws of the Domain

As has been stated in 4.1, it is not sufficient to have but one causal link from the evoking carbon to the chemical shift representation, because the direct first sphere neighbours as well as more distant neighbours of other spheres influence the electron density at the carbon in focus, and thereby also its chemical shift in the NMR spectrum. Thus, a variable is introduced per sphere to represent the influences of all atoms in that sphere. Because the strength of influences decreases with increasing distance, only two spheres are considered for a first approximation. Causal links are established from the sphere influences to the peak position.

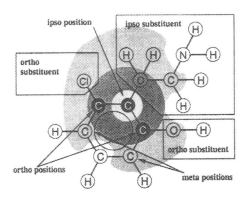

Figure 6: The carbons of the benzene ring are termed according to their relative positions. The carbon in focus is called *ipso* carbon, its direct neighbours are called the *ortho* positions. Like in figure 3 the first and second sphere are distinguished in different shades of gray.

As can be seen in fig. 6, there are always three atoms in the first sphere, two of which are the *ortho* atoms of the benzene ring. As this structural element is fixed given the framed task of recognising benzene substitution patterns, the respective atoms are invariant. Therefore their contribution to the first sphere influence is constant. So the first sphere is already covered by *aromatic carbon* variable: Its states correspond to the different variations of the first sphere. Their respective influences on the peak position are reflected as discretised numeric values in the states of the *first sphere influence* variable.

For the second sphere, there are again two benzene ring carbons (the so-called *meta* carbons next to the the *ortho* carbons) which are not taken into consideration because their contribution to the shift is constant. Beyond that, firstly there are the atoms attached to the *ortho* carbons (let them be called second sphere *ortho* atoms), which vary for different substitution patterns, and secondly, there are the second sphere atoms of the *ipso* substituent (second sphere *ipso* atoms). As for the latter, there is a dependency to be established with the *aromatic carbon* variable, because the valid number of second sphere atoms in the *ipso* substituent depends on the valence of the first sphere *ipso* atom. The second sphere *ortho* atoms, on the other hand, are independent. This again indicates that it makes sense to decompose the second sphere. Consequently, its influence also has to be decomposed into *ipso* and *ortho second sphere influence*. They add up to the total *second sphere influence*.

Beyond their influences on the observed chemical shift, all (first and second sphere) atoms depend on the molecular formula, so a causal link is established from each information variable representing the presence of a chemical element to the *aromatic carbon* variable and to the variables for the second sphere *ipso* and *ortho atoms*.

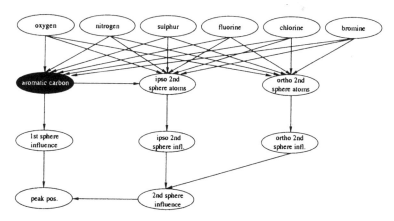

Figure 7: The model of the chemical shift of an aromatic carbon now contains mediating variables representing the contributions of the first and second sphere atoms to the position of the observed peak. Furthermore, the second sphere is subdivided into *ipso* and *ortho* portions. All atom combinations depend on the molecular formula, while all chemical shift increments depend on the atoms in the corresponding relative positions.

One question left open so far is how to design the states of the mediating variables. Concerning the shift influences, the traditional concept of increment tables proves helpful: An *increment table* is a list of substituents and their corresponding influences on the chemical shift of a certain carbon type.

Typically, the influences are given for complete substituents. For the model discussed here, these are generalised into first and second sphere partial increments. Assuming that hydrogen atoms in the second sphere do not have any influence, "standard substituents" where all open valences of the first sphere atoms are bound by hydrogen atoms (e.g. $-OH$, $-NH_2$, $-CH_3$) are used for the first sphere increment. The second sphere increments are derived by comparison of the "standard substituents" to substituents with also non-hydrogen atoms in the second sphere.

Despite due diligence, there is no guarantee of finding a certain peak in exactly the position where it is expected. In the first place, substituents may contain atoms beyond the second sphere, which also have an influence on the chemical shift of the respective carbon. However, it is not possible to incorporate infinitely many spheres, so there always remains an element of risk to encounter influences of distant atoms, as well as other chemical effects (see [16]) which are not covered by the model.

4.4 Assignment of Probability Values

To complete the Bayesian network, probability values have to be added to the model shown in fig. 7. The network is written down in the Bayesian Network Interchange Format (BNIF) [6]. Prior probabilities are required for all variables without parents (that is, the binary information variables concerning the chemical elements), and conditional probabilities $P(A|B_1, \ldots, B_n)$ are required for variables A with parents $B_1, \ldots, B_n$.

As stated in section 3, the numerical probability values can be computed empirically, derived from well-founded theories, or even be set to any value one could consider reasonable based on the given knowledge. The last method is quickly ruled out by two considerations: For one thing, entering every single probability value by hand would be quite time-consuming, but even more importantly, while it is usually easy to assess relative statements as "A is more likely than B" it is quite difficult, even for experts, to put the respective probabilities down to absolute numbers.

Still some of the conditional probabilities (those concerning *1st sphere influence*, *2nd sphere ipso* and *ortho influence*) are given by hand: The relevant events are influence terms corresponding to certain structural fragments. They are exclusively characterised by expert knowledge, which is derived from literature (e.g. [15]). Their values reflect whether it is possible that a certain combination shifts the peak position by a certain increment value. These increment values sum up to the subtotal *2nd sphere influence* and to the total chemical shift (*peak position*).

---

[6]http://www-2.cs.cmu.edu/~fgcozman/Research/InterchangeFormat/Old/xmlbif02.html

The remaining probabilities, including prior probabilities for the presence or absence of chemical elements, are determined empirically based on a set of typically expected molecular structures. They characterise the domain of application, as they determine the likelihood of molecules to be encountered in the domain. As to the presence of chemical elements, this approach reflects the real conditions better than just assuming an equal distribution, which would leave the system without any information on the chemical element's likelihood of occurrence in the given application. It reflects assumptions such as *"The user would mention it if there was fluorine present"* (which is rather unlikely). Anyway, the prior probabilities only play a role if incomplete or no molecular formula information is given.

A set of labelled spectra (molecular structure and experimental spectrum containing references to the evoking carbon for each peak) will be used for evaluating the Bayesian network.

5   Results and Outlook

Six identical networks are necessary to wholly analyse a substitution pattern, since each network is focused on only one position of the benzene ring. Strictly speaking, these networks are peak classifiers: Based on a single peak position (diagnostic evidence) and the molecular formula (causal evidences) it is determined which substituent is most likely to be present at the respective position.

First tests were carried out concerning peak classification. To allow for close investigation of the results, a reduced model with fewer states for the *aromatic carbon*, *2nd sphere ipso position* and *2nd sphere ortho position* variables was employed, keeping the size of the conditional probability tables manageable. This way the exact location inside the model where the system produced an error would be transparent to the developer. The reduction of the model was performed according to the test set, removing states related to structural patterns not present in the sample compounds.

Over 250 labelled samples were taken from digital NMR spectra of benzene derivatives. These spectra, kindly provided by BASF AG (Ludwigshafen), are real-world data which have been validated by multiple measurements. 83.3% of the peaks were classified correctly. Investigating in which cases the misclassifications took place, it turned out that all concerned larger substituents (more than three spheres) or compounds with a high degree of substitution.

The conclusion is that influences of more distant atoms (beyond the second sphere) should be incorporated: In aromatic systems such as the benzene ring, electron influences are propagated especially well, so that all substituents influence the chemical shifts of the ring carbons. Preparations are made to incorporate third and fourth sphere information.

Subsequent to the first classification step, the most probable *ortho* substituents are determined, entering the assumed *ipso* substituent as additional evidence. This leads to a three-membered ring fragment covering the *ipso* and *ortho* substituents. Not surprisingly, the classification error of this second step was again in the same order, because starting from a false *ipso* substituent of course leads to false corresponding *ortho* assessments. Furthermore, the combination of multiple influences throughout the benzene ring was sometimes mistaken for a single *ortho* substituent of similar effect even for correct *ipso* substituents, which is due to the fact that so far only the influence of the *ortho* substituent is covered by the model. Introducing third and fourth sphere information is again expected to improve this behaviour. Also knowledge on the likelihood of certain substituent combinations could be incorporated.

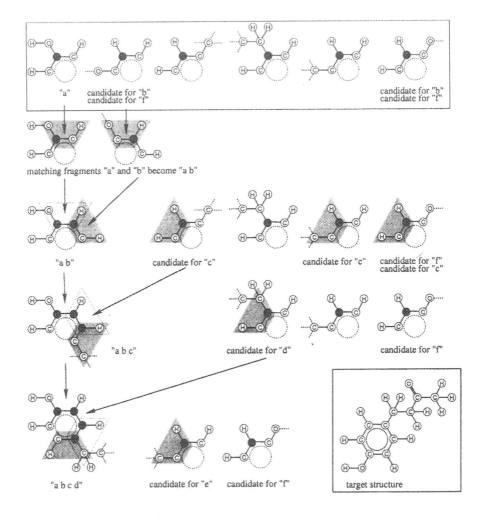

Figure 8: Step 3: Assembling the full substitution pattern: The three-membered ring fragments (box on the top) resulting from step 2 are given as input. Proceeding clockwise, matching fragments (parts that must match are shaded in gray) are added. If several fragments qualify, the one with the best probability score is chosen. Successful matches are shown by a dotted line.

In a third step, the desired substitution pattern is to be computed by assembling the six three-membered fragments to form a full benzene ring. It follows the ideas depicted in figure 8. The three-membered ring fragments along with the probability score from the first classification step are given as input. The most certain classification result is defined to be position "a". All fragments overlap, as "a" contains positions "b" and "f" as *ortho* neighbours, while "b" contains *ortho* positions "a" and "c", and so on. Using this interrelation, the full ring structure can be put together like a jigsaw puzzle.

This concept has been tested for a few sample cases. It worked perfectly when all peaks were classified correctly. If the *ipso* position or the *ortho* neighbours were misclassified, conflicts occurred when trying to assemble the benzene ring. In that case, the system may later correct its prior assessment by ruling out conflicting fragments and replacing the respective hypotheses with the second most probable ones. In some of the sample cases it was even possible to come up with the correct substitution pattern despite peak misclassifications even without including the second most probable hypotheses, just leaving out the conflicting fragment. Currently, an algorithm for this "molecular jigsaw puzzle" is under development.

The promising results obtained so far give rise to the expectation that, once models for the remaining three differently hybridised types of carbons are available, fully elucidating molecular structures for any kind of organic compound is not an utopistic goal.

References

[1] Meiler, J., Will, M.: Automated Structure Elucidation of Organic Molecules from ^{13}C NMR Spectra Using Genetic Algorithms and Neural Networks. J. Chem. Inf. Comput. Sci., **41** (2001) 1535–1546

[2] Beyer, H., Walter, W.: Handbook of Organic Chemistry. London; New York: Prentice Hall (1996) 42–47

[3] Benecke, C., Grund, R., Hohberger, R., Kerber, A., Laue, R., Wieland, T.: MOLGEN+, a Generator of Connectivity Isomers and Stereoisomers for Molecular Structure Elucidation. Anal. Chim. Acta, **314** (1995) 141–147

[4] Meiler, J., Meringer, M.: Ranking MOLGEN Structure Proposals by ^{13}C NMR Chemical Shift Prediction with ANALYZE. MATCH Communications in Mathematical and in Computer Chemistry, **45** (2002) 86–108

[5] Funatsu, K., Sasaki, S.: Recent Advances in the Automated Structure Elucidation System, CHEMICS. Utilization of Two-Dimensional NMR Spectral Information and Development of Peripheral Functions for Examination of Candidates. J. Chem. Inf. Comput. Sci., **36** (1996) 190–204

[6] Will, M., Fachinger, W., Richert, J. R.: Fully Automated Structure Elucidation - a Spectroscopist's Dream Comes True. J. Chem. Inf. Comput. Sci., **36** (1996) 221–227

[7] Smyth, P.: Belief Networks, Hidden Markov Models and Markov Random Fields: A Unifying View. Pattern Recognition Letters, **18** (1997) 1261–1268

[8] Elyashberg, M. E., Blinov, K. A., Martirosian, E. R.: A New Approach to Computer-Aided Molecular Structure Elucidation: the Expert System *Structure Elucidator*. Laboratory Automation and Information Management, **34** (1999) 15–30

[9] Jensen, F. V.: An Introduction to Bayesian Networks. UCL Press, London (1996)

[10] Pearl, J.: Probabilistic Reasoning in Intelligent Systems: Networks of Plausible Inference. Morgan Kaufman (1988)

[11] Bremser, W.: HOSE - A Novel Substructure Code. Anal. Chim. Acta, **103** (1978) 355–365

[12] Bilmes, J.: Graphical Models and Automatic Speech Recognition. Mathematical Foundations of Speech and Language Processing. Institute of Mathematical Analysis Volumes in Mathematics Series, Springer-Verlag (2003)

[13] Klingler, T. M. and Brutlag, D. L.: Discovering structural correlations in alpha-helices. Protein Science, **3(10)** (1994) 1847-57

[14] Borgelt, C. and Kruse, R.: Graphical Models. Methods for Data Analysis and Mining. John Wiley & Sons, Chichester, United Kingdom (2002)

[15] Ewing, D. F.: ^{13}C Substituent Effects in Monosubstituted Benzenes. Organic Magnetic Resonance, **12(9)** (1979) 499–524

[16] Atkins, P. and de Paula, J.: Atkins' Physical Chemistry, 7th ed.. Oxford University Press (2001)

Evaluation of a Mixed-Initiative Dialogue Multimodal Interface

Baoli Zhao, Tony Allen and Andrzej Bargiela
The Nottingham Trent University
{baoli.zhao,tony.allen,andrzej.bargiela}@ntu.ac.uk
www.ntu.ac.uk

Abstract

This paper presents the speech recognition accuracy testing and usability evaluation of a mixed-initiative dialogue multimodal interface for the ATTAIN* travel information system [1]. Experimental results show that although the speech recognition accuracy of the interface is less (sample accuracy rate 74.5%) than that of an equivalent directed-dialogue interface (sample accuracy rate 88.5%), the usability is seen to be significantly improved in terms of effectiveness, efficiency, learnability and user satisfaction.

1. Introduction

The main objective of this research is to investigate a robust speech-enabled query interface for the ATTAIN travel information system. In recent years, the use of speech and natural language interface technologies have shown great promise for significantly improving the usability of many computer based interactive applications [2]. The creation of a speaker-independent, speech-enabled interface system, especially one that could provide a natural language speech dialogue, was therefore thought to be of great benefit to future users of the ATTAIN system as it would immediately open up the system facilities to these users who are either unable or unwilling to use the existing WAP based interface. To develop the speech-enabled interfaces, Voice eXtensible Markup Language (VoiceXML) [3] is used. This language is based on web standards and can be used to easily create speech-enabled applications.

Our previous research has focussed on a creating a directed-dialogue speech-enabled interface for the ATTAIN travel information systems. As a result of this research, a directed-dialogue interface was developed and is presented in [4]. However, the previous usability test results show that the directed-dialogue interface only gave the lowest level of performance that is acceptable to the users. Although speech remains the most natural input method for communication with information systems, the previous interface had many problems in terms of usability performance and user satisfaction. In order to overcome the identifiable difficulties of the directed-dialogue interface, a multimodal interface has been developed that

---

* Advanced Traffic and Travel Information System

uses a mixed-initiative grammar. This grammar allows the interface to process natural language input, rather than directing the user through a rigid sequence of questions and answers. The multimodal aspect of the new speech-enabled system still requires speech to be used to input the required journey information but now uses text messages, as well as audio feedback, to present the results of the search back to the user. This overcomes the human short-term memory problem present in the initial version of the interface.

2. System Architecture

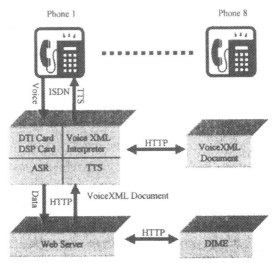

Figure1 ATTAIN Speech Interface Architecture

The present version of the interface can handle 8 users simultaneously interacting with the system. The users connect, using either land based or wireless telephones, to a VoiceXML Gateway through an ISDN line. A Dialogic Telephony Interface (DTI) Card connects the Voice Developer Gateway to the ISDN. A Digital Signal Processor (DSP) card is used in the Voice Gateway for Nuance's Automatic Speech Recognition (ASR) and text-to-speech (TTS) capabilities. The ASR and TTS software operate in conjunction with the DSP card.

The VoiceXML browser software (Motorola VoxGateway VoiceXML 2.0 voice browser) in the Gateway allows a user to navigate through a voice driven application via voice menus or commands. The software responds to these spoken commands from the user by presenting system information back to the user in an audible format.

The VoiceXML document application is delivered to the Voice Gateway from a VoiceXML document server. We also arrange (via the voice gateway) to have a Servlet interpreter of the VoiceXML language between the Voice Gateway and the ATTAIN system WWW server. This is to convert the VXML query language into the query format required by the existing ATTAIN system text based query format.

After the VoiceXML Gateway has accepted the voice input and recognized the words, it sends the user's information to the Servlet. This Servlet may use a variety of different mechanisms, such as CGI, ASP, JSP, Miva Script, but in our system it uses Java. The Servlet communicates with DIME [5] to get the required bus timetable information. It then generates a new VoiceXML document to pass this information back to the user in audio form, with an option to also send the information as a SMS message.

3. Operation Overview

The user dials a telephone number to access the system using either a fixed or mobile telephone. This number provides the user access to a VoiceXML browser that supports a mixed-initiative grammar.

Once connected, the user is introduced to the system through a welcome message and an opening prompt. The user can then give a very flexible answer. See Dialogue Flow 1.

System:	*Welcome to the ATTAIN travel information system in Nottingham.*
System:	*Please state your journey.*
User:	*I want to go from Arnold to Beeston.*
or User:	*I am going to Beeston.*
or User:	*To Beeston.*
....	

Dialogue Flow 1 The Opening Prompt

In the event that the user fails to give both origin and destination in their response, the system is able to incorporate this into its state and automatically request the unfilled data. See Dialogue Flow 2.

System:	*Welcome to the ATTAIN travel information system in Nottingham.*
System:	*Please state your journey.*
User:	*I am going to Beeston.*
System:	*Ok, you want to go to Beeston. Please state where you would like to travel from.*
User:	*Arnold.*

Dialogue Flow 2 The Mixed-initiative Detection 1

Likewise, in the event that the system only recognises one of the two given journey points, the system is able to incorporate this into its state and automatically request the unrecognised data. See Dialogue Flow 3.

System: *Welcome to the ATTAIN travel information system in Nottingham.*

System: *Please state your journey.*

User: *I want to go from Arnold to Beeston. (Unrecognised Origin)*

System: *Ok, you want to go to Beeston. Please state where you would like to travel from.*

User: *Arnold.*

Dialogue Flow 3 The Mixed-initiative Detection 2

Once the system has gathered all the mandatory data (origin and destination), it asks the user for confirmation and then launches a DIME query [6] to retrieve the required travel information. After the system has verbally presented the enquiry result back to the user, it then gives four menu options to accommodate different user preferences. See Dialogue Flow 4.

System: *I understand that you want to go from Arnold to Beeston, Is this correct?*

User: *Yes*

System: *Thank you. Please wait while I get the information you require. This may take a few moments.*

System: *Ok, you can get bus 36 at 10.23; it will arrive at Beeston at 10.46.*

System: *To listen to this message again, please say 'Repeat Message';*

To enquiry about another journey, please say 'Journey';

To send the result as a text message, please say 'Text Message';

To exit, please say 'exit'.

User: *Text Message*

System: *Ok, the result will be sent to your mobile 07901536567. Thanks for calling the ATTAIN travel information system. Goodbye.*

Dialogue Flow 4 The Sending Text Message Dialog

When a user calls from a mobile phone the user's telephone number is automatically known to the system. However, when a user calls the system from a fixed phone, the system requires the user to input his/her mobile number using either speech or keypad (DTMF).

4. Comparison between the Mixed-initiative and Directed-Dialogue Interfaces

In the directed-dialogue interface, the users did not like the way the application controlled the interaction all of the time; the user could not volunteer information. For example, they may wish to give the information in a natural single sentence (i.e. "I want to go from Arnold to Beeston."), but the directed-dialogue interface could not understand the volunteered information. In the mixed-initiative dialogue interface the user inputs are not constrained to a single data input as in the directed-dialogue interface. Users are able to respond with multiple data. In this way, the flow of the interaction is not controlled by the system, but is controlled by the user.

The implementation of a mixed-initiative dialogue is a tree wherein the root node is the opening prompt (Please state your journey). The number of branches from each node corresponds to the number of different types of response that the system allows the user to input at that point in the dialogue. In the directed-dialogue interface, we used a sequential decision process model and the system controls all of the interactions.

In the mixed-initiative interface, if the system detects error conditions (e.g., a repeated request for the same attribute), the system gradually reduces the allowed scope of user input by applying more and more input constraints and specific prompts. For example, after two attempts, the system will switch to a directed-dialogue mode where it will prompt the user for one piece of information at a time. See Dialogue Flow 5.

System: *Please state your journey.*

User: *I want to go from City Centre to Beeston*

System: *Sorry, I misunderstood what you said. Could you repeat your journey using your normal tone, and speed of talking. Please state your journey again.*

User: *From City Centre to Beeston.*

System: *I am still having a problem understanding you. I will ask you for information one piece at a time, just hold on for a moment.*

System: *please state where you would like to travel from.*

User: *City Centre*

System: *please state where you would like to travel to.*

User: *Beeston*

......

Dialogue Flow 5 The Error Recovery Dialogue

This mixed-initiative interface is also a multimodal interface in that it requires the use of speech to input the required journey information but uses text messages, as well as audio output, to present the results of the search back to the user. The directed-dialogue interface could only respond using verbal message, which the users found difficult to remember.

5. Accuracy and Usability Test

In order to compare the effectiveness of this new mixed-initiative dialogue system against that of the original directed-dialogue interface it was necessary to conduct a usability evaluation test similar to that performed on the original interface.

5.1 Participants Selection

Landaruer and Nielsen's previous research [6] showed that the number of usability problems found (T) in a usability test with n users is given by:

$$T=N(1-(1-L)^n) \quad (1)$$

Where N is the total number of usability problems in the design, L is the proportion of usability problems discovered while testing by a single user and n is the number of users. The typical value of L, found by Jakob Nielsen and Tom Landaruer, is 31%; averaged across the large number of projects they studied. Plotting the curve for L=31% gives the following result. See Figure 2.

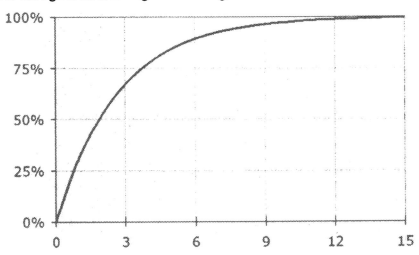

Figure 2 The Usability Problems Found Curve

Figure 2 clearly shows that we need to test with at least 15 users to discover all (99.62%) of the usability problems in a typical system [7]. For this usability experiment, we asked 20 users, 10 native and 10 non-native United Kingdom English speakers, to experiment with the system (none of them had previous experience of using such a system). They ranged in age from 18 to 70 years of age.

According to Landaruer and Nielsen's theory [6], 20 users should discover 99.99% of the usability's problems of this system.

5.2 Experimental Setup

A script of instructions was read to each participant and they were given an overview of the system. The users were initially informed of the purpose of the experiment and questionnaires were shown so that the users knew the key aspects of the system that they were expected to notice during the experiment. The users were not taught how to use the system. All the users were required to find out bus information including start journey time, arrive time, bus service number and bus changing information using the mixed-initiative speech-enabled interface. The origin and destination bus stops were randomly pre-selected from a 1355 bus stop names list. Each of the tasks were timed and recorded along with any comments made during the completion of the tasks. A questionnaire was given to participants at the end of each experiment. This asked the users to evaluate features of the system according to a 1-9 Likert rating scale [8]. Because it was possible that the test environment could directly affect system performance, we performed the experiment in two different environments: a quiet office and a noisy shopping centre.

For this experiment the confidence level of the recogniser was configured to 0.5. This is the confidence threshold required for the speech-recognition engine to decide whether the input speech matches a sentence from the grammar. The Timeout property was set to 5 seconds; this property specifies how long the interpreter allows the users to remain silence before they start to talk. The Complete Time Out property was set to 1 second; this property specifies how long the interpreter waits after the user stops talking before processing the speech input.

5.3 Statistics Methods for Test Results

As described by Sauro [9], adding confidence intervals to completion rates in usability tests will temper both excessive skepticism and overstated usability findings. Confidence intervals make testing more efficient by quickly revealing unusable tasks with very small samples. The risk of acceptance can be described using two elements: The Confidence Level and The Width of the Confidence Level (confidence Interval).

In order to evaluate the analytical data for continuous valued response items, we can estimate the true mean of a population using the formula for standard deviation and the student t distribution. As described by Sauro [10], this method is best for small sample size results. Equation 2 (overleaf) shows the expression used to calculate the true population mean from the results given in Table 1:

$$\mu = \overline{x} \pm t^* \left(\frac{s}{\sqrt{n}} \right)$$

(2)

$\overline{x}$ Mean of the sample

μ True mean of the entire population of users

n Number of users in the sample

s The standard deviation of the sample

t* t statistic = the excel function TINV(.05,n-1) [confidence level(.05) and degrees of freedom n-1]

5.4 Speech Recognition Accuracy Result

Our measurement of recognition accuracy depended on whether the desired end result occurred. For example, if the user said "yes", the speech engine returned "yes", and the "YES" action was executed, it is clear that the desired end result was achieved. However, if the engine returns text that does not exactly match the utterance (the user said "Yeah" and the engine returned "Yes"), yet the "YES" action was executed, we also say that the speech was recognised correctly because the dialogue processing was successful and system achieved the desired end result.

	Sample	Mean	95% Confidence Interval	Standard Deviation	t* (.95)
Accuracy Rate	20	74.5%	10.2%	21.8%	2.093
Rejection Rate	20	21.1%	10.2%	21.8%	2.093
Substitution Rate	20	4.4%	3.8%	8.2%	2.093

Table 1 The Overall Accuracy Rate

Table 1 shows the accuracy rate in detail for the twenty users in the usability test. To evaluate the results we used the standard deviation with student t distribution method. Overall there was a mean sample rejection rate of 21.1% and a mean sample substitution rate of 4.4%. This gives a mean sample accuracy rate of 74.5% (μ=74.5%±10.2%) that is worse than the directed-dialogue interface's average sample accuracy rate of 88.5% (μ=88.5%±5.8%). Even though we can claim with 95% confidence that the best true population mean accuracy rate of the mixed-initiative interface could be 84.7% (74.5%+10.2%), this is still lower than the directed-dialogue sample mean. As both interfaces have the same number of bus stop names (1355), it is necessary to consider what caused this drop in recognition accuracy. In the directed-dialogue interface, the grammar was constrained to one keyword input at each point in the dialogue thereby maximising the underlying ASR performance. The mixed-initiative dialogue interface is required to process a wider range of inputs capturing all possible user initiatives. This requires a larger and more complex grammar that produces a reduced ASR performance. A mixed-initiative system is thus a trade-off between the degree of initiative allowed and the ASR performance achieved.

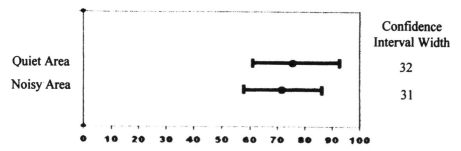

Figure 3 The Accuracy Rate in Different Test Environment

To analyse the results further, we separated the results on the basis of environment, as shown in figure 3. From the experiment results, we are 95% confident that the true population mean accuracy rate is between 60.4% and 92.4% in the quiet environment and between 56.8% and 87.8% in the noisy area. By comparing this data, we can see that the ASR performance is not strongly affected by the users' calling environment. It is therefore possible for the users to call the system from any environment, e.g. their homes, their offices, the mall, the airport, or their cars.

5.5   Usability Attributes Result

	Sample Accuracy	Completion Time (sec)	Efficiency Level	Satisfaction Level	Learnability Level	Re-learnability Level
Mixed	74.5%	126	7.6	7.0	6.8	7.1
Directed	88.5%	111	5.7	5.3	6.2	6.4

Table 2 The Performance of directed and mixed-initiative dialogue interface

The mean intelligibility scores for the two speech-enabled interfaces are presented in Table 2. To accomplish the task using the mixed-initiative dialogue interface, the average user spent more time (126s) than using the directed-dialogue interface (111s). However the average user still thought that they accomplished the task more efficiently using the mixed-initiative dialogue interface. The users gave a mean score of 7.6 ($\mu=7.6\pm0.7$) for the efficiency level of the mixed-initiative dialogue interface compared to the directed-dialogue interface's 5.7 ($\mu=5.7\pm0.9$). It would appear that time to complete and recognition rate are not critical factors as far as user perceived efficiency is concerned. A better alternative is to relate user perceived efficiency to the number of operations performed during the task. For example, allowing single user utterances containing multiple data inputs gives an impression of greater efficiency even if the recognition rate is lowered and the average time to complete is increased.

Looking at the satisfaction scores, it is apparent that the users were more satisfied with the mixed-initiative interface. All the users scored over the neutral satisfaction threshold and the average score was 7.0 ($\mu=7.0\pm0.6$). This confirms that the mixed-initiative dialogue interface was better accepted by the users than the original directed-dialogue interface's 5.3 ($\mu=5.3\pm1.0$).

The results also indicate that the mixed-initiative dialogue interface was easier for a user to learn than the directed-dialogue interface. With a score of 6.8 ($\mu=6.8\pm0.7$) compared to 6.2 ($\mu=6.2\pm0.8$), we can see that it is easier for a new user to become acquainted with the mixed-initiative dialogue interface than with the directed-dialogue one. By questioning the users, we were able to identify several user behaviours that were implicitly learned during system usage (e.g. voice loudness, absence of extraneous utterances, etc.). Consequently the users gave the mixed-initiative interface a re-learnability score of 7.1 ($\mu=7.1\pm0.8$). This is also an improvement on the directed-dialogue interface.

Finally, the mixed-initiative dialogue interface can be seen to be more effective in accomplishing the task. In both the mixed-initiative and directed-dialogue interface experiments, all of the users 'successfully' got the bus information that they wanted. However, in the case of the mixed-initiative interface, 100% of the users said they could complete their journey following the enquiry result. The mixed-initiative interface users did not need to remember or write down the result, because all of the result was saved on their mobile. This multimodal approach completely overcame the short term human memory problem evident in the directed-dialogue interface.

5.6 Results according to user age

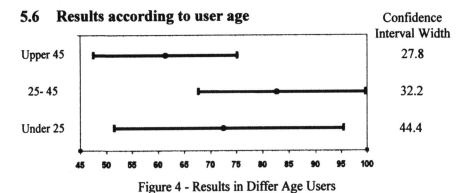

Figure 4 - Results in Differ Age Users

It is interesting to perform an analysis of variance in performance due to age, see figure 4. Subjects were chosen to be representative of a broad range of ages. We divided the users into three groups, ages under 25, ages between 25-45 and ages above 45. We can see that the older subjects have difficulty with speech recognition. We are 95% confident that the true population mean accuracy rate is between 47.3% and 75.1% for the older age people. This is much lower than the middle age group (68.8%-99%) and the younger individuals (51.4%-96.2%). Older people who spoke too slowly caused this problem. The timeout property of the speech recogniser was not set long enough to wait for the older people to finish a long utterance. When we design the next interface, we need to consider the potential hearing loss, reduced memory capacity and slow talking speed of older individuals.

From figure 4, we are also 95% confident that the true population mean accuracy rate is between 51.4% and 96.2% for the younger individuals. This is a very wide spread and needs explanation. From our observations during the experiment, we found that some of the younger individuals did not speak in a normal manner. After they discovered that the mixed-initiative dialogue interface could understand a full sentence, some of them tried to challenge the system with special English sentences that the system failed to recognize. In addition, some of younger individuals spoke very quickly with strong accents. Because this is their natural way of speaking, we cannot expect that they will change their talking manner. Therefore in any future interface, we should give clear prompts to avoid the young users giving over long sentences. In real life, the majority of buses users are the elderly and young people, so we should give the behaviour of these two groups of people more consideration in any future dialogue design.

5.7 Error Recovery Test Result

In the mixed-initiative interface, if the system detected a recognition error in the opening prompt (Please state your journey.), then the system would ask the user to repeat what they said by playing a different prompt. If the system still has difficulty recognizing the second attempt, the system would switch to a directed-dialogue mode where it will prompt the user for information one piece at a time.

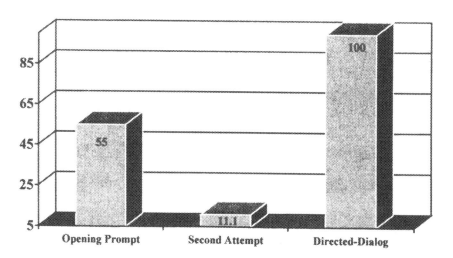

Figure 5 - Results in Error Recovery

Figure 5 shows the percentage of users who completed the tasks in the different error recovery levels. We can see that 55% (11 out of 20) of the users were able to complete their query at the initial prompt level. However of the 45% of users who failed the opening prompt stage, the system could only recognize 11.1% (1 out of 9) of user utterances in the second attempt level. The same recognition error was repeated when the user spoke the similar words or phrases again, even though the system has supplied a progressive assistant prompt message. However, when the system reverts to the directed-dialogue format following the second attempt failure it can be seen that all of the remaining user responses were correctly recognised.

Previous research work had suggested that a good strategy for recovering from speech recognition error is to allow the user a second try [11]. From the above experimental result, we can see that in our system asking the user to simply repeat is not a good error recovery method. In any future version of this interface we intend to go directly to a directed-dialogue error recovery level once one recognition error has occurred at the mixed-initiative level.

6. Conclusion and Discussion

In this paper we have discussed the implementation of a mixed-initiative dialogue multimodal interface. The interface gives the user control over the dialogue. From the users' usability test results and feedback, we can see that the mixed-initiative speech-enabled interface gives a level of performance that is acceptable to the user. However the interface still has problems in terms of ASR performance and input method.

In the mixed-initiative dialogue interface, the mean sample ASR accuracy rate is 74.5% ($\mu=74.5\%\pm10.2\%$). This has the potential to be improved upon. The current interface only returns a single utterance string as the result of each speech-recognition event. If the user's response is not clear, the result will be the one utterance that the speech-recognition engine judges to be the most likely. However, instead of returning the single most likely utterance, it is possible for the speech-recognition engine to return a list of the most likely utterances. Confidence-scoring post-processing can then be investigated as a way of improving the speech recognition error handling. As described by Pitrelli and Perrone [12], confidence-scoring post-processing uses a recognition verification strategy: the computer calculates a measure of recognition confidence, and if it is above a threshold it can accept the recognition result, thereby automating the processing. When the confidence value is below the threshold, the result can be automatically "rejected", meaning that the recognition result is assumed to be unreliable and the item needs to be re-entered. Confidence scoring may consist of a function of appropriate parameters drawn directly from the recognition process, or it may be considered a learning task in which a classifier is trained to use an array of such parameters to distinguish correct recognition from incorrect. We aim to use a post-processing approach to confidence scoring, in which confidence is measured following recognition. It may also be possible to use confidence measures to eliminate the need for the confirmation stage if the system can automatically determine that it is 'confident' in its recognition results. Subsequent usability experiments on the new interface will be carried out after the system is fully optimised in terms of performance.

Keypad input is required in situations where the ASR persistently fails to recognise what the user has said because of the user's ambiguous pronunciation. The user will be stuck at this point without access to a different input modality. Keypad input would be the best alternative input method. When the system detects "trouble" conditions, the system gradually reduces the allowed scope of user input by applying more and more input constraints and specific prompts. After two attempts, the system switches to a directed-dialogue mode where it continues to prompt the user for one piece of information at a time. If system still cannot recognize what the user has said, we could ask the user to input the data using the phone keypad. When the user spells a bus stop name on his/her telephone, instead of simply looking up a hypothesized word in a lexicon, the system must remain open to the possibility that the hypothesized word is misspelt. An intelligent spelling checker must be built. If the spelling checker is not robust enough to identify all the words from the misspelling, the system would need to initiate a disambiguation sub-dialogue to resolve the ambiguity.

In the near future, it is also anticipated that the ATTAIN travel information system be extended to apply to apply to the London Metropolitan area where over 45,000 location references are needed to provide a comprehensive coverage of the London city locations. Compared with the current speech-enabled ATTAIN interface for Nottingham (which only contains 1355 location references), the London speech-enabled ATTAIN interface will require far larger vocabularies and a variety of grammars. In order to support this extension, the dialogue of the speech-enabled interface must be optimized to handle grammar and lexicon elements that contain references to more sophisticated grammar and lexicon modules. The impact of this on dialogue management and system usability needs to be determined, and mechanisms for dealing with any differences devised. For example, the study of Hataoka and others [13] state that an automatic generation scheme for lexicons and grammars could handle such an issue. An intelligent component to help automatically generate the lexicons and grammars will be investigated.

Acknowledgements

The Authors would like to acknowledge the contributions of their project partners from MASC Company, Nottingham City Transport, Nuance and Motorola.

References

1. NTU: Advanced Traffic and Travel Information system.
   http://dcm.ntu.ac.uk/RTTS/Projects/grr32468/attain.html, accessed on
   12/08/2004
2. Miller, M.: VoiceXML: 10 Projects to Voice Enable Your Web Site. John
   Wiley & Sons, 2002
3. W3C: Voice extensible Markup Language (VoiceXML) versiton 1.0.
   http://www.w3.org/TR/2000/NOTE-voicexml-20000505/, accessed on
   12/08/2004
4. Zhao, B., Allen, T. & Bargiela, A.: Directed-dialogue Speech-enabled Query
   Interface for the ATTAIN Travel Information System. In: Proceedings of
   PREP, Hertfordshire, 2004
5. Kosonen, I. & Bargielar A.: A Distributed Traffic Monitoring and Information
   System. In: Journal of Geographic Information and Decision Analysis 1999,
   3(1) 31-40
6. Landaruer, T. K. & Nielsen, J.: A Mathematical Model of the Finding of
   Usability Problems. In: Proceeding of INTERCHI, Amsterdam, Netherlands,
   1993
7. Nielsen, J: Why You Only Need to Test With 5 Users.
   http://www.useit.com/alertbox/20000319.html, accessed on 02/08/2004
8. Komorita, S.: Attitude content, intensity and the neutral point on a Likert
   scale. In: Journal of Social Psychology 1963, 61,327-334
9. Sauro, J.: Restoring Confidence in Usability Results.
   http://www.measuringusability.com/conf_intervals.htm, accessed on
   12/08/2004
10. Sauro, J.: You don't need a large sample of users to obtain meaningful data.
    http://www.measuringusability.com/sample_continuous.htm, accessed on
    12/08/2004
11. Boyce, S. & Gorin, A.: User Interface Issues for Natural Spoken Dialog
    Systems. In: Proceedings of International Symposium for Spoken Dialogue,
    Philadelphia, 1996
12. Pitrelli, J. F. & Perrone, M. P.: Confidence-Scoring Post-Processing for Off-
    Line Handwritten-Character Recognition Verification. In: Proceedings the
    Seventh International Conference on Document Analysis and Recognition,
    Edinburgh, Scotland, 2003
13. Hataoka, N., Obuchi, Y., Mitamura, T. & Nyberg E.: Robust Speech Dialog
    Interface for Car Telematics Services. In: Proceedings of 2004 IEEE
    Consumer Communications and Networking Conference, Las Vegas, 2004

AUTHOR INDEX